# GENETIC
## TESTING&SCREENING

### CRITICAL ENGAGEMENT AT THE
### INTERSECTION OF FAITH AND SCIENCE

*Roger A. Willer, editor*

KIRK HOUSE PUBLISHERS
Minneapolis, Minnesota

# GENETIC TESTING AND SCREENING:
Critical Engagement at the Intersection of Faith and Science

Roger A. Willer, editor

DIVISION
FOR CHURCH
IN SOCIETY
EVANGELICAL LUTHERAN CHURCH IN AMERICA

Library of Congress Cataloging-in-Publication Data
    Genetic testing and screening: critical engagement at the intersection of faith and science / Roger A. Willer, editor.
        p.      cm.
    Includes bibliographical references and index.
    ISBN 1-886513-11-2
    1. Religion and science.   2. Philosophy and science.   3. Willer, Roger A., 1955-
    BL240.2.G45   1998
    241'.64957—dc21

Kirk House Publishers, PO Box 390759, Minneapolis, Minnesota 55439
Manufactured in the United States of America

# TABLE OF CONTENTS

# PREFACE

The Division for Church in Society of the Evangelical Lutheran Church in America (ELCA) is pleased to make available this reliable and accessible guide into Christian reflection on genetic testing and screening. The book is a Lutheran contribution to an intensifying ecumenical dialog. It places you the reader at a vital intersection of faith and science, helps you understand the issues, and invites you to join the conversation on what we as individuals, church, and society should do in relation to this rapidly developing area of scientific and technological endeavor. Pastors and other church leaders, Christians who live their vocation in medical or biotechnological professions, persons who have faced or will face questions related to genetic testing and screening, and citizens concerned about justice and the common good will find here a most helpful resource.

On behalf of the Division, I thank the Rev. Roger A. Willer for so ably directing this project, and Dr. John R. Stumme, Associate Director for Studies, for assisting with the project. I am deeply appreciative of the competent and dedicated writers who have so generously given of themselves and have worked together for almost two years to prepare this book for our church. A special word of thanks goes to Dr. Kevin Powell for assisting with the medical part of the glossary.

The authors, it should be noted, are expressing their own views. The book is not an official statement of the ELCA but is meant to promote deliberation within and beyond the ELCA.

The Rev. Charles Miller
*Executive Director, Division for Church in Society*

# INTRODUCTION

## *Roger A. Willer*

Like the ocean crashing upon a shoreline, the emerging knowledge of genetics and its technological applications are impacting American society with nearly tangible force. The major crests of this new knowledge rivet public attention as front page news and become the material of thoughtful musing and conversation as well as grist for late night comedians. Even highly theoretical breakthroughs ripple through the news media and into social awareness. But like beach walkers entranced by the large swells, we may be inattentive to the rising tide lapping about our feet. While the potential of human cloning, for instance, is a momentous issue, few of us would ever face the decision whether to clone; yet many people will—if they have not already done so—encounter genetic testing and screening. It is largely through genetic testing and screening that the nonspecialist will personally confront the personal, social, theological, and pastoral dilemmas that attend genetic developments. It is through genetic testing and screening that most people will—if they have not already done so—personally realize that the tide of genetic knowledge is now an inescapable part of the situation in which we live.

The procedures of genetic testing and screening available today are being established steadily into medical protocol, the court system, and the workplace. Sustained by the "big science" represented in the Human Genome Project (see Glossary), this humanly-generated "tide" rises steadily in the name of knowledge, healing, and profit. The potential benefits are clearly immense. Genetic knowledge can lead to preventative medical therapy, allow informed choice, set free the wrongly accused, and spin off whole new industries that respond to the ailments and misfortunes of life. Yet, as Ecclesiastes 1:18 reminds us, "those who increase knowledge increase sorrow." While we

> ### What are genetic testing and screening?
>
> For the purposes of this text, they indicate any technological procedure that analyzes a sample of human body fluid or tissue for the presence or absence of specific genetic material. Currently the most common medical applications involve screens or tests that detect the heritable basis of disease, defect, or abnormality during pregnancy or in ▶

may celebrate these new powers, their application also brings vexing personal crises and social dilemmas.

Some of these are unprecedented. For instance, the coined term "toxic knowledge"[1] designates the unprecedented possibility that an adult or child may know decades ahead of time about the inevitable onset of, or strong predisposition to, a disease or disorder for which there is no therapy. The purest example is the genetic test for Huntington's disease which can indicate its inevitable onset, even though information about severity and timing remain approximate. More common instances of toxic knowledge include the growing number of tests for a statistical disposition for some forms of cancer or heart problems. Since each human on average carries about half a dozen genetic sequences which, if activated, could cause crippling or lethal conditions, the quantity of toxic knowledge in our lives is bound to increase. On the societal level, genetic knowledge creates the possibility of a new underclass: the genetically "deficient," a class of those discriminated against on the basis of their genetic make-up. Might contemporary examples of job and insurance discrimination due to genetic information point to wide range discrimination to come?

Other quandaries that attend the use of genetic testing are long standing but now intensified; for example, selective abortion.[2] Genetic testing means that prospective parents must now decide whether they want to know an increasing quantity of detail about any new life in the womb. Should they want to know about severe genetic abnormalities for which no therapy can be given? If they do know, is it ever morally proper for them to decide to abort that new life? By what criteria does one make that decision? How shall such a couple make sense of their trust in the goodness of God's creation or their parental calling before they even hold a child in their arms? While such dilemmas may be obvious, others are especially troubling because they are not. Some of our authors, for instance, will argue that the dangers lie concealed in the way our society uses technology or within the very language and mindset brought to these issues.

# Origin, Convictions, Method

In awareness of this "rising tide" and the attendant need for conversation and action, the board of the Division for Church in Society of the Evangelical Lutheran Church in America (ELCA) authorized this writing project. ELCA members with backgrounds in science, business, medicine, ethics, and theology were invited to address the implications of genetic testing from their vantage points. The result of this initiative and subsequent work is the *"Critical Engagement"* with genetic testing and screening published here.

The designation *critical engagement* indicates, first of all, that the church ought to self-consciously come to terms with genetic testing and screening. The ELCA and its predecessor bodies that together formed the ELCA in 1988 have produced a variety of pertinent statements and publications concerned with bioethics and other related topics. What is sometimes called the genetic revolution, however, addresses fresh and powerful questions to the church. What is it that we in the church should teach about this new technology? What word does the church have for those who are responsible for its development? What are the most informed models of care for pastors and congregations who minister to those wrestling with unprecedented situations. For which of the resulting public policy issues should the church advocate? The church must come to terms with these questions but can do so satisfactorily only by engaging scientific, medical, and business thinking.[3]

At the same time, the idea of critical engagement carries the equal conviction that faith-informed perspectives ought to be heard in the public forum. The church has significant and distinctive things to say about a society wrestling with the questions and the meaning of genetic developments. This work, then, is simply part of its call to witness in society.[4] The church's conversation will be inaccurate and incomplete if it does not engage and learn from scientific, medical, and business thinking, but public debate will be thin and dangerous if it does not give attention to the wisdom of faith traditions. The intersection of conversation about genetics requires both "secular" and faith-informed knowledge.

## Related ELCA Resources

**ELCA Social Statements:**

"Church in Society: A Lutheran Perspective," 1991.

"Abortion," 1991.

"Caring for Creation: Vision, Hope, and Justice," 1993.

**ELCA Message:**

"End-of-Life Decisions," 1992.

**Studies from predecesor church bodies:**

"The Ethics of Prenatal Diagnosis," by Edmund N. Santurri, 1986.

"Genetic Manipulation," by James H. Burtness, 1986.

"Genetic Screening and Counseling," by James M. Childs, Jr., 1986.

*Single copies are available for no cost from the Division for Church in Society (800-638-3522 ext. 2712).* ■

Critical engagement further signifies that, in principle, the emerging genetic knowledge and its application are to be affirmed; *but* it simultaneously indicates that people of faith must consider any particular instance critically. This means Christians must decide about any specific instance according to criteria informed by faith and Christian sources. The engagement with these new powers must always maintain a tension between acceptance and resistance, as the writers here repeatedly demonstrate. Such a position distinguishes this book from those who reject in principle these new powers as "playing God" and, at the opposite end, from those who optimistically or unreflectively hold that whatever science discovers and the market will bear is acceptable. The writers, especially in sections two and three, take on the exacting work of discerning and proposing the criteria necessary for such a stance. Their proposals are intended to serve as stimulation for church conversation in the dimension of its calling as a community of moral deliberation.[5]

Critical engagement, finally, recognizes that genetic developments are occasions in which God is at work. Genetic testing and screening are part of God's creative enterprise and evoke religious concern at every level. This belief does not pronounce blessing on any particular aspect, for sin is just as assuredly present. But because God encounters us precisely in such ambiguous situations, we are called to be attentive to God's presence and will. We are called to decide and to minister in these developments with the best of our faithful understanding.

Some readers may disagree with one or more of these convictions that undergird this book as a critical engagement. But since discussion with a diverse audience is part of the assignment, conversation about that disagreement would be fulfilling the task. This *Critical Engagement* thus invites readers to join the conversation by considering, debating, and engaging this book from bottom to top, from its underlying convictions to any specific proposal.

Since genetic testing and screening is but one arena of the vast genetic developments promised at the dawn of a new century, some may find the concentration on it surprising. Yet as already noted, it is the gate through which most people will meet its challenges firsthand. Moreover, genetic testing is *the* pivotal technology for applying genetic knowledge. Even "sensational" technology such as genetic engineering would finally depend on plain vanilla genetic testing to make possible its engineering of selected cells or fertilized ova. The choice of genetic testing thus presents the writers a reasonably manageable topic with unforced openings to much larger concerns. This book, then, is not confined solely to biomedical ethics but engages a wide range of issues at the intersection of faith and science. It becomes an occasion for the writers to reflect on life in contemporary society with its increasingly staggering powers and a place to offer their best thinking about how Christians, congregations, and others may or should respond.

Simply put, this book intends to be a tool for education, conversation, and action. The authors speak from within the Christian Lutheran tradition and as participants in the larger social conversation about genetics; they speak at the intersection of religion, society, and science and intend to assist readers to be more astute participants in that debate. Yet, this volume's aim is not just conversation, for it intends also to equip people for action: for making personal decisions, for living in compassionate care for one another, and for advocating just medical, corporate, and government policies.

The book's method follows from its intention to join in and evoke conversation within the church and the wider society. The writers from various disciplines were invited into a collaborative process. Between May of 1997 and January of 1998, they spent three weekends and innumerable e-mails discussing the overall project and critiquing drafts of one another's chapters-in-progress. The chapters represent their own thinking but the engagement with one another appears in references to another's work as well as in certain common themes and messages that emerge from the whole. To read this book is to eavesdrop on them as they encounter the issues, other thinkers, and one another in the awareness that we live in a society that increasingly practices genetic testing and screening.

This anthology does not offer an official ELCA position. As Lutherans the writers naturally gravitate to resources from their tradition, although they call upon a wide array of sources as they develop their positions. If the ELCA were to address these matters through an official policy development process, this book intends to provide fuel for that conversation. But prior to adoption of any official position, many more people within the church must together think through these concerns in a variety of settings in order to determine what positions are the most faithful ones.[6]

## Chapter Descriptions

The book begins with a section sketching the facts, issues, personal stories, and market forces involved in genetic developments, material that may be new to many readers. In addition, it provides this material because a moral principle is at work: anyone who confronts these matters ought to have the opportunity to gain a working knowledge of genetics so that they can make informed decisions. The authors in Section One also do more: They take the opportunity to make what is sometimes called the "Sunday-Monday" connection. They reflect, in other words, out of their faith about their topic and work.

In Chapter One, Kevin Powell, a pediatrician, targets two equally important audiences. The first is the nonspecialist who needs a working knowledge of genetic vocabulary and concepts; the second is the specialist who may know genetics but desires a sharper awareness of the moral and social questions implicit in or perhaps overlooked in these "facts." Powell identifies and interweaves the scientific concepts and the moral questions with the hope of providing a primer, that is, a collection of basic material for a shared conversation between these sometimes disparate clusters of people and concerns.

Conversations about genetics sometimes may become fact and issue dominated, but Kirstin Finn Schwandt, a genetic counselor, reminds the reader how personal these matters really are. Schwandt sketches stories of ten families (their names have been changed) whose lives are significantly altered by the enhanced knowledge that genetic testing brings. In this way she underlines for us the genuine anxieties and sorrows, moral quandaries, and personal crises that may be forgotten amid concentration on technical and theoretical considerations. Her chapter also provides an introduction to the new profession of genetic counseling for those unfamiliar with it. Along the way she demonstrates the importance of fostering a team approach among professionals in dealing with genetic dilemmas.

John Varian, chief financial officer for a biotech firm, takes us into an arena that has strategic impact—an impact sometimes overlooked because it is so obvious—on this topic: the marketplace. Varian's chapter provides an insider's view of the dynamics through which scientific breakthroughs are transformed into available procedures. He offers a crucial perspective on the stated values of the industry, the economic forces at work, and the ethical issues that must be balanced against profit motives. His underlying message is that many individuals within the industry want to take part in a meaningful dialog about genetic testing and screening, something his chapter should help further.

The chapters in Section Two are reflections in theology and culture—broadly understood—focused by the kinds of realities and concerns described in Section One. These reflections address a wide range of the issues currently being debated, or, as some of the authors insist, that *ought* to be debated. These issues include worldviews, concepts of nature, the cultural nature of genetic knowledge and use, racism and sexism, social policy, abortion, individualism, language, biomedical decision making, and care giving. Many of these are addressed by several writers from their varied vantage points. In each case the author provides careful analysis and then offers proposals and lays down challenges with implications for society, church, and the individual.

Philip Hefner, a theologian, explores the "big picture" of worldview or social mindset in which the use of genetic knowledge occurs. In his reflective and suggestive style, he examines prevailing perspectives about nature and medicine that "condition" (unreflectively inform) our thinking about genetic testing and screening. Hefner then constructs an intentionally "ambivalent" response that clarifies both the desirable and troubling dimensions of these mindsets. The second part of his work sets forth the implications and challenges for the task of theology, living the faith, and being a vital congregation in a society that practices medicine affected by genetics. Hefner's broad-ranging reflection ultimately centers in a call for congregations to devote themselves to fostering "Christian friendship."

Elizabeth Bettenhausen, a social ethicist, turns our attention to themes often excluded in the genetic debate: to social dignity and personal identity, as well as to group interests, resources, benefits, and burdens. Her provocative question "Whose Body?" becomes the thread upon which she weaves incisive questions about social policy and the way society uses genetic testing and screening. She asks and analyzes, for instance, who defines what is taken as scientifically, medically, or socially "normal" and "abnormal"—and when and why. Bettenhausen encourages an interpretation of Lutheran ethics that counters individualistic moralities—moralities that neglect our "embodiment." Her chapter offers lines of analysis that can enable Christians to engage astutely in the needed public debate and action to counter these dangers. Such efforts, she concludes, will be guided by Luther's criterion of the "benefit and advantage of the neighbor" as enlivened by a preferential option in favor of "the least of these."

Using the metaphor of an approaching and massive storm system, Ted Peters, a theologian, considers what dangers may be brought upon American society by mixing genetic powers with social and economic pressures. He forecasts the prospect of "free market eugenics," "perfect baby syndrome," genetic discrimination, widespread selective abortions, and the treatment of children as commodities. In the face of this likely downpour, he calls upon the church and people of faith to enlist in social policy advocacy and to make personal decisions based on love and dignity for those affected. As the guiding moral principal for this, Peters proposes a norm (see Glossary) of imitation based on 1 John 4:19: "God loves each human being regardless of genetic make-up, and we should do likewise."

In the last chapter of Section Two, Hans Tiefel, an ethicist, also begins with an analysis of social mindset and shares Peters' concerns. Tiefel, though, concentrates his constructive work on the personal decisions that individuals and families face in medical situations. He contrasts two perspectives on these questions: that which he calls American individualism and that of biblical-liturgical faith. Tiefel critiques individualism's liabilities, giving special attention to what he holds is its affinity with the bloodless language of biological science, an affinity that he claims exposes prenatal life to fearful dangers. His constructive work contrasts this individualism with a biblical-liturgical tradition that ascribes human dignity to a transcendent source, envisions relationships of solidarity, and speaks a language of love understood as care. Under this lens he considers how differently decisions will look about carrier testing, prenatal screening, and tentative pregnancy.

In Section Three we turn from theology of culture to proposals oriented to professional confrontations with genetics in clinical and pastoral settings. Robert Roger Lebel, clinical geneticist, begins by asking what intellectual synthesis might satisfy the seemingly competing demands of fidelity to the Gospel and the evolutionary theory that underlies genetic knowledge. Lebel's proposal, indebted to scientist and theologian Pierre Teilhard de Chardin, conveys how he as one Christian practitioner has "put it together." Whether finally persuaded or not, the reader will find a thought provoking perspective on the matter of faith and evolution. This perspective also generates a moral norm for consideration: Human lives should be guided by the criterion of a "creative and generous response that builds up the body of Christ." After laying this foundation, Lebel reflects on factors in genetic decision making and genetic technology, as well as upon one of Schwandt's cases. In so doing, he allows us to glimpse how one Christian geneticist thinks about the problems he confronts in the clinic.

Larry Holst, a hospital chaplain now retired, concentrates his chapter on two couples for whom genetic testing has parted their "veil of innocence" by exposing previously unknown medical problems. Holst details how emotionally charged, morally ambiguous, and theologically provocative the resulting dilemmas can be for both the couple and the care-giver. Through these reflections Holst offers a perspective for pastors or—with some adaption—any care-giver who wants to serve persons in genetic crisis. The perspective calls for sensitive listening and gentle spiritual guidance toward the goal of clarifying moral options and making decisions consistent with the individuals' Christian allegiance.

# Conclusion

The metaphor of "the rising tide" expresses figuratively how inescapably genetic testing and screening are becoming parts of the situation in which we live and in which the church is called to carry on its ministry. For the sake of that ministry, the church needs to wade into this tide. Just as vitally, our society needs a church and a people who greet the situation with informed thinking and with discernment for compassionate and just action. This book will have fulfilled its mandate if it equips the reader to join in such a critical engagement.

# CONTRIBUTORS

**Elizabeth Bettenhausen** is a social ethicist and theologian who divides her teaching time between Hartford Seminary, the University of Massachusetts at Boston, Project Hope (G.E.D. classes), and Baldwin Elementary School. Her work in bioethics includes course offerings while associate professor at Boston University (1979-1988) and initiating the Lutheran Church in America's (LCA) study on bioethics as Secretary for Social Concerns in the Department for Church and Society for the LCA (1974-1979). Her more recent publications include a 1994 Lutheran World Federation paper entitled "Creation" in *Concern for Creation: Voices on the Theology of Creation* (ed., Mortensen, Tro & Tanke, 1995), and "Ethical Issues in Post-Menopausal Pregnancy and Birth" (*IN/FIRE ETHICS*, 1994). She is a member of University Lutheran in Cambridge, Massachusetts.

**Philip Hefner** teaches systematic theology at the Lutheran School of Theology at Chicago and is Director of the Chicago Center for Religion and Science. He is also Editor-in-Chief of *Zygon: Journal of Religion and Science*. In the area of religion and science, he has authored *The Human Factor: Evolution, Culture and Religion* (Fortress, 1993) and *Natur-Weltbild-Religion* (Munich: Institut Technik-Theologie-Naturwissenschaften, 1995). He is a member of Augustana Lutheran in Chicago, Illinois.

**Lawrence E. Holst** served as the chair of the Department of Pastoral Care at Lutheran General Hospital for 35 years, retiring in 1995. Holst has edited several books, written numerous articles, and lectured in the fields of pastoral care and clinical ethics throughout his career. He coauthored *Ministry to Outpatients: A New Challenge in Pastoral Care* (Augsburg, 1991). He has served in various capacities on biomedical committees and was active in the foundation of the Park Ridge Center for the Study of Health, Faith and Values. He now resides in Seabrook Island, South Carolina and is a member of St. Matthew Lutheran, Charleston.

**Robert Roger Lebel** is a community-based clinical geneticist with Genetics Services, S.C. serving the Western Chicagoland area. His numerous degrees include masters in zoology, theology, ethics, and medical genetics as well as his M.D. from the University of Wisconsin Medical School, Madison. He is a Founding Fellow of the American College of Medical Genetics and helped draft the code of ethics for geneticists of the Council of Regional Networks for Genetics Services under the Maternal and Child Health branch of the Department of Health and Human Services. He is a member of Faith Lutheran in Glen Ellyn, Illinois.

**Ted Peters** teaches systematic theology at Pacific Lutheran Theological Seminary and the Graduate Theological Union in Berkeley, California. He is a research scholar at the Center for Theology and the Natural Sciences. On the topic of genetics, he has authored *For the Love of Children* (Westminster/John Knox, 1996) and *Playing God?* (Routledge, 1997); he edited *Genetics: Issues in Social Justice* (Pilgrim, 1998). He was a principal investigator for the National Institutes of Health on "Theological Questions Raised by Human Genome Initiative" (1991-1995). His wider work in theology includes *God—The World's Future: Systematic Theology for a Post-Modern Era* (Fortress, 1992) He is editor of *Dialog, A Journal of Theology*. He is a member of Christ Lutheran in El Cerrito, California.

**Kevin Powell** is a pediatrician for Carle Clinic in Urbana, Illinois. He is a clinical assistant professor at the University of Illinois College of Medicine and serves on the hospital ethics committee. Prior to his entrance into medicine he worked as an engineer in industry and has two patents in biotechnology. He earned a Ph.D. in Medical Engineering jointly from MIT/Harvard Medical School. His M.D. degree is from Tufts University School of Medicine. Kevin is a member of the steering committee for the ELCA Work Group on Science and Technology. He attends St. Andrew's Lutheran in Champaign, Illinois.

**Kirstin Finn Schwandt** is a full-time, community-based genetic counselor in Bloomington, Indiana. Her Master of Science degree from the University of Wisconsin-Madison was in medical genetics with an emphasis on counseling and ethical issues. She is a member of the National Society of Genetic Counselors. Her background in genetics includes several years as a genetic research lab assistant. She is a member of St. Thomas Lutheran in Bloomington.

**Hans O. Tiefel** teaches at the College of William and Mary in Virginia, where he is professor and chair of the Religion Department and offers a range of courses in religion and ethics. He has published essays on medical ethics in *The Journal of the American Medical Association* and the *New England Journal of Medicine*. He also authored *The Nontreatment of Seriously Handicapped Newborns*, an essay in the series on Procreation Ethics sponsored jointly by the American Lutheran Church, Lutheran Church in America, and Association of Evangelical Lutheran Churches. He is a member of St. Stephan Lutheran in Williamsburg, Virginia.

**John Varian** is vice president and chief financial officer of Neurex Corporation, a biotechnology company located in the San Fransico Bay Area. He has spent most of his 17-year career working on financial aspects of the biotechnology industry, with companies such as Anergen, Inc., Ernst & Young, and Arthur Andersen. He has been involved in numerous public financings, including initial public offerings, and has established strategic alliances with major pharmaceutical companies. Varian has served as guest lecturer at various universities including University of

California Berkeley and the University of California Los Angeles. He is a member of St. Mark Lutheran in San Fransico.

**Roger A. Willer** is an ELCA pastor who has served in the part-time position of project director and editor of this writing project on genetic testing and screening for the Division for Church in Society's Department for Studies. He has previously served congregations in Ohio and is currently engaged in Ph.D. studies in theology at the University of Chicago. His study program has concentrated on work at the intersection of theology, science, and ethics, including regular participation in the Advanced Seminars of the Chicago Center for Religion and Science. He is a member of Reformation Lutheran in Eastlake, Ohio.

# SECTION ONE

# UNDERSTANDING GENETIC TESTING AND SCREENING

# A BASIC GUIDE: FACTS AND ISSUES

## Kevin Powell

The genes that make us human creatures are numerous and complex. It has been a century since a monk named Gregor Mendel first started studying characteristics of plants (yellow peas, green peas, smooth peas, wrinkled peas) and identified rules for the inheritance of these characteristics. It has been a half-century since James Watson and Francis Crick published their landmark article identifying *deoxyribose nucleic acid* (DNA) as the double helical shaped, chemical messenger that carries this genetic information. Every month research in genetics now produces thousands of pages of new information. Despite its complexity, most of the key concepts of genetics can be easily understood once the technical vocabulary is hurdled. One purpose of this chapter is to orient nonscientists to the vocabulary and concepts of genetics.

In addition, this chapter aims to raise awareness among scientists about the ethical, legal, and social issues created by our increasing knowledge of genetics. While humans share over 98 percent of their genetic information with other primates, what makes us human is far more complex than our genes. Sequencing all human genes has been referred to as "the Holy Grail" of modern biology. Within the next decade the Human Genome Project may place that Holy Grail before us. However, this new scientific knowledge alone will not answer the deeper, philosophical questions that have plagued humankind for centuries. What does it mean to be "created in the image of God?" What is the relationship of humankind to the rest of creation? Pondering the worthiness of humankind, the Psalmist rhetorically asked God, "What are human beings that you are mindful of them?" (Psalm 8:4). The answer to these questions does not lie in our genetic sequence. But unveiling the sequence may profoundly impact our understanding of those questions.

The two purposes of this chapter interlace, building a bridge between two very different cultures of scientific knowledge and religious understanding. With this bridge to encourage conversation, I hope to promote a positive response to an important practical question: "Given an increasingly powerful ability to control small bits of creation, will humans act with wisdom?"

# The Basics

## Protein and Gene

A quick reading of the nutrition label on packaged foods identifies most food to be made up of carbohydrates, fats, and proteins. Humans are indeed what they eat. Carbohydrates have few functions besides being the primary source of energy for the body. Fats are primarily the body's way of storing excess energy. Proteins are the most fascinating components of the body because of their diversity and range of tasks.

There are many types of proteins. Some are structural proteins. Collagen is a protein that gives elastic strength to cartilage and ligaments. Some proteins are enzymes. Factor VIII is an enzyme important for blood clotting. Some proteins have specialized functions. Hemoglobin is the red colored protein in blood that carries oxygen. Each hemoglobin molecule, tremendously complex and made up of thousands of atoms, is designed to carry a mere eight oxygen atoms from the lungs to the rest of the body. Another complex, specialized class of protein is immunoglobulin, also known as antibodies, which protects the body from disease. Nonscientists need not understand all these scientifically named things, but should understand that the diversity of protein plays a critical role in allowing cellular life to exist and evolve.

Chemically, proteins are chains of amino acids, linked together like beads of a necklace. Human metabolism uses 20 different amino acids. Think of these as 20 different colors for the beads. The necklace may range from only a few beads long to several thousand. The order in which these colored beads are arranged, called the sequence, determines how the protein will function. A protein's sequence developed over eons of evolution. The sequence is determined by a blueprint or a recipe called a gene.

Evolutionary survival is enhanced by the ability to transmit useful genes to successive generations. A very complex system developed to accomplish this, but its function is similar to carpenters apprenticing their sons or mothers teaching their daughters how to cook, with each generation passing on the family's secret recipes. The recipes are constantly being improved by trial and error. These trials are called mutations. Too many mutations produce too many deaths in the short run. But developing new protein recipes through these mutations enhances long-term survival. Even more beneficial is sharing recipes with others of the same species. That occurs during sexual reproduction. Both the male and the female give a copy of the recipes, or genes, to their offspring. Two gametes, a sperm and an egg, each containing a copy of recipes from different people, combine to produce offspring with two nonidentical copies of the genes. The birds also do this. The bees do this for the flowers. Even lowly bacteria have a method for exchanging genetic information, and bacteria are very promiscuous.

## Encoding the Genetic Information

The recipes for proteins are passed from cell to cell written in the chemical called deoxyribose nucleic acid (DNA). Within most cells is a nucleus. Inside the nucleus are chromosomes. Chromosomes are long strands of DNA that look like a rope ladder that has been twisted. This twisted ladder then coils, much like a telephone cord, with special proteins to enable the coiling. These coils then coil on themselves, like a telephone cord that has been twisted into knots. In this coiled up form these chromosomes, made up of DNA, store the protein recipes called genes. When the time is right, the chromosomes uncoil and the rungs of the ladder are again visible to the apparatus of the cell that makes protein. Each rung of the DNA ladder is one letter in the recipe.

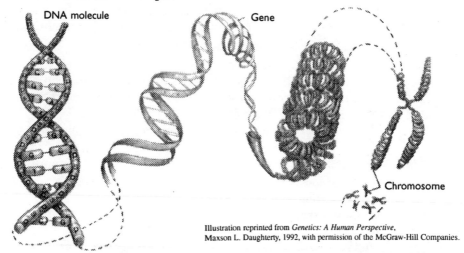

Illustration reprinted from *Genetics: A Human Perspective*, Maxson L. Daughterty, 1992, with permission of the McGraw-Hill Companies.

The language for these protein recipes is a special code. Think of it this way. There are only four letters in the alphabet, C, G, A, and T. All words are exactly three letters long, so there is no need for spaces between words. Each three-letter word (called a *codon*) corresponds to one of the 20 amino acids, or 20 colored beads in the necklace, that makeup a protein. Each protein recipe, or gene, is like a sentence. Some sentences are only a few words long. Many are thousands of words long.

Viruses, like the common cold or HIV (human immunodeficiency virus), are very simple germs. They contain just a single paragraph worth of DNA, as few as three sentences long. A virus is simply a strand of DNA encapsulated in a protein to carry it from cell to cell. The virus even contains the recipe for that encapsulation protein.

Larger germs, like the *E. coli* bacteria, contain many more recipes. These recipes are collected in a cookbook called a chromosome. *E. coli* has only one cookbook that is over 4 million letters long containing over 3,000 recipes. In animals, there are two copies of most chromosomes in each cell. Human beings have an estimated 70,000 useful genes or recipes, collected in 46 chromosomes or cookbooks. These 70,000 proteins allow humans to function at a much more complex level than that of viruses or bacteria. Altogether, these human chromosomes contain three billion letters. (Each letter corresponds to a "base pair," but nonscientists need not master this complexity.) The information contained in this encyclopedia of 46 cookbooks is called the genome. The Human Genome Project, a 15 year, three billion dollar research project, seeks to determine a typical sequence for those three billion letters. Most pages of those cookbooks, perhaps 90 percent, contain gibberish (the scientific term is nonsense) left over from evolution. The useful recipes are scattered among this nonsense and are not easy to identify.

The 46 chromosomes of the human genome are numbered by their size, #1 being the largest and #22 the smallest. There are two copies of each of these first 22 cookbooks. These duplicate copies of chromosomes have a special name, called *autosomes*. Forty-four of the 46 chromosomes are autosomes. The remaining two cookbooks are special sex chromosomes given labels X and Y rather than being numbered. If both sex chromosomes in a particular human being are the large cookbooks, labeled X, the body is female. If there is one copy of the X chromosome and one of a smaller version labeled Y, the body is usually male.

At the right time in the reproduction of cells, chromosomes can be seen with a microscope. A photograph of the chromosomes can be taken, and the chromosomes can be counted and arranged in order. This is called a *karyotype*. Karyotypes do not look at single genes, but at whole chromosomes. The technology of identifying, locating, and sequencing individual genes is exceedingly complex. Fortunately, those details are not critical to understanding the implications of the new technology.

## Male or female?

If you have a Y chromosome, but the genes do not function properly, are you male? Consider the plight of a person with the syndrome of *gonadal dysgenesis* due to androgen insensitivity. In this person, the body has a gene for making testosterone, the main male hormone, but it lacks a good copy of the gene to make the hormone receptor that allows the testosterone to work. The result is a person who has testicles, but they never develop properly. No penis is formed. The external genitals are by default female in appearance. There is a short vagina but no womb, so the person is infertile.

The body is tall, statuesque, female-shaped with large breasts and clear, acne-free ▶

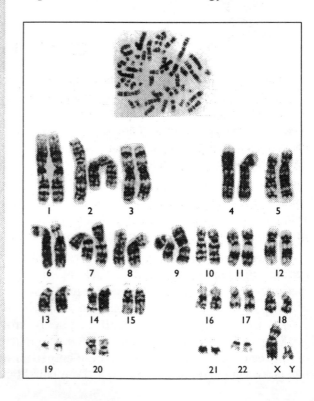

## Transmitting the Genetic Information through Reproduction

Once encoded in DNA, the recipes must be passed on to the next generation. Human sexual reproduction combines one copy of each of the 22 autosomes (cookbooks) and one sex chromosome from each parent, producing a child with 46 chromosomes, half from each parent. Much of the personal and moral complexity of genetic testing and screening arises because the natural process of transmitting genetic information, the protein recipes, from generation to generation is fraught with errors. The biological details of these errors are explained below. The next chapter contains more examples from the paradigm of a genetic counselor assisting people who are struggling to cope with the results of these errors.

# Genetic Errors

Just about anything imaginable can and does go wrong in transmitting the genetic information. Using the encyclopedic cookbook analogy, whole volumes of the cookbook may be missing. Cookbooks get collated incorrectly or incompletely. Pages get put in upside down. Recipes are missing ingredients. Letters get deleted and words get misspelled. Nature is an excellent typist, but the genome is 100,000 times longer than this chapter. Mistakes happen, many of them lethal. In fact, it is estimated that 60 to 80 percent of all human conceptions die before birth, most within the first two weeks after conception, largely due to genetic errors. This phenomenon is called *fetal wastage*. The survivors grow up to be humans with many health problems related to their genes.

## Chromosome Errors

We can think of these errors in several categories, the first at the level of the chromosome.

### Whole Chromosomes

There may be extra or missing copies of whole chromosomes. It is not the chromosome

skin. In short, on the outside, this person may be indistinguishable from a Playboy centerfold. Is this person a male or a female? It is not so simple. In sports, this person, who has been raised a girl by unsuspecting parents, may not be allowed to compete on women's teams because of the chromosomes. Most such women are diagnosed at puberty because they do not menstruate. Pastoral care may be critical at this point to help the person understand "her" sexual identity at a critical time in adolescence. But what happens if the woman is already married, age 20, and now because she cannot bear children she sees a doctor who discovers this genetic problem? The doctor must explain to her that she has internal testes, not ovaries. She can never bear children. She must have surgery to remove the dysgenic testes that often develop cancer. But what happens to the marriage?

According to Genesis 2, God created both male and female. This passage has been cited as justification for various gender roles and in condemnation of homosexual behavior. But science indicates God did not create just male and female. There are a few other variations. This alters the paradigm, like the earth revolving around sun and not visa versa. When scientific revelations conflict with dogma, religion must respond. For instance, can religion define what it means to be male or female? ■

that causes the problem but all the genes on that chromosome. Most errors this large are lethal and result in spontaneous pregnancy loss. There are a few exceptions, mostly involving the sex chromosomes. Having only a single copy (called monosomy) of the X chromosome produces a woman with Turner Syndrome. She is typically less than five feet tall and may have other physical anomalies, such as a broad chest, webbed neck, and angled elbows, which hint at the diagnosis even without genetic testing. She may have normal intelligence. She cannot bear children. Generally speaking, though, embryos missing any other chromosome do not survive until birth. Extra chromosomes (called trisomy) are also usually incompatible with live birth. Exceptions are trisomy 13, 18, 21 and extra sex chromosomes X and Y. Most fetuses with trisomy 13 and 18 miscarry, but a small fraction survive to birth and some have been known to live a few months. They have many physical problems and profound mental retardation. The typical child with trisomy 21, also known as Down's Syndrome, is characterized by slanting eyes, a large tongue, and mild to profound mental retardation. This child also has a high risk (about 50 percent) of severe congenital heart malformations. Extra sex chromosomes, like XXX or XYY Syndromes, usually cause relatively minor problems.

### Partial Chromosome/Translocations

Sometimes a section of one chromosome is lost. A syndrome called *cri du chat* is characterized by an infant with a weak, kitten-like cry and developmental delay caused by missing a small segment of chromosome 5. Sometimes sections of two chromosomes get switched. For instance, chromosomes 3 and 14 can get entangled during reproduction, and as they separate the tip of one chromosome 3 gets spliced onto the tip of 14 and vice versa. This is called a translocation. Using the cookbook analogy, imagine that the last 50 pages of cookbook 3 are removed and placed at the front of cookbook 14. They are replaced with the first 100 pages removed from cookbook 14. In most cases, this will not harm that particular child, since it is a balanced translocation. There are the correct number of copies of each recipe (except perhaps the recipe right at the splice) though they are in different cookbooks. However, when that person, say a father, has a child, say a daughter, random chance will control whether he gives her a correct set of recipes. Recall that humans carry two copies of chromosomes 1 through 22. Only one copy of 3 and 14 will be in error. Children by chance inherit a single copy of each chromosome from each parent. The girl may inherit the correct copies of father's chromosomes 3 and 14.

Or she may inherit both translocated chromosomes, resulting in a normal growth for her but problems for her future fertility. Or she might, for instance, get a correct copy of chromosome 14 plus a translocated chromosome 3, which is missing 50 pages of recipes belonging to chromosome 3 and has an extra copy of the first 100 pages normally on chromosome 14. This partial monosomy/partial trisomy will likely cause her to have birth defects, if she survives to birth at all.

## Single Gene Errors

In many diseases, a single error in a single gene coding for a single protein is known to be the cause of disease. Single gene errors come in many forms. Common types of single gene mutations include point mutations (a "genetic misspelling"), deletions, and repeated copies. Two concepts help understand these mutations.

### Genes and Alleles

The first concept is the difference between a *gene* and an *allele*. (Note—this book tries to use the terms allele and gene properly, but mass media frequently use gene when they mean allele.) For example, using the cookbook analogy again, within most cookbooks is a recipe (a gene) for chocolate chip cookies. However, this recipe may have variations. Each specific variation is an allele. So while most of my relatives share what we call Aunt Patra's chocolate chip cookie recipe, my neighbors' family and their relatives use a different recipe they associate with their great grandmother Isobel. These are both recipes (genes) for chocolate chip cookies, but there are the Patra allele and the Isobel allele. Alleles tend to be named after people or places where they were discovered, or by technical nomenclature like the delF508.

Nature is constantly evolving new recipes by mutating the genetic sequence. Analogously, recipes are often modified—just add a little more flour or substitute margarine for butter. Sometimes the new recipe is a flop. Imagine substituting salt for sugar in the recipe—the cookie would be uneatable. That recipe variation (that allele) would be judged as causing disease. Sometimes, these modifications just produce variability—there are as many different recipes (alleles) for chocolate chip cookies as there are different eye colors. It is not always clear whether a genetic variation represents disease or just diversity. This is a value judgment, not a purely scientific one. I prefer soft chocolate chip cookies, but others might prefer crisp or chewy ones. Similarly, an allele of a "growth factor gene" that affects a person's height or weight may or may not be considered a disease. Sometimes mutations produce entirely new cookies— imagine substituting raisins for the chocolate chips. Evolution progresses via this type of mutation.

### Dominant and Recessive

The second concept to master involves *dominant* vs. *recessive* genes. Recall that there are two copies of chromosomes 1 through 22 in each cell nucleus. Therefore there are two copies of each gene on those chromosomes. Each copy of a gene is called an allele. In some cases, one bad allele is enough to cause trouble despite the presence of one correct allele. If so, the trait carried by that gene is called dominant. In other situations, one good copy and one erroneous copy of a gene do not cause disease. The one good allele works well enough. In this case, the gene and its consequent condition, trait, or disease are termed recessive. For recessive conditions, the disease is seen only if both alleles are erroneous. The presence of one good and one bad allele is called a carrier state.

All humans, among their 70,000 genes, carry 10-15 lethal recessive alleles that are hidden by the good copy. We are all carriers of these lethal diseases. It is not plausible to purify the entire human race of recessive genetic diseases through any eugenics program of genetic screening. These recessive genes cause no problems unless we are unlucky enough to parent a child with someone else carrying a lethal allele of the same gene. Incest and inbreeding are more likely to produce a match of two recessive alleles.

### Examples

The following are representative examples of single gene mutations. They illustrate how genes may have different alleles and how diseases can be either dominant or recessive.

**Deletion.** Cystic fibrosis is a recessive disease caused by improper production of a protein that regulates the movement of chloride ions through cell membranes. This defect causes mucus in the body to be very glue-like, producing lung infections and digestive problems. The most common genetic error is an allele called delF508. The 508th word in the recipe is missing. As a result, the protein is missing a single amino acid, called phenylalanine or labeled "F" for short. From a necklace 1,480 beads long, a single bead is missing. But this tiny change alters the structure of the protein, which prevents it from functioning properly. It is the failure to make the correct protein that leads to the disease. Scientists have sequenced this gene. This means they know the exact order of the necklace. They also know that genetic errors anywhere in the long sequence for this protein can and do cause the disease cystic fibrosis. The delF508 allele is present in three fourths of all children with cystic fibrosis. But one fourth of cases are caused by other mutations (alleles). This complicates genetic testing and counseling. As a fine point of vocabulary, note that there is really no "cystic fibrosis gene." There is a gene for a particular cell membrane protein. If both alleles (the particular copies of that gene in an individual) are erroneous, the person has a disease called cystic fibrosis. However, media often uses the term "cystic fibrosis gene" as shorthand.

**Single Point Mutations.** Even misspelling a single letter in a single word can produce disease. In sickle cell disease, the allele of a gene that codes for hemoglobin—the red, oxygen carrying protein in the blood—has the middle letter of the sixth word of the recipe (the middle base pair of the sixth codon of the gene) mutated. A different amino acid is therefore inserted into the protein as it is made. This mutation changes the solubility of the hemoglobin. This leads to disease symptoms, such as severe joint pain, shortness of breath, increased infection, and anemia.

**Trinulceotide Repeat Sequences.** Some chromosomes have areas where the same sequence of three base pairs (letters, like CGG) repeats itself many times, as many as 10 to 100 times. Fragile X syndrome, a common form of mental retardation, is caused by an overlong repeat sequence at the tip of the X chromosome.

## Multifactorial Syndromes

Many syndromes and diseases are caused by more than one gene. News media often report the discovery of a gene that causes a common problem, like alcoholism or Alzheimer's disease. However, these diseases are caused by many factors, some genetic, some not. For instance, a gene identified as causing early onset Alzheimer's disease accounts for only a small fraction of all Alzheimer's cases.

# Why Do Scientists Study Genetics?

All this technical information points out that genes are both a fundamental source of our complex existence and a source of much suffering. Alleviating this suffering motivates many of the researchers in the field of genetics and medicine.

bad allele and the same for mom's allele. There is, therefore, a 25% chance of the child inheriting the disease, a 50% chance of the child inheriting one good allele and one bad allele (producing a healthy carrier of the disease, like both parents), and a 25% chance of inheriting neither disease-causing allele. These are random chances. It is certainly possible to have an unlucky family with three children, all of whom suffer from the disease. ■

### To test or not to test?

Huntington disease is caused by an increase in the size of trinucleotide repeats on chromosome 4. The disease is autosomal dominant, which means that if even one copy of the prolonged genetic sequence is inherited, the person will eventually express symptoms. The symptoms are loss of coordination, then uncontrolled, involuntary body movements, and progressively worsening dementia. The age of onset, whether at 30, 40 or 50 years, seems to be partly related to how many extra repeats are present. The person is otherwise unaffected until that age. She has usually seen relatives or one of her own parents ▶

deteriorate and die from the disease. She may have children of her own by then. Even before the gene was sequenced, the inheritance pattern was recognized. Each child had a 50:50 chance of inheriting the disease-causing allele from his parent.

If at age 21 you knew you had a 50:50 chance of having this gene, which would then ultimately debilitate and kill you, would you want to be tested to know for sure? The test is now available. Some people choose to have it done, others choose not to. It is a personal choice. Many medical ethicists and geneticists will not let parents test their children, so that the child can make the decision about testing himself as an adult. As with many genetic tests, if one member of a family decides to get tested, the results may reveal the status of other family members. Pastoral counseling may help people cope with these results. ■

Genetic research is not done by mad scientists like Dr. Frankenstein. The desire of most researchers is to provide better care and comfort for the sick. There are numerous other motivations for scientists. Some scientists seek to always advance technology "because we can" in the name of progress. In government funding of scientific research, this motivation frequently dominates. Others are motivated by scientific curiosity, or "because it's there." Profit is a key motivation (see John Varian's chapter in this book). Others are motivated by the sense of being created co-creators with God (see Hefner, p. 77). Others look for power or control. Still, most researchers of genetic technology, as in most medical technologies, are motivated by a desire to help people. Genetic conditions cause a lot of suffering. A scientific response to suffering is to increase knowledge so that we can control and manipulate the world. To scientists, genetic technology is a means to achieve control that might alleviate suffering. However, even when created with altruistic intentions, technology can produce bad results. The eugenics movement of the early twentieth century is an example of this (see Peters, p. 116).

## History of Gene Selection and Manipulation

Genetic testing and screening takes place in the context of human endeavors to control the world around them. History provides perspective on this context. While genetic technology has great import for human medicine, the greatest impact of genetic engineering may be in agriculture, which manipulates the genes of plants and animals. Recall that the primary goal is to control the transfer of genes to offspring. This can be done in three ways: by controlling mating, by selective harvesting or destruction of the offspring, or by more directly manipulating the gene at the level of the cell, chromosome, or gene itself.

The earliest recorded human manipulation of genes is in the Bible. In Genesis 30, Jacob names as his wages all the striped and speckled sheep and goats as well as all the black lambs. Laban, as he had previously done, attempts to cheat Jacob by first culling the flock of such animals, leaving only the solid colored animals. Jacob purposely bred the stronger animals with each other for himself and the feebler ones for Laban (verses 41-42). Furthermore, Jacob prospered from the birth of speckled animals. A reason for this is given in verses 37-39. But Jacob was an intelligent man cunning enough to outwit Esau and Isaac for a birthright and a blessing. He was a shepherd with many years of experience. It is interesting to conjecture that he may have also recognized how to crossbreed sheep for speckles, a recessive genetic trait.

## Animals

Control over genes in animal husbandry has previously been achieved through selective mating. The thoroughbred racehorse industry is based on mating the fastest studs and mares. Dairy farms may have hundreds of cows but only one bull. Today, for safety reasons, the bull is often kept elsewhere and the prize cows are artificially inseminated. Cross-species mating has also been practiced. Horses and donkeys are mated to produce mules, whose traits of temperament, load carrying capacity, and endurance are more suited to certain domestic tasks. However, the mules are sterile. Certain laboratory mice have been exhaustively inbred to produce litters with almost identical genes. These hairless mice are important for medical research. Genetic engineering now extends this control of mating from the level of a set of chromosomes to the level of a single trait. For instance, a rat growth gene has been transferred into a mouse, making a much larger laboratory mouse.

## Plants

Since the beginning of agriculture, smart farmers have chosen seeds from the best plants of the harvest to plant the following spring. Grafting vines, mentioned in the Bible (Romans 11:16-24), yields grapes or olives with genetic traits of the graft, not of the vine root. By carefully controlling cross-pollination in pea plants, Gregor Mendel discovered the basic principles of genetics. Luther Burbank advanced this practice of botany, developing many new strains of plants. For many years, most seed corn grown in the United States has been specially hybrid for superior yields and drought resistance. Now gene-splicing technologies offer new methods to improve agriculture. Soybeans are available for large scale farming in 1998 with a gene giving them increased resistance to herbicide.

Recall that sexual reproduction diversifies and improves the gene pool. One of the risks of reducing diversity is catastrophic crop failure. But this risk is not specific to genetically engineered crops. In the 1970s, a large portion of the Florida corn crop was lost due to a blight that struck the commonly used hybrid. The great Irish potato famine of the 1840s was due to a blight that wiped out half of the country's crop for five years. All Irish potatoes may have descended from a single plant that Christopher Columbus brought back from the New World. The entire crop was therefore sensitive to the same blight. Loss of genetic diversity is a potential risk of any program of genetic screening. While these events have already happened in plants, the risk applies to human eugenics as well.

New technology can also decrease risk. Gene banks can be used to store plant strains that will otherwise disappear. This practice creates a social justice issue. An enterprising company can cheaply purchase a few pounds each of hundreds of strains of potatoes growing in South America. The farmers previously producing these strains may be induced to plant a common strain that grows more productively. If or when this common strain becomes unusable due to blight or changing environment, the company could test its bank of strains for a suitable replacement. Those few pounds of potatoes could be worth a fortune to the company, but not to the farmers who originally developed them. New technologies often have great impact, positive and negative, on the distribution of wealth, power, and social justice. Later chapters in this book address concerns about similar effects from genetic technology applied to humans.

## Human

Historically, the choice of mates in humans has also been subject to selective pressures. Marriages have been and continue to be arranged for a variety of reasons, including power, royalty, and wealth. Marrying outside of one's religion is addressed in the Bible. Taboos banning marriages between races or between royalty and commoners predate modern eugenics. Even in societies where marriages are not arranged, many social customs facilitate people meeting other people with similar values and traits. Technology extends this idea. For example, there is a sperm bank from Nobel Prize winners.

Selection of children after conception has also gone on from distant times and the issue is not inherent to genetics. Infanticide is a frequent theme in Greek myths. Abortion based on sex is common practice in a few countries, notably China where it currently plays a role in ten percent of pregnancies. An ultrasound examination of fetal anatomy—not expensive genetic screening—is the usual method of determining sex. Genetic testing and screening expands the role of prenatal diagnosis as discussed in more detail later in this and other chapters.

In some ways, modern genetics is not a new kind of technology but simply an extension of previous animal husbandry motivations and methods. Consider an analogy with the technology of warfare. Conventional bombs can level a city as effectively as nuclear weapons. Bombs have killed far more people than nuclear weapons. The starvation and poverty created by occupying armies have killed far more than the actual combat. Are nuclear weapons truly a different kind of killing technology or is it just a matter of degree? Is genetic testing and screening any different than breeding based on observable traits such as ethnicity or skin color?

# Potential Misunderstandings of Genetic Information

The history of genetic manipulation shows how technology can increase humankind's power to control the world. Depending on one's goals, this increased power may increase either good or evil. Even with laudable goals, harm may also come from people who misunderstand how genetics truly affects health and behavior. The following are some examples of how this may occur.

## Variability

Genes control many characteristics of a person, but this control is not absolute. It varies based on other factors, such as interactions with other genes, the environment, and sometimes random chance. Consider hair color. Basic biology textbooks usually divide hair color into dark and blond. Blond hair is a recessive trait. If a person inherits one or two dark alleles, he has dark hair. If he inherits no dark alleles, his hair is blond. But the degree of darkness of dark hair is controlled by other genes, so the color may range from brown to black. Blond hair also has various shades. These characteristics, or traits, are observable expressions of the gene's function. Sometimes the expression cannot be observed. If the man also inherits alleles causing albinism, he cannot make pigment and will have white hair regardless of whether he inherits dark or blond alleles. Geneticists use the term "penetrance" to refer to the frequency, or percentage of all cases, that a given gene actually manifests its trait. People with the same gene sequence are said to have the same genotype, while those who have the same observable trait are said to have the same phenotype. Another term, "expressivity," quantifies the degree to which the gene shows itself or the severity of the disease. One does not have to master this scientific vocabulary to understand the idea that there is not a one-to-one correspondence between genes and outcome. While this variability in expression is easily seen by the hair color example, it is true for most other gene expressions.

## Determinism

Genetics should not be used to avoid responsibility for behavior. A common excuse for sin could become, "It's not my fault, the obesity (or alcoholism, depression, or criminal tendencies due to excessive aggression) is in my genes." Our genome is not a deterministic system. Genetic tendencies do not equal predestination. Identical twins have identical DNA but don't act the same. For instance, some types of schizophrenia are inherited. But when one twin has schizophrenia only half of the other twins show the disease. A person's future is still subject to environmental influences, random events and other factors. As another example, inheriting an allele associated with breast cancer like BRCA1 increases a woman's lifetime odds for developing breast cancer from about 9 percent (the background rate) to 40-80 percent. Certainly a much higher risk, but not a death sentence. However, this increased risk may be important to insurers. Genetic information could be used to discriminate against people by denying them health care coverage, rather than empowering them to make better decisions regarding their health. Laws are being created to help prevent this (see Varian, p. 62, and Peters, p. 120). Perhaps more important than this is how the person with genetic "defects" is perceived and treated by society.

## Value Judgments

While scientific terms may describe observable variations due to gene expression, they do not truly define what is an abnormal or a disease state rather than just normal variation. Those are value judgments that involve more than scientific input. Genes controlling things like hair, eye, and skin color are commonly labeled normal variants representing genetic diversity. Other gene expressions cause such suffering and premature death that they are labeled diseases. Sometimes this label is subject to interpretation. Many members of deaf communities view their lifestyle as a variant rather than a handicap. Some deaf couples, seeking to bear a deaf child, desire prenatal testing to determine if their potential child will inherit deafness. Couples where both parents have inheritable forms of dwarfism have done the same (see Schwandt, p. 45).

Researchers are also searching for a gene that "causes" homosexuality. One research report suggested such a gene might be approximately located in a certain area on the X chromosome, though a specific gene or location has not yet been found. It is not known if homosexual tendencies are influenced by a single gene or many. It remains unclear how much environment influences expression of the gene. Even if located, the presence of a gene will not necessarily answer moral questions. Whether a gene's expression is considered a normal variant or a disease state is a value judgment supplemental to the scientific identification and sequencing of the gene.

## Toxic Knowledge

Genetic technology is a two edged sword. While offering new options, it also requires new, difficult choices to be made that people previously did not face. Scientists, who tend to be more interested in acquiring knowledge than the general population, are developing new tests to gather more information that create new informed choices. This is most clearly seen in prenatal diagnosis. Several chapters in Section Two address the social impact of these new choices while various chapters throughout this book consider aspects of the personal crises they create.

# Prenatal Diagnosis

An increasing amount of information is being gathered about the fetus before birth. Not all of this information involves genes. Prenatal ultrasounds can locate many anatomic birth defects, like holes in the heart or blocked kidneys. Any abnormality may trigger further testing, like amniocentesis. New technology confronts prospective parents with new choices.

## Screening

Pregnant women undergo many screening blood tests during pregnancy. The term "screening" means that all pregnant women have the lab work performed even if they have no symptoms. This differs from genetic testing, which means that there are specific indications for the testing of that particular woman. One screening blood test is the triple screen, which measures the level of three chemicals in the pregnant woman's blood. They are alpha fetoprotein (AFP), human chorionic gonadotropin, and estriol. These levels may indicate an increased risk for the presence of birth defects in the fetus. Some of these birth defects are not genetic, so the issues raised transcend genetics, but genetics has markedly increased the number of tests available. The triple screen often leads women into more genetic tests.

For instance, the AFP level is high in cases where the fetus has a neural tube defect, either spina bifida or a meningocele. Spina bifida means the lower end of the spinal cord did not form normally. In some cases the defect is very mild, perhaps causing a mild limp and bedwetting. In severe cases, the legs are paralyzed. Intelligence is normal, though minor brain surgery may be necessary to install a shunt to prevent hydrocephalus (excess water in the brain.) Defects at the upper end of the spinal cord are meningoceles. Again, mild cases may require surgery but otherwise produce near normal intelligence and functioning. In severe cases, such as anencephaly, most of the brain is missing. Most children with anencephaly, if not miscarried or aborted, die shortly after birth because the brainstem cannot even control breathing and heart rate. The severity of neural tube defects can be estimated by ultrasound. They are common birth defects, occurring in about one or two out of 1,000 births. If a woman has had a prior child with a neural tube defect, the risk increases to about 30 out of a 1,000. This suggests that a yet unidentified gene increases the risk. However environment and random chance must be playing a role in the defect, since 97 percent of subsequent children are born normal. Eating enough folate before becoming pregnant, either in a vitamin or in a diet rich in green vegetables, also significantly lowers the risk.

One problem with the AFP screen is that it is inaccurate (the technical term is nonspecific.) It is very sensitive, detecting almost all cases of neural tube defects. However, out of 1,000 women who take the screening test, the screen will identify 50 women requiring further testing, though only one will actually have a problem. The other 49 had false positives. The only way to determine who has the real problem is to do more tests, usually an amniocentesis and a high-resolution ultrasound.

The triple screen also identifies fetuses at increased risk for having a chromosomal problem, such as Down's Syndrome. Down's Syndrome is caused by trisomy 21, the presence of a third copy chromosome 21, usually by itself though sometimes a portion of chromosome 21 is attached to another through translocation. Down's Syndrome occurs in one out of 2000 births in teenagers. The risk increases with maternal age, reaching over one out of 10 births to women in their mid-forties. Based on maternal age and the results of the triple screen, these odds can be better estimated. Women can then choose, if they consider the risk high enough, to have another test when they are four to five months pregnant to determine if Down's Syndrome (trisomy 21) is present in the fetus. This test is an amniocentesis. The results are very accurate at identifying the genetic defect. However the test cannot identify whether the future child will have mild, moderate, severe, or profound mental retardation. Harder still is helping the parent(s) decide what to do with this information. Here the medical science crosses into the moral value realm of religion. Most but not all women do decide to abort. Twenty years ago, women did not have to face such a choice, nor did they have the opportunity to do so. This is the double-edged sword of technology.

## Genetic Testing

Prenatal genetic diagnosis consists primarily of three steps. The first step is obtaining a sample of the DNA of the fetus. The second is using some technique to identify the presence or absence of some gene or genes. Finally, a value judgment must be made based on the acquired information.

### Sample Acquisition

The most common method for obtaining fetal DNA is through amniocentesis. A long, thin needle is inserted under ultrasound guidance through the mother's abdomen into the womb and into the sac of fluid that the fetus floats in. This fluid contains fetal cells with DNA. The procedure is relatively painless, involving a needle poke and maybe some cramping for the mother. For technical reasons, amniocentesis is typically done only after 15 weeks gestation and some lab tests take up to two weeks to perform. There is a risk of causing miscarriage, about five times per 1,000 procedures. Two further disadvantages of this technique are that the woman will already be showing her pregnancy and any abortion will be a more complex second trimester abortion.

Another technique for gathering fetal DNA is called chorionic villous sampling. Done when the woman is about 10-12 weeks pregnant, a bit of what will become the placenta is suctioned off with a catheter. The risk of miscarriage is higher, ranging from 5 to 30 times per 1,000 procedures. Results are back in time for a first trimester abortion. This technique is more often recommended when the risk of genetic defect is 25 percent or more.

The latest technique is embryo biopsy or blastomere sampling, used in conjunction with in vitro fertilization. On the third day after the egg is fertilized, while still in the petri dish, the embryo is about 8 to 16 cells in size. One of these cells can be removed and the embryo will still grow normally. The baby will not be missing an arm or leg. This one cell can be tested to determine if the embryo in the petri dish should be implanted in the mother or discarded. The technique is limited to those genetic tests which can be performed on a single cell sample and have results available within 24 hours.

A potential future sampling method is obtaining fetal blood cells directly from maternal blood. The placenta, which forms a barrier between the maternal and fetal circulatory systems, has occasional leaks whereby small amounts of fetal blood mix into the maternal circulation. The fetal cells can be obtained risk free along with the many other blood tests pregnant women get. First performed 15 years ago, the technique remains unperfected.

### Testing

Once a sample of DNA is obtained, by any of the above methods, it must be tested for the presence or absence of a genetic condition. Many techniques are available. Sometimes the cells are cultured, and chromosomes in dividing cells can be examined and counted under a microscope. This is called a karyotype. Only missing or extra chromosomes or large fractions of them can be detected. Down's Syndrome is identified by counting three copies of chromosome 21 per cell. The sex of the child will become known from the karyotype, though the parents can choose not to be told the result. Ultrasound is a much simpler method than karyotypes for determining the sex of the fetus.

Individual genes cannot be seen with a microscope, so special probes are needed to identify them chemically. Exact copies of some genes are available and exist as vials containing purified DNA sequences. This is called a gene clone (not to be confused with a clone of a total organism). Gene clones can be labeled with radioactive or fluorescent markers and used to identify the presence or absence of a corresponding gene. There are many variations of this methodology.

For many diseases, the gene has not yet been isolated or cloned yet its existence has been shown and its approximate location in the genome mapped onto a particular area of a particular chromosome. There are complex technologies that use methods like restriction fragment length polymorphism (RFLP) to test several family members as well as the fetus. The RFLP analysis combines knowledge of the approximate location of the gene of interest with knowledge of who in a given family does and does not carry the disease. The RFLP analysis computes the risk, usually 90 to 99 percent accurate, that the fetus has the disease-causing allele. This technique only works if enough family members are available and willing to donate blood for the test. The analysis may reveal undesired information. It may identify family members who are carriers of the disease. It may identify nonpaternity, situations where the mother's husband is not the biological father of the baby.

## Value Judgments

Science can identify genetic variations. Labeling those variations as defects is a value judgment. These values involve defining what it means to be human, defining what is a worthwhile quality of life, and clarifying the sort of life the woman chooses to create for herself and her children. For thousands of years religion has sought to provide a basis for such values.

Prenatal diagnosis frequently generates information that is used to decide whether or not to have an abortion. Presently we are in a window of time where diagnostic tests are available but therapies are not. There is hope for such therapies though they may take years if not decades to develop. This situation creates moral dilemmas as some researchers spend their lives studying genetics with the hope and intent to cure disease but actually contribute primarily to prenatal testing and abortion. Their situation is perhaps analogous to atomic scientists who studied fusion with the intent of providing cheap, pollution free energy, but found their research primarily used to design more powerful bombs. If science is truly a vocation for Christians, the church must minister to scientists faced with dilemmas like this.

The church must also minister to the pregnant women who are having the tests. Once the genetic information is available, difficult decisions about the elective abortion of a fetus with birth defects must be made within a few days. Even if not aborted, there is a grief process involved as the parents accept that their child may not be what they hoped for.

The issues of prenatal diagnosis have been around for decades. Genetic screening and testing markedly increases the power of the prenatal diagnosis. Genetic testing in the near future may be able to identify many traits of the fetus, ranging from life threatening conditions to potential tendencies toward obesity to eye color and adult height. Science provides knowledge to create such technology. Theology must provide wisdom to use it morally.

# Current State of the Art

Genetic testing and screening are primarily done to diagnose disease. While prenatal diagnosis is a common use of the technology, some adult diseases are also diagnosed with genetic tests. Some genetic diseases are treatable with medicines and lifestyle changes. Curing genetic diseases is more difficult.

For example, women with only one X chromosome, which is called Turner Syndrome, are typically less than five feet tall. Experiments are in progress testing whether daily shots of extra human growth hormone during childhood can increase the adult height of women with Turner Syndrome. These trials are done with the expressed intent of treating disease, but some doctors and ethicists find only a blurred boundary between treating disease and eugenics, the attempt to improve human traits. If extra growth hormone is used for a child with a known genetic defect that causes short stature, should it also be available for children who have inherited genes (not yet identified) that cause everyone in a family to be short? Would that be treating a "disease" or eugenics? The moral issues intensify when the primary "treatment" of a disease identified prenatally through genetic testing and screening is abortion.

Gene therapy and cloning are beyond the scope of this book, but they do represent the next steps in the advancement of medical technology. Genetic testing and screening can only identify the disease. Gene therapy seeks to introduce new genes directly into living humans in order to cure disease (though it might also be used for eugenic purposes.) Over 100 research trials using gene therapy are underway in humans. There have been a few promising trials but no clear successes yet. Current human gene therapy trials have been somatic gene therapy: Genes are introduced into body cells but excluded from eggs and sperm. In germ-line gene therapy the genes would be passed onto grandchildren and future generations. This has been accomplished with laboratory animals for research purposes but it is not currently performed on humans.

Despite the lack of success so far in human gene therapy, gene manipulation already provides great benefits to medical care. Transferring whole chromosomes between cells has been possible since the 1970s. This technology allows creation of monoclonal antibodies, which are used in millions of diagnostic tests every year, from rapid strep throat tests to pregnancy tests to AIDS tests. Gene splicing has allowed the hepatitis B vaccine to be produced in vats of yeast culture rather than being obtained from human blood. This process made the vaccine safer and less expensive. Today, (since 1992) most newborns receive the vaccine before they leave the hospital. Gene splicing has also made human insulin available to diabetics, replacing the previously used pork and beef insulin, which were slightly different. Transferring whole cell nuclei, containing its entire genome, from one cell to another is possible. This process has been accomplished with the fetal cells of several animal species during the last few years. It has recently been achieved using the adult cells of "Dolly," the ewe in Scotland. All of these technologies are properly called cloning by scientists, though mass media tend to imply only the last named technology when they use the word clone.

Genetic manipulation has long been practiced at the level of mating and breeding whole organisms, plant or animal. As these examples show, genetic manipulation is now possible and operational at the cellular, chromosomal, and single gene levels, more so in agriculture than in humans.

# Conclusion

Many diseases are related to genetic conditions. These diseases cause much suffering. Despite the chaos of errors in reproduction and the lack of genetic determinism, people still seek to gain increased control over their lives. That is after all the primary utility of technology. Having created this technology with the compassionate goal of alleviating suffering, we cannot and should not try to put the genie back

## Seeking the Shephelah

During the reign of Saul in the Old Testament, the Israelites lived in secluded mountain villages. They were an agrarian and shepherd society. The Philistines were a technologically advanced society who lived on the seacoast, were seagoing merchants, and possessed metalworking technology that the Israelites lacked (1 Samuel 13:19-20). Between Israel and the gentile world were foothills called the Shephelah. God did not command the Israelites to remain isolated from other cultures. As a light to other nations, they interacted with them in these foothills. During a time of conflict, a Philistine warrior named Goliath, clothed in state of the art bronze ▶

armor and carrying bronze weapons, challenged the Israelite army (I Samuel 17:4-8). David responded to the challenge. Saul offered David his armor (a rare commodity in Israel) to wear, but David rejected that technology in favor of what he knew best, the staff and sling (I Samuel 17:38-40). David slew Goliath. Then within a generation all of Israel was manufacturing metal tools. Wisdom lies not in the technology itself, nor in its rejection, but within how the technology is used to the glory of God. That wisdom is found neither in cities on the hill nor in the sea level temples of technology. Wisdom is developed at the interface of science and faith, the modern Shephelah. ∎

in the bottle. As genetic technology revolutionizes medical care it becomes crucial to understand how the technology affects our relationships with others. How do we perceive someone who has a genetic "defect" when all people have some level of genetic defect? What do we think of parents who choose to bring "defective" children into the world rather than abort? How does actively choosing to do this differ morally from the much more frequently made passive choice of having children the parents cannot afford to raise?

From the viewpoint of genetic science, people are not born with equal health. Scientists are motivated by compassion to help others who are suffering from genetic diseases. These efforts increase social justice. The tradeoff is that genetic technology also increases power and places that power in fewer hands, which may decrease social justice. Science continues to increase knowledge. Religion must increase wisdom of how to use this knowledge. These two functions cannot operate independently, but must interact.

# PERSONAL STORIES:
# CASES FROM GENETIC COUNSELING

## Kirstin Finn Schwandt

*Steve and Mary were sitting in the waiting room of their doctor's office. Their wedding day was three weeks away, and they needed to have the obligatory blood tests performed. As Mary looked around, a pamphlet on a table across the waiting room caught her eye. Her interest was aroused by the title: "What you should know about your family history before having children." She and Steve had talked with their pastor in their premarital counseling session about what family and children meant to both of them. They both agreed they wanted to start a family about a year after they were settled in their recently purchased home. Mary opened the pamphlet and began to read. It contained a short list of questions about her family and medical history. She answered "no" to all but one on the list. The pamphlet explained that if you answered "yes" to any of the questions, it is suggested that you speak with your physician about it because he or she might recommend an appointment with a genetic counselor. Mary's mind drifted. She had never been concerned that her younger brother's mental retardation would put her own childbearing at risk. Could the problem with **his** chromosomes affect **her**?*

Medicine is being influenced and aided by genetic advancements in wonderful ways that can scarcely be imagined. However, this opening vignette suggests, as do the others that follow, the ambiguous impact of the new techniques of genetic testing and screening. People challenged with genetic-based health problems are real people, people who are often stunned, fearful, and marginalized by information revealing their genetic makeup. Usually they hear about their genetic problems for the first time from their physician. For most, genes and genetic risk factors do not seem real. When people are told that they have a genetic-based health problem, they may feel overcome by a sense of personal doom. Anger and fear only increase when they learn that DNA cannot be "fixed" or "replaced." They may question the value of knowing about a genetic risk factor. Why indeed should people be burdened with this genetic information when the foregoing generations have survived without it? Why, they may ask, do we use this technology when we cannot solve the genetic problems we can diagnose?

These concerns are valid. Physicians can test now for problems that currently cannot be cured. The first cures may not be available for several decades. However, the human struggles depicted in this chapter will show that genetic information can empower people to undertake life planning, to find support groups, and to live life fully.

This chapter also hopes to engender compassion and respect for those people making decisions based on genetic information. As a genetic counselor, it is my position that no one, particularly a physician or pastor, should impose personal values on those confronted with health care decisions, but rather should support, comfort, and encourage. Often professionals can unwittingly and subtly suggest their outcome preferences in the guise of advice. Many patients tend to accept the suggested outcome, instead of independently examining their beliefs, religious and otherwise. Everyone needs to come personally to a decision that is right for them and this struggle is initially tough. Most of us are unskilled and inexperienced in the complex decision-making based on new and complex medical information. In the end, however, few people remain uncertain or wavering. When medical professionals provide an ethically neutral decision-making environment and the information necessary to make it, most people can arrive at a satisfactory decision.

The stories in this chapter—composites of real situations—are intended to serve this book as a kind of primer. They are designed to encourage you to think about the ethical implications of genetic testing and screening and are intentionally left open ended.

Finally, in this chapter I hope to acquaint readers with the relatively new field of genetic counseling and the resources available through these medical professionals. People in genetic-based health crisis need a team approach, and a genetic counselor is an important member of that team. A genetic counselor is trained to translate confusing and potentially frightening genetic information into terms accessible to the patient, and to provide resources for support, decision-making, and coping.

## Reflecting with a Genetic Counselor

How much do you know about *your* family history? Some people know very little and others can recite the birth date and cause of death of all their relatives. The reasons for our lack of knowledge of ancestors' health problems are varied. Perhaps too many loved ones were lost to cancer, and it is just too emotionally difficult to ask more questions about their deaths. Or perhaps you are concerned about the personalities of your family members, not their ailments. Unless you are worried about something in your family history, you are not likely to know health details.

Is there a pattern of similar illnesses in your family that has caught your attention? Family history can be frightening for some. If your father had Alzheimer's disease at a young age, you may fear that the same fate will befall you. This thought can be so terrifying that you may try to push it out of your mind and not bother to speak to a physician about it. On the other hand, you might be the type of person who copes by gathering lots of information. For such people, it might be comforting to know about family medical history, especially if you know you can try to ameliorate symptoms. For example, if diabetes is prevalent in a family, lifestyle changes can help. Some people like to know everything, while others prefer ignorance.

However, sometimes people face a medical decision which requires them to learn something about their genes that they do not particularly want to know. Even if a patient does not seek out family risk factors, a health care provider may be the one to bring up the topic. If your health history reveals that your father died of a heart attack at age 40, your physician is likely to monitor you closely for signs of heart disease. Alternatively, for some diseases, your physician might now offer you a blood test to determine if your DNA suggests you are prone to develop them. While such genetic tests are currently rather limited, the number of available genetic tests will continue to grow. How will you decide if you want to know what possible "defective" genes you inherited from your parents and what new combination of DNA spells out your future? Even more difficult, do you want to know what genetic disorders may eventually face your unborn child?

These kinds of questions are becoming commonplace as primary care physicians keep abreast of daily genetic discoveries. In attempting to provide for your health care needs, they may refer you to a genetic counselor or an M.D. geneticist who is trained specifically to help you understand the value and implications of possible genetic testing. Because of genetic complexities, genetic counseling and education *should* be an integral part of all genetic testing and screening.[1] Guidance from these professionals is available for informed decision making.

The American Society of Human Genetics Ad Hoc Subcommittee on Genetic Counseling described genetic counseling as: "a communication process which deals with the human problems associated with the occurence, or risk of occurence, of a genetic disorder in a family. This process involves an attempt by one or more appropriately trained personas to help the individual or family to:

1. comprehend the medical facts, including the diagnosis, a probable course of the disorder, and the available management;

2. appreciate the way hereditary contributes to the disorder, and the risk of recurrence in specified relatives;

3. understand the alternatives for dealing with the risk of recurrence;

4. choose the course of action which seems to them appropriate in view of their risk, their family goals, and their ethical and religious standards, and to act in accordance with that decision; and

5. to make the best possible adjustment to the disorder in an affected family member and/or to the risk of recurrence of that disorder."

(Epstein et al., 1975) ∎

Genetic counselors try to help people to interpret and cope with these kinds of questions and with genetic information. They may explain to a couple the risks that their next child will have the same birth defect as their first child. They may also give test results to an individual indicating that he or she carries a gene for a serious, degenerative disorder. Genetic counselors do not tell people what decisions to make. For example, if the patient declines testing or chooses to terminate a pregnancy, it is his or her choice alone. The genetic counselor's code of ethics mandates this approach. If sorrowful or bad news enters the picture, some appointments may concern only the patient's feelings. If that is the case, the person or family may bring up how their religion fits into the picture. If the person draws strength from faith, I believe it should not be ignored, but explored. However, while genetic counselors receive some training in the area of emotional issues, their main role is as experts in *genetics*. When individuals are having emotional difficulties in accepting certain aspects of the information received from a genetic counselor, it is time to refer them to other professionals.

# Ten Cases About Genetic Testing and Screening

Genetic counselors and medical geneticists see many people struggle with genetic decision making each day. The following stories from the clinic will not only serve as a genetic primer, but will provide a glimpse of that struggle and the ethical challenges posed by genetic testing and screening. The conflicts faced by persons in these cases commonly occur. To encourage further reflection I will offer genetic information and personal thoughts after presenting each case. However, because the process of decision making is all-important, no resolution is offered. The questions raised do not necessarily have immediate answers. As these stories are discussed in subsequent chapters, the goal is to bring chaplains, pastors, congregations, people affected by genetic information, and people in the genetics community to a greater mutual understanding about genetic testing and screening. All helping professions must work together to support persons dealing with genetic health problems.

## 1. A Prenatal Screening Test for Birth Defects

The triple marker screen, although routine in most obstetricians' offices in this country, is often drawn without properly explaining the implications to pregnant women (see Powell, p. 30 for explanation). Because the intent is to identify pregnancies at higher risk for birth defects, this screening test is offered to all women regardless of family history. Emotional repercussions arise when a "screen positive" result is relayed to the patient, who may not have even understood what the screen was about.

*Some blood had been drawn during Sarah's regular visit to her doctor about a week ago when she was 16 weeks pregnant. Sarah was anxious about the results, but her obstetrician had told her not to worry. If the test showed an abnormality, she could learn more about it at that time. When her doctor called her that evening, she could tell by the tone of his voice that something was wrong.*

*"Sarah," he said, "the results of your triple test came back 'screen positive.' You might want to consider having amniocentesis performed."*

*Sarah did not hear much else that he said other than the fact that her baby might have Down's syndrome. She tried to explain it to her husband, Allen, but she realized that she really did not understand what the results meant. That night she cried a lot. Allen tried to comfort her, but both did not sleep much. The next morning Sarah called her obstetrician's office and asked to speak with her doctor so that he could explain the results to her in more detail. Later that morning a nurse returned her call with the message that Sarah should call the hospital to make an appointment at the prenatal diagnosis clinic.*

*Sarah called for an appointment and was told that she needed to see a genetic counselor. She was not familiar with genetic counseling, but she managed to get an appointment for that afternoon. Allen took off work so he could join her.*

Genetic counselors hold a master's degree and are certified by the American Board of Genetic Counseling and/or the American Board of Medical Genetics.

The National Board of Genetic Counselors Executive Office can provide referrals to genetic counselors with expertise in many areas:

- Cancer genetics
- Neurogenetics
- Psychiatric Genetic Disorders
- Prenatal Genetics
- New Reproductive Technologies
- Pediatric Genetic Disorders
- Birth Defects
...and more.

If help is needed locating your nearest genetic counselor, contact:

The National Society of Genetic Counselors Executive Office
233 Canterbury Drive
Wallingford, PA 19086-6617
(610) 872-7608 ∎

*At 3:00 p.m. they were introduced to Jill, the genetic counselor. Jill explained to them that the triple screen test had come back with a one in 16 risk that their baby might have Down's syndrome. The results did not mean that the baby with certainty had an extra chromosome number 21; it just meant there was an increased risk, and the only way to find out was to have amniocentesis.*

*As they talked with the genetic counselor, they realized that they, by having the triple screen test, were now confronted with possibly knowing before the birth of their baby that it had Down's syndrome. Sarah was not sure she wanted to know.*

*Allen, on the other hand, was wondering if the anxiety of not knowing whether the baby was normal would be too much to think about for another five months. Together they discussed with the genetic counselor whether or not they might think about termination if they found out the baby had trisomy 21. Sarah and Allen had never even thought about it. They were not sure what they would do. They did not even really know what children with Down's syndrome were like. Could they raise a child with mental retardation and other health problems?*

*Allen and Sarah were overwhelmed at the thought of having to make the decision to terminate a much-wanted pregnancy. Jill suggested they think about the amniocentesis more before making any decision. The genetic counselor explained the procedure step by step.*

*That evening the couple talked more about the triple screen test results, this time armed with enough information to make an educated decision. In the end they decided they would go through with the amniocentesis. When they had the chromosome results, then, and only then, would they be able to think about what they should do.*

*The amniocentesis was performed two days later. Allen and Sarah waited impatiently for the results of the chromosome studies. They tried to keep themselves busy, occasionally saying a prayer together. As far as this couple was concerned, life could not go on until they had the answer.*

*The genetic counselor called them early the next week. "I'm sorry I have to give you this news," said Jill. "I know you were hoping to be reassured by the results. The baby has an extra chromosome 21. This confirms Down's syndrome . . ."*

*Sarah was shocked, even more so than when she had received the results of the triple test. Jill suggested that she and her husband come for another appointment. Sarah agreed. She knew the information on Down's syndrome would be beneficial, but she also wondered how much she really wanted to hear it at this point.*

*The couple tried to think of others with whom they might be able to talk. They had little previous preparation for making this decision. What would Jesus tell them to do? They knew that this information could help them prepare for the birth of their baby with Down's syndrome; abortion did not necessarily follow a result like this. Would God be disappointed if they decided that termination was the best option for them? Perhaps they could look into adoption. Jill had told them that it would not be a problem for her to find a family who felt a calling to take care of severely developmentally disabled children. Sarah was already 18 weeks along in her pregnancy, so they had only a few weeks to make a decision.*

After an abnormality has been confirmed by amniocentesis following a screen-positive triple test, the decision making has only begun, and the questioning continues. Decision making must include not only the emotional and financial resources of the parents, but the effect this child will have on the whole family and the anticipated quality of life. Parents need support both before and after the decision is made, whatever the decision might be.

In my experience, most people also value spiritual guidance. Let me observe in this regard that one of the challenges for church people is where to find it. While one cannot turn directly to the Bible for answers, it can provide an entry into meditation and prayer. The Book of Psalms is a particularly rich resource. Martin Luther put it well when he wrote of the Book of Psalms, "Whether in joy, fear, hope, or sorrow, it teaches you to be equable in mind and calm in word."[2] Unfortunately, all too often people want immediate and easy solutions to problems and forget to take time for prayer and reading the Bible. In the familiar lines of Psalm 46, it is God who is our refuge and our strength, a very present help in trouble (Psalm 46:1-2).

## 2. Prenatal Diagnosis Based Upon Advanced Parental Age

Deciding whether or not to use prenatal testing and diagnosis is usually difficult for mothers over the age of 35. The reason is the risk of the testing itself. A woman more than 35 years old should not be forced to undergo one of these procedures. However, her physician might highly recommend it depending on her age risk, which increases gradually each year. While the chromosome results may be reassuring, couples may forget to look ahead to the possibility that a genetic disorder might be detected in their baby.

*The Richardsons got a late start on having children. They both wanted to establish their careers first, so they delayed things. Then, when the time was right, they found that getting pregnant was not easy, and they went though years of infertility treatments.*

*Finally, Jan, now 40, and David, 54, were going to have a baby. They were both very excited. Then, at their first doctor's appointment, their obstetrician mentioned to them that due to their age, they were at increased risk for having a baby with trisomy 21, 18, 13, an extra X, or a single gene disorder. Suddenly, their joy was overshadowed. Their doctor explained that they could use CVS or amniocentesis as a way to know prenatally about the maternal age risks. However, they were also told that no tests currently existed to check for paternal age risks.*

*The Richardsons almost wished that they did not know about the risks to the pregnancy. Jan felt they would have accepted whatever child God had given them. David partially agreed, but reminded Jan of his sister's experience:*

*"Do you remember that my sister had CVS because of her age and they discovered that the baby had Klinefelter's syndrome? It meant her son had an extra X chromosome instead of just an X and Y."*

*Jan replied, "I remember vaguely. But do you really think it was of value for her to know ahead of time?"*

*David's memory was coming back as they spoke. "I think it helped my sister. She was able to learn all about Klinefelter's syndrome. The genetic counselor who gave her the results even found a family that just had a baby with the same syndrome, so she found some other support. She never would have terminated the pregnancy, but she's the type of person who is empowered by knowledge."*

*"I guess," Jan said, "but I'm not sure what is the right decision for us. After all that we have been through trying to conceive a child, I'm just not sure."*

Many people are starting their families later—some because of careers, and others are just waiting longer. New technologies now available for helping infertile couples may also delay childbearing. Whatever the reason, more and more people may be faced with prenatal decision making. Because the prenatal diagnostic procedures are not risk-free, many couples are hesitant to take the risk of losing a chromosomally "normal" pregnancy (see Lebel, p. 161). Although the risk for miscarriage is approximately 0.5 percent, any risk may be too much, especially for women who have experienced previous multiple miscarriages.

While this risk of the test may appear to be daunting, knowing prenatally if the chromosomes are abnormal is of great value for some, regardless of the risks of the procedure or age. Questions can help lead the couple toward the answer that is right for them. Could they imagine having responsibility for a disabled child in their old age? Would they find the experience personally rewarding? Could their family adapt to the life-altering impact? The answers to these questions often help the couple prepare for a baby that will have special needs at birth.

The ability to know prenatally whether or not a child will have a birth defect may raise difficult questions for some Christians. If a baby is born with a chromosomal abnormality, most people feel obligated to love and take care of the child. Should that belief change when a fetus is prenatally diagnosed with a chromosome abnormality? Perhaps the parents feel that preventing the birth of the child is the most loving decision. On the other hand, the couple may decide to continue the pregnancy, believing God will provide the strength required to take care of such a child. What they believe about God can shed light on such choices.

## 3. Newborn Screening for Genetic Disorders

Newborn screening is performed on almost all babies within the first few days or weeks of life. In some states, screening is mandatory. Blood is analyzed by collecting a few drops on filter paper after puncturing the baby's heel with a needle. The genetic disorders revealed by these tests are mostly biochemical, or inborn errors of the metabolism. The panel of tests differs from state to state, but the most common screens are for PKU (phenylketonuria), sickle cell anemia (a disease caused by chemically altered hemoglobin molecules), congenital hypothyroidism (a deficient thyroid hormone), and galactosemia (inability to digest milk sugar). These tests provide early identification of disorders so that treatment may begin, thereby lessening serious complications.

*Elizabeth had given birth to Samantha a little over a week ago and already she was making multiple trips to the pediatrician. The next appointment was scheduled to discuss the results of some blood tests Samantha had when she was only a few days old. All Elizabeth could think of was, "What next?" She was already struggling to deal with life as a single mother.*

*At the appointment, Dr. Summers informed Elizabeth that her daughter had PKU and that she was going to have to be referred as soon as possible to a metabolic clinic specializing in this disorder. Little did Elizabeth know how much her life was going to change.*

*At the metabolic clinic, Elizabeth was introduced to a biochemical geneticist and a genetic counselor. After long discussions with these two specialists, Elizabeth realized that she and her daughter were going to see a lot of them. Samantha would have to have frequent blood tests, and Elizabeth would need careful instruction about the restricted diet and the special formula. Eventually, she would have to learn to make meals free of something called phenylalanine so it would not build up in her daughter's body and cause mental retardation. Her daughter had this autosomal recessive disorder because she had inherited one non-functioning gene from Elizabeth and another one from the man she used to call her husband.*

*Nonetheless, newborn screening brought with it a positive approach to the situation. If Samantha could stay on the strict food plan with the help of a dietitian and have frequent monitoring of the amount of phenylalanine levels in her blood, there was a good chance that she would not be mentally retarded. In addition, Elizabeth now knew that she no longer had a 25 percent chance that she could have another child with PKU because she would probably not meet up with another carrier, and, more important, would know to have any partner tested for carrier status.*

PKU is just one example of a disorder that can be effectively treated if identified early. In the absence of newborn testing, irreversible damage to the infant's body may occur by the time symptoms appear and a diagnosis is made. However, not all of the genetic diseases tested for by newborn screening can be treated. Although parents may often have little choice when it comes to knowing gene status through this panel of screens, in this story, the knowledge clearly benefitted Samantha and her mother.

## 4. Genetic Testing to Prevent the Birth of a "Normal" Child

The technology is now available to identify prenatally babies with many genetic disorders. Individuals typically use this type of testing for reassurance that a child is unaffected or to terminate an affected pregnancy. However, the reverse is also possible. A parent with a particular genetic trait may want children just like himself or herself, including an abnormal trait. For example, some couples with Achondroplasia want a child with the same dwarfing disorder. Thus, they would want to prevent the birth of a child who instead has a functioning gene for normal height and would be of "average" stature. Many people would object to this decision, but this case is a real story that represents the complexities that come with genetic knowledge.

*Phil and Rose met each other three years ago at a national meeting of "Little People of America." A year later they were married. They both knew that they wanted to spend their lives with someone of short stature. Many modifications had been necessary to make daily life manageable for them—everything from lowering kitchen counters to having furniture special ordered. As Rose got to know Phil better, she realized that not only did she love him, but also she loved the fact that life would be easier together. Phil knew what it was like to have a physical disability and therefore he and Rose faced the same daily challenges. He also agreed with her that having Achondroplasia was not a defect, just a different way of life.*

*Rose had learned from the geneticist who specialized in bone disorders that the reason she was a dwarf was that she had inherited a gene with a new mutation—which was not present in either of her very tall parents but only in one of their reproductive cells. Now she had that mutated gene in every cell in her body, including half of her eggs. It meant that she could pass the gene to her children. She and Phil too could have offspring with Achondroplasia.*

*Phil and Rose had decided it was time for Rose to try to become pregnant. They had talked about it extensively. They knew that they had a 50 percent chance of having a child with Achondroplasia because it was an autosomal dominant disorder. They were also at a 25 percent risk for having a child with a lethal form of the disorder if the zygote received both "mutated" genes, and a 25 percent chance that a child would be of "normal" stature.*

*Together they scheduled genetic testing of the fetus to determine if it carried the gene for Achondroplasia. If the gene was not present or present in a double dose, they decided that they would terminate the pregnancy. They are adamant about having a child with the same dwarfing characteristics as themselves because they view short stature as an alternative lifestyle rather than a disabling condition.*

Should genetic testing be used in a way that allows parents to "pick" the child that they want? God created us to be free human beings. On the other hand, did God also create us to function only within rigid "normal" confines? If God said "Before I formed you in the womb I knew you" (Jeremiah 1:5), where does genetic testing fit in?

If some individuals have a right to terminate a pregnancy because they view a disorder as debilitating, does a couple have the right to select for a disorder because they view it as *not* debilitating? Is it all a matter of perspective? How can anyone truly define whether or not disorder is bad enough that a child should not be brought into the world because of it? Is every person created equal in only God's eyes? What about the couple who has six daughters and gets pregnant again in the hope of having a boy? Through genetic testing, they would be able to learn if the fetus is a girl and to terminate a "normal" female.

Genetic counselors cannot share personal perspectives with the patients, but they can raise difficult questions in the hope that the "right" decision will be made. A pastor or friend, on the other hand, may voice their perspective, although they too must honor boundaries (see Holst, p. 186). Unconditional love should guide the advisor discussing these decisions: "This is my commandment, that you love one another as I have loved you" (John 15:12). God does not value one person's genetic make-up over another. God cares about how each person lives life and treats others. Surely this includes how genetic-based decisions should be made.

## 5. Access to Genetic Testing

People who have had genetic testing know that it can be costly. The expense comes from the fact that most analysis is not performed in mass quantity, and the results require careful interpretation. Sometimes insurance companies will not cover genetic testing because they deem the test to be medically unnecessary. Even if all or part of the testing is covered, the individual may not want an insurance company to pay for fear that if the company is allowed to know the test result, health insurance may be terminated. Having a gene that will lead to a disease later in life may motivate the insurance company to drop a policy or decline coverage later based upon a preexisting condition. If an individual lacks insurance, testing may not be affordable. Issues of cost, therefore, will lead to issues of access to genetic services.

*Clark is a prominent businessman. In fact, he was just promoted to C.E.O. of a petroleum company. He was surfing the Internet on his laptop computer when he came across a web page of a biotech laboratory that offers a panel of 50 gene tests that will identify diseases to which you may be predisposed. Knowing this information may allow for lifestyle changes or early treatment.*

*The testing costs thousands of dollars, but money is no object for Clark. Like everything in his life, he wants the best—especially the best medical care so he can live as long as possible and enjoy the profits of his work. Clark orders the test kit off the Internet. He knows his friend Edward, a physician, will draw the blood for him.*

In the forseeable future, genetic testing will most likely be provided in groups of tests called *multiplexing*. This testing would enable one laboratory to provide answers to multiple genetic questions in a single analytical process. For example, this testing process could examine dozens of disease susceptibility genes and therefore let a person know to what illnesses he or she may be prone and what disorders will probably develop. ∎

*Jim works at the quarry right outside of town. When he is not cutting stone, he likes to spend time at the local library. Recently, the librarian helped him to learn how to use the Internet on the public computers. Sometimes he spends hours surfing the net.*

*One day, Jim came across a fascinating web page. It happened to be the same web page that Clark had discovered. Jim was intrigued. He did not remember much about genetics from high school biology, but he did learn a lot from watching television. Genetics was frequently mentioned in the media. Jim printed a page so he could find some books on the subject and learn more. He had always wished he could have gone to college, but there simply was a lack of money, not to mention that he felt he needed to stay home and help take care of his ailing mother.*

*With time, Jim felt he learned some basic genetic principles. Multiplex testing seemed like a wonderful idea—until, of course, he read the fine print that listed the cost. Jim would never be able to afford the test in his lifetime.*

As with most new technology, genetic testing such as multiplexing will be costly. Therefore, it is likely that only the wealthy will have access to such testing. Is this just? Does this imply the coming of a genetically impaired underclass? If a test is not available to all who need and want it, should it be available to anyone at all? If a society is committed to developing technology that allows genetic fortune-telling, should everyone be permitted to look into the crystal ball? In a world of scarce resources, an answer is not self-evident.

A Christian view of justice as "faith always active in love" can apply here. Christian love, according to Martin Luther, must be directed not to those who are at the *highest risk*, but to those who are in *greatest need*. Love must be "most active among the poor, the needy, the evildoers, the sinners, the insane, the sick, and the enemies."[3] Genetic testing should be used to improve human life for those who are most needy. In this view, justice for everyone must underlie the distribution of resources devoted to genetic testing and screening with a preference to those who have the least.

## 6. Unavailable Genetic Testing: Research in Progress

The goal of the Human Genome Project is to map and sequence the entire genome of approximately 100,000 genes. This project involves the coordinated efforts of several national and international organizations. In this country, financial support comes from the National Institutes of Health and the Department of Energy. Although it is conceivable that the project will becompleted in the next ten to fifteen years, the full benefits of that work will not be available to the public in the form of genetic testing for many years.

*Marcella and Daniel have a 13-month-old daughter, Angela, who was born with a genetic disorder. Features of this syndrome include severe heart defects and liver problems. This syndrome is passed on in an autosomal dominant fashion and can be either inherited (from a parent) or sporadic (occurring for the first time).*

*The couple was told by Angela's specialist that it cannot be determined by a physical exam if either parent carries the gene. Symptoms can be mild or even nonexistent in some individuals. Marcella and Daniel were not too concerned at the moment. The physician reassured them that the gene testing would be available before too long. The couple wanted to figure out whether another child could be at risk for this disorder sometime, but they became caught up with all of Angela's medical needs. The answer did not seem urgent, but then Marcella learned she was pregnant. Panicking, the couple made an appointment to see a genetic counselor.*

*The genetic counselor, Eric, explained to the couple that he could try to contact the researcher who was looking for the gene. Later that week, Eric contacted Marcella.*

*"I spoke with Dr. Harris about your situation. Unfortunately, he has not been able to locate the gene yet. He did say that he would like to include you in his studies if you would be willing to provide him with some blood samples."*

*Marcella was distraught, "I do not want to have another baby with this syndrome. I cannot take a 50 percent risk. Is there anything else that can be done?"*

*Eric shared all that he knew, "This researcher thinks the discovery will be made within the next 12 months. I know this does not help you with this pregnancy. About the only other thing we can offer you would be an extensive ultrasound to take a look for abnormalities in the baby's heart and other organs. To get the best information, the ultrasound should be done after 18 weeks of pregnancy."*

*The couple wanted answers. They were angry at the medical profession. Marcella and Daniel had invested so much time and so many resources on Angela that the thought of terminating the pregnancy entered their minds. Their marriage was already under incredible stress. In fact, Daniel had mentioned to Marcella that if they had another child with the same genetic disorder, he would leave her. Marcella knew the ultrasound could not be diagnostic; and even if it were normal, there would be no guarantees. Pregnancy was no longer a joy for her, but a burden.*

How should people with a high risk of genetic disease be supported? Many people assume that because of all the media hype over genetic discoveries, the genetic basis for every disease can be identified, and every disease can be eventually cured. At the time of this writing, genetic testing is available to identify approximately 500 disorders. Even when tests are available for hundreds and hundreds of genetic disorders, treatments or cures will not be available for decades. Nonetheless, genetic counselors can offer support even when testing is unavailable. For example, they may be able to connect the individual with a research group searching for the gene in question. In addition, genetic counselors may be able to provide a link to local, regional, or national support groups.

Many Christians have yet a deeper concern: "Will the availability of more genetic tests only bring us closer to 'playing God' as medical researchers attempt to rid humans of genetic imperfections?" How far do they go? Can perfection be found? Is it a desirable goal? Who will define perfection? It seems to me that Psalm 8:4-5 suggests that humans were not created to meet an ideal of perfection or to assume godlike control of the earth: "What are human beings that you are mindful of them, mortals, that you care for them? Yet you have made them a little lower than God." Perhaps the delicate balance can be found in which medical researchers move away from playing God to helping humanity.

## 7. Carrier Screening for Genetic Disorders

Screening for carriers of the sickle cell anemia gene in the African-American population began in the early 1970s. If a person has sickle cell anemia (two hemoglobin gene mutations), abnormal hemoglobin exists in red blood cells. This abnormality of structure in the hemoglobin causes many symptoms, including episodes of excruciating pain, anemia, and susceptibility to infections. A carrier has *no* symptoms, but genetic testing will show that one hemoglobin gene is abnormal. From the beginning, the campaign to screen for sickle cell anemia headed in the wrong direction, failing to clarify the purpose of the testing. Many African-Americans believed that they were being stigmatized. Many Caucasians misinterpreted the screening test. Some employers and life insurance companies discriminated against *carriers*, wrongly labeling them as having the disease.

In the 1970s, little benefit resulted from identifying carriers. Prenatal diagnosis and treatment were not available. The information could be used, however, for reproductive planning. If both parents were carriers, the only option then was to take the 25 percent risk of having a child with the disease, or to forego having children. For African Americans, it seemed like a form of racial eugenics, a deliberate plot to eliminate a race under the guise of eliminating heritable diseases through encouraging "superior" individuals and discouraging "inferior" people from reproducing.

Today prenatal diagnosis is available for sickle cell disease, and early detection is advantageous because penicillin prophylaxes reduce infant and childhood mortality. However, the suspicion remains among African-Americans who, in the 1970s, suffered discrimination on the basis of their genotypes.

*Derek was in his sophomore year, majoring in history at the state university. For a change of pace he had registered for an introductory biology course this fall. He had expected it to be interesting, but not life altering. What started it all was the assignment to draw out his family history. Since he did not have all the facts, he called his mom for more information. He learned that he had two cousins with sickle cell anemia. His mother had not shared this information with him before because that side of the family was estranged from them and she did not think it was crucial that he should know. She reminded him of her view that the sickle cell anemia screening program was a mistake. She even went so far as to tell Derek that she had managed to avoid having him tested as a newborn because she did not want him to be labeled a carrier.*

*The news shocked Derek. Not only did he carry the general risk of one in 12 that every African-American has for being a sickle cell carrier, but, with this family history, he was at an increased risk. His mind was filled with questions. If he ended up being a carrier, was he "defective"? Would a woman want to marry him if she knew he was a carrier? He needed to talk to someone about this, but he had no idea where to go.*

*Derek remembered the history of sickle cell screening with its perceived discrimination. Many African-Americans were discriminated against because of their test results. Yet he felt he wanted to know if he was a carrier. Derek knew intellectually that the results would not change who he was as a person, but emotionally he was concerned.*

African-Americans are not the only group at high risk for a genetic disease. Almost one in twenty-five Caucasians of Northern European descent is a carrier of the gene for cystic fibrosis. Similarly, carriers of the gene for Tay Sachs disease are frequent in the Ashkenazi Jewish population. In fact, everyone is at risk for any number of disorders. Each human being is estimated to be a carrier of approximately a half dozen deleterious genes. However, a carrier of a "defective" gene is not a defective person, just an at-risk person.

It seems to me that it is our duty as Christians to take what God has given us, including our intelligence and physical being, and to make the best of it. Everyone has a talent and a purpose. Too often talents remain undeveloped and unappreciated, and the purpose is underestimated. Nonetheless, movement in the general direction of fulfilling that purpose is success. Martin Luther emphasizes the words of Paul's letter to the Romans about how Christians ought to conduct themselves: "They must teach, preach, rule, serve, give, suffer, love, live."[4]

## 8. Genetic Testing for Predisposition to Cancer

As many as one in ten women will develop breast cancer. Many women secretly worry that they will become a victim to this killer. Yearly gynecological exams focus on the proper way to perform monthly self-examinations. All women over age 40 are now urged to get an annual mammogram. All of these precautions are taken in hopes of detecting breast cancer at a curable stage.

Only a small number of the women, perhaps five percent, who will develop breast cancer have a genetic predisposition to it. Thus, the gene test is useful to a select group with strong family histories of breast and/or ovarian cancer. These women usually have several close relatives who were diagnosed with cancer before age fifty (premenopausal).

At this writing, two major genes associated with inherited breast and ovarian cancer, BRCA1 and BRCA2, have been discovered in this high-risk group. Testing for these genes is now available through several laboratories. Testing, however, is not for everyone. Although these two genes connected to breast cancer have been isolated, their connection to the disease, either in their functioning or mutated state, is not fully understood. Thus, the gene test is not as useful as women would like and are led to believe by the media.

*Rachel, 27, has a strong paternal family history of breast cancer. Her grandmother died at 45, one aunt died at age 39, and another at age 35. She has heard much in the news about genetic testing for breast cancer. At her last annual exam she asked her physician about the test, who agreed she was a candidate and thought she should consider it. The laboratory would need only a blood sample. Her physician told her he could draw the blood and send it off for her.*

*The fear of getting breast cancer was constantly in the back of Rachel's mind. Yet something was wrong in the simplicity of the procedure. She decided to call the laboratory's toll-free number to see if she could get some written information on the gene test.*

*When the materials on BRCA1 and BRCA2 arrived, she was surprised to learn that the laboratory recommended a pre-test consultation by a genetic counselor. They even provided a state-by-state listing of names of professionals who specialize in cancer counseling.*

*Later that month, Rachel met with Jackie, the genetic counselor. It was a productive appointment, but she was overwhelmed. Whether to have the test seemed unclear now. Jackie explained to her the difference between BRCA1 and BRCA2. She also described how the genes are sequenced to show mutations in the DNA. It would have been helpful to have DNA from an affected relative, but none was available. Rachel thought the lab would be able to tell her "yes," she would get breast cancer, or "no," she did not need to worry anymore.*

*Rachel did not get the answer she expected. First, she learned that the test might reveal a mutation that is known to increase the risk for breast cancer. Although the risk is higher than the general population, much research remains to be done before the precise nature of the risk is clear. If she had the gene, she would not have a 100 percent chance of getting breast cancer. Some experts say there is an 80 percent risk; others say it is closer to 40 percent. Researchers may find that different mutations lead to different risk figures. Second, the test might reveal no mutations. While this is a good result, it would not eliminate Rachel's general risk or the possibility of a yet unidentified gene on another chromosome for which we cannot yet detect mutations. Third and last, Rachel learned the test may show an unidentified mutation whose significance is unknown. It could be a harmless change in the DNA, or it could be a marker of potential disease.*

*Although Rachel thought about the possibility of carrying the gene for breast cancer, the genetic counselor brought up many more facets to the decision. She was not sure how she might handle a result indicating that she was at a high risk for developing breast cancer. The other possibility was that she might be at risk for developing ovarian cancer as well. Would a prophylactic mastectomy be an option for her? What about the prophylactic removal of her ovaries which could not be done until she had finished childbearing? Would she even want to have children if there was a 50 percent risk of passing the gene on? She also had to consider the views of her fiancé. Worst of all, her sense of self-worth was jeopardized with the thought of having a "defective," disease-causing gene. Did she carry the family "curse?" The genetic counselor had given her the name of a psychologist who deals specifically with difficult issues raised by testing, but she was not sure if she was comfortable with going to a psychologist. What she really wanted to do was to talk with the pastor of her church. Perhaps he could help her sort through her fears and anger. How could God create something as wonderful and mysterious as genes and then allow them to change into awful diseases?*

Breast and ovarian cancer are just two diseases involving known predisposition genes. The list will only continue to grow. More and more tests will be available. Physicians will offer testing to patients who do not really want to know the results. Furthermore, most physicians lack time to spend with patients, discussing the meaning and implications of the test, much less the available options.

For some individuals, testing is the right choice. However, the wishes of people who do not want to know their gene status must be respected. The recognition that data are lacking on the long-term personal impact of this knowledge of cancer risk is also important.

As with evil, we may ask: Why did God create something as wonderful and mysterious as genes and then allow them to change into awful diseases? This question, of course, seems to imply that God is imperfect. When the story of genetic mutations is fully understood, it will be clear that God is not responsible for genetic imperfections any more than for evil and other earthly imperfections. Christians affirm that all things work together for the glory of God. All living things are inter-related and were created by God with magnificent intricacies, including the complexities of DNA. Understanding of our place in creation begins with awe and respect. Even God himself was delighted: "God saw everything that He had made, and indeed, it was very good" (Genesis 1:28). It seems to me that the basic goodness of creation is not destroyed by a few "defective" genes. Most important, flawed genes do not make the whole person flawed. Although our genetic make-up may make life more difficult, it should not prevent us from leading fruitful Christian lives.

## 9. Late Onset Disorders: Testing in Adults and Children

Huntington's disease is an adult-onset disorder that slowly causes the neurologic system to degenerate. This disease causes a progressive degeneration of brain cells, which in turn causes severe muscle spasms and personality disorders. Most individuals first exhibit its symptoms between the ages of 30 and 50; death occurs ten to twenty years after the onset of symptoms. No treatment or cure exists. Genetic testing is available that will predict with reasonable accuracy whether Huntington's disease will develop at some point in the person's life. For someone who has a parent with the disease, the risk is 50 percent for inheriting the gene (see Powell, p. 25).

As with other late-onset disorders, the decision to be tested as an adult is not an easy one. Fortunately, guidelines exist in many genetic centers. Huntington's disease stands apart from other disorders because of all the work that was done to prepare appropriate testing procedures. Most protocols for it include some level of genetic counseling, along with other medical appointments (neurological, psychiatric). These steps are taken to ensure that an individual is ready to be tested and that support and coping systems are in place at the time test results are received.

Problems can also arise because other family members may also be at risk. Some may want to be tested, and others may not. Sometimes whole families are tested together. Regardless, family tensions can surface in the form of direct conflict or complete withdrawal.

*Huntington's disease is known to run in the Decker family. Grandpa Samuel Decker recently died at age 60 from Huntington's after a long and horrible ten years. He left behind two sons and a daughter, who were all asymptomatic. They all had children themselves before they realized that they were at risk. No one in the family has yet been pre-symptomatically tested for the gene.*

*At the traditional Thanksgiving Decker family gathering, Kurt, the son of Robert, Samuel's oldest child, announced that he had already had blood drawn to see if he carried the Huntington's disease gene. The relatives were horrified.They had an unspoken understanding that no one would get tested pre-symptomatically. Whoever got the disease would be taken care of by the other family members. God would help them through with whatever they were dealt.*

*The person who was most upset by Kurt's decision was his sister, Cindy, who was four months pregnant. She felt Kurt was being selfish and not thinking of anyone else in the family. He could have at least discussed it with her and their parents. Cindy had come to the conclusion that she did not want to be tested because she was afraid that if she was found to carry the gene, she would have decided not to have children. She wanted to live as normal a life as possible. Her father, Robert, felt the same way. After all, if her father had decided not to have children, she never would have been born. She felt she had lived a wonderfully fulfilling life so far; she was glad to have been born.*

*By the Christmas holidays, the whole Decker family anxiously awaited Kurt's results. Since there was a growing animosity, no one really knew if he was going to share the news even though they had expressed to him he should not tell them.*

*Kurt did get the test result, and it was positive. Now he knew that his father was going to get Huntington's disease and that Kurt's only child as well as his sister were at a 50 percent risk. He was not sure how he could bear the burden of this news. Kurt and his wife would probably not have any more children. He thought about all the aunts, uncles, and cousins who were at risk. He questioned his own worth as a human being. Should he have his newborn daughter tested? The idea that he might have passed on Huntington's made him sick to his stomach.*

Testing for such autosomal dominant late-onset disorders affects the entire family, regardless of whether or not all members are involved in the testing. (Genetic counselors and other individuals can assist in promoting conversation among relatives.) What happens when one individual wants to be tested and others do not? Sometimes the results can even affect unborn and very young members of the family. Because it is possible that the testing of one individual may reveal the gene status of another, everyone needs to be aware of the impact of testing on the family unit. Although genetic disease can be predicted, human reactions cannot. Will Robert be overcome by guilt when he discovers he has passed on the gene for Huntington's? Who can this family turn to for support? Will faith in God be strengthened, or will they become bitter and stray from their religious beliefs? Will the family grow closer together or farther apart? In this and many other situations, support systems should be available and in place *before* genetic testing is initiated.

Although prenatal and childhood testing is available, the National Society of Genetic Counselors (NSGC) recommends that children should never be tested for Huntington's disease. Other types of genetic testing in children are also discouraged. In fact, some laboratories are beginning to prohibit testing for certain disorders on individuals younger than eighteen years of age. The reason is obvious: children cannot understand the implications of genetic testing. Once tested, most children cannot cope with what the genetic disease may mean for the future. Clearly, the negative psychological effects of genetic information could cripple a child emotionally.

Are there circumstances under which it might be permissible to test a minor? Parents ultimately have the power to make all decisions for their children; yet, most are unprepared to make a decision on genetic testing for their children. It is urgent that medical professionals develop a consensus for the testing of minors for genetic diseases. In the case of incurable, adult-onset disorder many of them would argue that testing should not be performed on children until they are at least eighteen and can decide the issue for themselves.

Another "touchy" aspect of childhood testing is one that many parents may not even consider. Could the discovery of a disease-causing gene in one child lead to preferential treatment to a sibling who lacks the gene? Inadvertent discrimination within the family can occur. In addition, trauma to the child can result when parents feel guilt for having passed on the gene, or see the child as a reminder of their own genetic disease. Whether it is adult or childhood testing for a late-onset disease such as Huntington's, the possibility for causing irreparable harm through potentially "toxic knowledge" is real. These realities suggest that early testing may lead to early unnecessary damage to children.

In struggling with these issues, it is helpful to remember something that Luther held close to his heart: all things, including children, are gifts from God.[5] Thus, it seems to me that, for Christians, a decision about childhood genetic testing should be based solely on whether or not the God-given gift of that child's life would be benefitted. If any question remains, it should be put off until the child is ready in mind and in spirit to undergo the testing.

## 10. Testing for Disorders with Questionable Genetic Component

Many people have had a brush with psychiatric disorders in some form or another, be it a mild bout of depression or knowing someone with obsessive-compulsive behavior. Perhaps a mother and daughter both exhibit the same panic attacks. Is this pattern familial? No one yet understands why some people develop a psychiatric disorder while others with the same genes remain mentally healthy.

*Sharon and her husband Jeff visit their local obstetric and gynecology clinic for an infertility consultation. For the past five years, they have been trying to conceive a child. In the course of taking their medical history, their physician learned not only about their medical history but also about their social history. What Dr. Brown learns, she does not like.*

*As a teenager, prior to meeting Jeff, Sharon had been institutionalized for mental instability, during which time she had been taking various forms of birth control medication. Fortunately, psychotherapy and drugs substantially reduce her psy-*

chotic episodes. *Now in her thirties, Sharon is able to live on her own, but she has a difficult time staying employed, and depends heavily on welfare and Medicaid. Jeff also has spent many years with a therapist and needs daily medications to control his manic depression. Some days he is on top of the world and other days he feels as if it is the end of the world. The couple tells the physician that together they can deal with their mental illnesses.*

*The physician decides to order some basic fertility tests on Sharon and Jeff and asks them to come back in a week to discuss the results. In the back of her mind, all she can think about is, "What negative genetic potential this couple has. Should I really help them try to have children?"*

Many people, even medical professionals, may have a strong bias against people with mental illness. They may make moral judgments about the ability of these individuals to overcome their problems. Consequently, an individual with a mental illness may not receive the same level of care as someone with a genetically predisposed cancer.

Schizophrenia and manic depression are the two most common psychiatric disorders. Much research has been done to look for genetic causation, but no triggering genes have been found. Twin, sibling, and adoption studies have demonstrated that if a psychiatric disorder runs in a family, other members are at increased risk, suggesting a genetic component. However, nothing currently would enable us to be able to provide predictive testing.

This case raises the warning for all of us about bias. For Christians, the ministry to which Jesus calls us is to treat everyone with dignity and respect. Love begins with overcoming biases.

# Conclusion

While genetic counselors are key members of the medical care team, they are not usually trained to focus on the faith-related needs of patients. Some will not take the time to discuss how religion can coexist with the diagnosis of a genetic disorder. In addition, spiritual issues often fall by the wayside because a counseling session is devoted to the exchange of information. Many patients are left with unanswered questions like, "Why do bad things always happen to me?" Others are searching for a divine answer to their genetic problems. Most patients seem to yearn to do some soul-searching, and to want someone there to listen.

If the church chooses to be present to people struggling with genetic choices, it must become genetically literate in order to understand and respond. Science and technology have brought us into an era which requires profound responsibility. For Christians, this is not an affliction but a gift from God. This gift offers opportunities for great good or for radical abuse. God has given us the freedom and responsibility to make such decisions. Christians are called to participate in genetic decision making, both in personal and societal realms. As servants of Christ and stewards of the mysteries of God (1 Corinthians 4:1), this responsibility requires preparation. There is much to learn, especially about how to be good stewards of scientific information. In taking up the responsibility to participate in the genetics revolution, readers are challenged to begin by seeking further information on genetic screening and testing.

1. Use this book to become informed. Many common genetic disorders are presented here.

2. Read some of the many excellent books now available on the subject.

3. Ask for help. Someone in every major town in the land is willing to talk about these issues.

4. Commit to standing with, not deciding for, those afflicted with genetic-based health problems.

In addition, the church must be prepared to contribute to ethical decision making in government and the health care industry. Based on the stories in this chapter, the following issues are urgent:

- What is the value to parents and to the unborn baby for prenatal genetic testing?

- Under what circumstances should genetic carrier testing be done?

- Is it morally acceptable to terminate pregnancies in order to work toward conceiving a child with the traits you want?

- Should all people, regardless of financial resources, have access to genetic testing?

- Should genetic information be used by anyone other than the physician and patient?

- How can public misconceptions about available genetic technologies be prevented?

- Should children ever be tested because of the potential for harm to the child?

- Do the psychological implications of offering testing for late-onset disorders outweigh any benefits from the testing?

- Will discrimination occur when testing for psychiatric disorders becomes available?

- Should we make genetically flawless offspring a societal goal?

- Can we afford the cost to produce a genetically healthy populace?

- Will genetic testing lead to a genetic-based class system?

- Who will decide what is genetically valuable?

How we answer these questions will radically affect our understanding of ourselves, our society, and our faith.

Finally, the church needs to act as well as to discuss. As Luther stated in his devotional letter on *"Whether One May Flee From a Deadly Plague,"* "We are bound to each other in such a way that no one may forsake the other in his distress, but is obliged to assist and help him as he himself would like to be helped."[6] Sadly, people who are afflicted with a genetic disorder or who are burdened with genetic questions suspect that they are being punished by God, and rarely seek help from clergy. In Luther's view, this attitude is like saying that "anyone who falls into deep water dare not save himself by swimming but must surrender to the water as a divine punishment."[7] Anyone who leaves his neighbor to his misfortunes, according to Luther, is a murderer in the sight of God.[8] On the other hand, the church should not be tempted to give easy answers, suggesting God will take care of everything. God is not "Mr. Quick Fix." Easy answers encourage people to drop all reflection, inquiry, and sharing as well as promoting isolation and an attitude of powerlessness. Blaming God or self for bad outcomes eventually leads to despair. The trap of easy answers is deadly.

In order to be present to those in need, the church must be prepared with love and compassion for those who are faced with new and fearful problems and decisions. We must make it clear that the church will be present to all who seek help in whatever struggles lie ahead. Finally, the church knows, and must help us all know, that God does not judge us on our genetic make up, but only on our lack of compassion and love for those afflicted with pain, fear, and despair.

I hope that the stories told in this chapter will open new understanding and care for people struggling with the burden of useful but frightening genetic information. I also hope that we who are the church will be challenged to prepare for the public discussions and personal decisions ahead.

# GENETICS IN THE MARKETPLACE: A BIOTECH PERSPECTIVE

## John Varian

Genetic mutations which predispose individuals for certain diseases are being discovered at an astounding pace. The only way individuals can determine if they have a particular genetic mutation is if a test for the mutation exists. Typically, genetic tests can only become widely available to the public if a company decides to "develop" the test for the medical marketplace. Development of a genetic test is expensive, time consuming, and risky. This development is occurring primarily at "for profit" companies in the biotechnology industry. "For profit" companies are responsible to their investors to provide a return on investment in the form of a profit. This chapter is intended to provide the reader a view of the dynamics surrounding genetic test development that exist in the biotechnology marketplace and considers some issues which must be balanced against profit motives. It also attempts to express how a person of faith working in the biotech industry integrates the day-to-day work life with a set of Christian values. In doing so, this chapter provides an overview of:

- The status of genetic test development in the biotech industry;
- The composition of the biotech industry and our industry position on genetic testing;
- How people of faith view some of today's moral and ethical questions;
- The economics of genetic test development;
- Some examples of the usefulness of tests already available;
- Some of the evolving more complex ethical issues;
- Discrimination issues which exist, as well as some on the horizon;
- Developments in our understanding of the impact of genetics on behavior;
- A discussion of a completely new field known as pharmacogenomics which provides for "customized" drug development;
- Some final thoughts on how directly our genetic makeup determines our fate.

# Initial Factors

In writing this paper, I was greatly assisted by input from G. Steven Burrill, CEO of Burrill & Company, a Merchant Bank, and a member of Calvary Presbyterian Church in San Francisco, as well as Franklin Berger, Vice President in the Research Department of J. P. Morgan Securities, Inc., and a Vestryman at St. James on Madison Avenue in New York City. ■

## The Power of Information

Medical information about each of us has always existed and more is constantly being added. When my daughter was born recently, my wife's obstetrician generated information about her, and her pediatrician soon began to add to the data. When she goes to school, more will exist. If she undergoes a hospital procedure, even more will be amassed, and with every physical examination she undergoes, more will pile on until a mountain of medical data will exist on her as it does on each of us. This information can help protect our health or it can potentially be used against us in a discriminatory manner. Genetic information is a small but rapidly growing portion of all the medical information gathered on each person.

The ability to identify and test for genes that predispose individuals for particular diseases is a powerful tool that allows us to begin to treat these diseases at their root cause. While better genetic information is not in itself the answer, genetic tests can provide more accurate and useful information that are additive to current diagnostic tests. Currently in the United States, over one trillion dollars, or 15 percent of the Gross Domestic Product, is spent on health care. Very little of that amount is spent on prevention. Most treatment today focuses on alleviating symptoms rather than eradicating the disease itself. With much better information from more accurate and earlier tests, we can begin to spend our health care dollars to prevent and more appropriately treat disease.

## The People of the Industry

Genetic testing also creates new challenges with which society must deal. The individuals who make up the biotech workforce very much reflect society as a whole. We are not uniform in our views and beliefs. Some may portray us as "mad scientists" bent upon the advancement of medical technology regardless of its impact on society; but in fact, we break down very much like any group composing any town, business, or congregation.

My experience indicates that the biotech industry includes a significant percentage of people of faith. There appears to be an almost universal view that those of us who have chosen this industry did so because we want to accomplish something purposeful with our careers. We want to be able to look back and know that people's lives were changed for the better due in part to our individual efforts.

In 1997 my company, Neurex, formally recognized a statement of our values and beliefs as follows:

- We are here for the benefit of the patient first and foremost.
- We will display quality, innovation, and excellence in everything we do.
- We will operate with integrity and honesty in all internal and external interactions.
- We will accomplish our goals through teamwork and share our successes.
- We will strive to be profitable in order to allow us to fund development of future therapeutics.

These adopted values are not unusual. If you canvassed others of the 1,300 biotechnology companies, you would find similar sets of values and beliefs. Of course, there are many in our industry who do not abide by these beliefs in their actions. Those of us in the biotech industry who grapple with decisions about genetic testing are not perfect, but many of us carry strong faith-based moral beliefs which we bring to the issues we face. My message is not "Trust us," rather, "Engage us in meaningful dialogue on genetic testing."

America does not exist in a vacuum, and different societies will deal with genetic testing differently. Even if we do not like the jet airplane or the internet, they exist. Genetic testing and the development of therapeutics based on genetic markers will happen. The worldwide Christian church should make an effort to be part of the decisions around these new developments, and not merely loom overhead as a voice of condemnation.

Genetic test results are only a piece of the puzzle patients must solve to make decisions regarding their medical care. Their medical history, other medical information, their lifestyle, economics, employment, insurance, ethics, values, and faith are all factors. The real question is: "How can the church best position itself to provide input to the industry and the individual from a Christian point of view and influence decisions in a positive fashion?"

## To Develop or Not to Develop . . .

For a person of faith working in the biotech industry, today's issues surrounding genetic test development are fairly simple. Currently the only significant genetic tests being developed in the industry relate to a person's genetic predisposition for certain diseases. These tests for ailments fall into two categories:

- Diseases for which effective preventions or treatments currently exist.
- Diseases that cannot be prevented and for which no treatment options exist.

I believe it is morally appropriate to develop a genetic test under either scenario. Of course, if preventative measures or treatments exist, such tests allow for the earliest possible diagnosis, providing the patient and physician the best opportunity to avoid or lessen the negative impacts of the disease. If no preventative or treatment options exist, I believe it is still morally appropriate to develop such a test.

Most of us have read and seen commentary on people who have a genetic mutation associated with Huntington's disease. The disease is devastatingly insidious in that patients lose motor and mental capabilities over a long time period and then die horribly. In addition, this disease is hereditary; individuals know they have a 25 percent or 50 percent chance of contracting Huntington's if certain family members have been afflicted. By making a test for Huntington's available, we in the industry are moving the choice of "to test or not to test" into the hands of the patient and their physician, where it belongs. A recent study concluded that 95 percent of people tested had reduced anxiety as a result of the test even though many were found to be carriers of the genetic mutation.[1] It is difficult for each of us to decide what we would do if faced with this question. Importantly, although it is truly a profound dilemma, many of us believe that it is clear that neither the biotechnology industry, federal regulators, nor the church are better suited to make the choice than the individual. If we withhold genetic tests from individuals, we are making such a choice for them.

Genetic tests and existing diagnostics will not typically provide "yes" or "no" answers regarding disease development. They are not by nature "good." They can, however, add early and better information to the armament of information gathering techniques and often in a less invasive way.

For instance, if a genetic test for prostate cancer were available, it might provide useful information in addition to the current test for Prostate Specific Antigen (PSA). Knowledge that an individual does not carry a genetic marker for prostate cancer may affect whether he chooses to have the dramatic prostate surgery that is often chosen following an ambiguous PSA test result.

# Privacy

Those of us in the biotech industry who believe in the utility of genetic testing base our stance on one absolute condition: that the results of such tests are kept strictly confidential; only the patient and his or her physician should have access to the results. The biotech industry believes that legislation should protect Americans equally, and therefore it should be legislated federally rather than state by state. Our industry's position on privacy would result in a radical change in the current private insurance system. The Biotechnology Industry Organization (BIO) stated its position as follows:

> BIO supports the creation of federal standards to protect the confidentiality of an individual's medical information, including the results of genetic testing.
>
> Genetic testing provides important opportunities to improve patient health. These tests can be used to diagnose the presence of disease. Equally, they can provide information that can be used to reduce the risk of future disease and enable earlier and more effective treatment if and when disease occurs.
>
> The recent acceleration in the development of new genetic tests has helped focus public attention on the broader issue of the need to protect the pri-

vacy of medical information in general, including but not limited to genetic information. Genetic testing provides information that is comparable to that which may be obtained by using other diagnostic methods. As such, it forms part of the continuum of medical information. For example, testing for the presence of a gene yields information that is similar to testing for the protein that is encoded by that gene. Even something as basic as a family medical history, which provides the physician with information critical to the diagnosis, prevention, and treatment of disease, can be misused to discriminate against an individual or family.

These examples highlight the need to protect the privacy of, and safeguard against misuse of, all personal medical information, regardless of the method by which it is obtained. For this reason, BIO believes that Congress should enact a comprehensive bill with respect to the privacy of all medical information, including genetic information, rather than a bill that treats genetic privacy issues in isolation. Legislation focusing exclusively on genetic information runs the dual risk of failing to address the larger issue of medical privacy while inappropriately stigmatizing genetic information in the public's mind.

The recently enacted health insurance reform (Kassebaum-Kennedy) law serves as an example of an approach that recognizes the comparability of genetic information to other types of medical information. This law prohibits insurance companies from refusing health insurance coverage to individuals on the basis of their medical history, including "genetic information." BIO strongly supported inclusion of genetic information and enactment of this provision of the law. We support a similar approach to genetic and medical privacy issues.

BIO believes that medical information that identifies a particular individual should not be released without that individual's consent. At the same time, standards to protect the confidentiality of medical information should ensure that legitimate and vital medical research is encouraged and facilitated. For example, privacy standards should not impede the conduct of clinical trials (including the reporting of results to the Food and Drug Administration ) nor should they impede the use of anonymized samples in research.

Finally, privacy standards should be national in scope to ensure legal uniformity and consistency throughout the States, and to avoid impeding medical research and interstate commerce with a patchwork of inconsistent laws.

Insight into the genetic and other biological bases of disease holds great promise for alleviating the suffering associated with many human diseases. BIO believes that information resulting from clinical genetic testing and genetic research must be treated responsibly, and safeguarded against its discriminatory misuse, if these new advances in medical knowledge are to achieve their full potential for improving human health.[2]

It appears that the political will is also present to protect genetic privacy. A July 14, 1997, *New York Times* article stated that:

> President Clinton called on Congress today to block insurers from holding people's genes against them by denying people coverage or increasing their premiums because of their family histories or the results of genetic tests. Mr. Clinton marveled at advances in gene testing, but warned that some people were not being tested because they feared what the results might mean for their insurance. "Americans should never have to chose between saving their health insurance and taking tests that could save their lives," the President said in the East Room in the White House. Used properly, he said genetic tests could "save millions of lives and revolutionize health care." The government forbids insurers to use genetic information to deny or limit coverage to people in group plans. Today Mr. Clinton endorsed bills, opposed by insurance companies, to extend that protection to people who buy their own insurance.

Again, predicated on privacy, many of us in the industry believe it is not a moral dilemma to create a genetic test for commercialization. While writers in other chapters in this book disagree about privacy, I believe that by doing so we are merely making available a tool that patients and physicians can choose to use or not. (see Peters, p. 120; Tiefel, p. 132).

# The Economic Question

While there are other moral questions which are more complex that we in the industry must consider (discussed later in this and other essays), it is important to consider the economic issues that exist in the marketplace because they are key factors in any moral consideration. The fundamental reality is that for a genetic test to become widely available, a company must determine that the economics of developing the test are compelling. We will consider both therapeutic and diagnostic developments in this regard.

> A genetic test is considered a "diagnostic" test and the companies that develop these tests are classified as diagnostic companies. Only 26 percent of the world's 1300 biotechnology companies are diagnostic companies. The remaining 74 percent are primarily classified as therapeutic companies, that is, they develop therapies to treat disease.[3] ∎

## Therapeutic Drug Development

The economics related to the development of a therapeutic product are daunting. It is estimated that it costs $280 million to take an idea for treatment through clinical trials, Food and Drug Administration (FDA) approval and to the patient. Astoundingly, only one out of 10 potential products that start testing in humans makes it to the market. For companies to attract money from investors for a potential breakthrough drug, the investors must be convinced that the return on the $280 million spent to develop a successful drug is sufficient. The return on investment must also be large enough to encourage investors to put up this huge sum of money when there is a 90 percent chance of failure.

Imagine a biotech company executive coming to your door and asking you to invest your savings. She would propose: "Invest your money in our new product. We're about to spend seven years testing this drug in thousands of people. If it looks like it works, we'll present the data about the drug to the FDA which will take a couple of years to look at it. Even if the data are good, they may still say no. If they do say yes, we'll be able to sell it and hopefully sell enough of it at a high enough price to give you back your money plus a profit."

After telling her she should knock on someone else's door, you will have an increased understanding of why those little pills you take cost a ridiculous $1 per day and why certain therapeutics cost tens of thousands of dollars per treatment.

The only way new and innovative medicines will continue to be invented is if the reward for the successful products is high enough to offset the huge risk and cost to develop these products. This was demonstrated during the year that National Health Care Reform was under heated debate, when on a relative basis, no money was raised by biotech companies.[4] The reforms proposed that year by the Clinton Administration included two provisions that froze drug development cold, since either or both would have reduced or eliminated any potential reward for product development. First, under the proposal, the Secretary of Health and Human Services (HHS) had the right to set prices on new, breakthrough drugs; and second, if the company that developed the drug did not agree to the price, the Secretary of HHS could "blacklist" the medicine so that no American could be reimbursed for its cost. Price controls on new drugs may sound appealing in the short-term, but they would also mean a virtual end to new and innovative drugs.

## Genetic Diagnostic Test Development

The economic issues related to development of a genetic diagnostic test are very similar. The chance of failure is lower, the dollar amounts are smaller, and the time frame is shorter, but the same issues of risk, reward, and return on investment exist. For a company to consider moving forward with development of a genetic test, certain criteria must be met.

### Capital Strength

Although less than the approximate $280 million needed to develop a therapeutic product, developing a new genetic test is still extremely expensive. It is estimated that it costs approximately $30-40 million to bring such a test to market. A diagnostic development program is a major and risky business decision. The tough economics of genetic test development in the "for profit" world is actually a positive for those of us concerned about development of potentially "inappropriate" genetic tests. There are many decision makers who must agree to advance the development of any test. The magnitude of the investment dictates that formal approval is required from internal management from each discipline (research, development, finance, marketing), the company's Board of Directors, and the financial community (venture capitalists, institutional investors). The fear that a single or a few misguided individuals could bring an immoral genetic test to the marketplace is difficult to support. The economics actually creates checks and balances that work to avert such a possibility.

## Risk and Reward

Before developing a genetic test, the potential developer must be convinced the potential rewards outweigh the risks for the company. None of us would open a new shoe store on a street where ten other stores already more than meet demand. None of us would risk the time, money, and effort to develop a new sandal for our shoe store if those other ten stores could immediately copy it and sell it for less. These same questions exist when we consider developing a new therapeutic or genetic test.

## Proprietary Position

The developer of the test must have a proprietary position, that is, patents, licenses, and so forth, for the test. If the genetic markers being tested for are not "owned" (internally discovered or licensed from the discoverer) by the test developer, others could develop the same or similar test and undercut profitability. At first blush, you might think a reduced price for a test is good, but without the profit incentive, the test will never be developed for use. In absence of a proprietary position, the test will most likely never become widely available.

## Regulatory Environment

We are protected from "sham techniques" in genetic testing by strict regulatory guidelines and oversight. Test developers must provide strong clinical evidence that the test is accurate and reliable. They must also demonstrate that their testing process itself is of high quality, consistent, and dependable. The cost to develop a commercial genetic test includes the cost of the research and, to an even greater extent, the expense of setting up the clinical laboratory where such tests are conducted. These laboratories allow full sequencing of any gene selected for testing and are subject to strict quality control standards. Oversight of these laboratories is covered by the Clinic Laboratory Improvement Amendment that is administered through a federal government agency in addition to various state regulatory agencies.

# Commercial Genetic Laboratories

To illustrate these economic dynamics at work, we can take the case of one of the more visible genetic testing companies in the biotechnology industry: Myriad Genetic Laboratories, Inc., of Salt Lake City, Utah. Myriad is commercializing a test derived from a key discovery that mutations in what has been named the BRCA1 (BReast CAncer) gene result in a predisposition for breast and ovarian cancer. Combined with the discovery of the BRCA2 gene, Myriad can identify certain individuals with a higher than normal chance of getting breast or ovarian cancer.

If a mutation exists in either of these genes, the likelihood of developing breast or ovarian cancer increases as follows:

|  | Likelihood—General Population[5] | Likelihood with Mutation[6,7,8] |
|---|---|---|
| *Breast Cancer* | 7-10 percent | 40-80 percent |
| *Ovarian Cancer* | 1 percent | over 30 percent |

In the case of this genetic test, knowledge is power. A negative result could help put the patient's mind at ease. A positive result allows the patient and physician to develop a customized observation regime. For instance, the American Cancer Society (ACS) currently recommends that a woman have her first mammogram at age 40 and begin annual exams at age 50.[9] Unfortunately, in women who have this genetic predisposition, 50 percent of all cases of breast cancer occur by age 46.[10] It is easy to understand why the standard ACS recommendations should be radically adjusted for women who carry a mutation in the BRCA1 or BRCA2 gene. Breast cancer can be effectively treated 95 percent of the time when it is detected in stage 1. When caught in later stages, the chances can drop to 20 percent or less.[11] Knowing the genetic predisposition also lowers the threshold for taking action.

An example of this is cited by Jay Moyes, Vice President and Chief Financial Officer at Myriad. In this case a radiologist reviewed a mammogram and said it "looked okay." The physician informed the radiologist that the patient was positive for the BRCA1/BRCA2 gene mutation, causing him to look further. A very minor looking spot that the radiologist would normally have ignored was biopsied, found to be cancerous, and surgically removed. In this case, the knowledge of genetic predisposition very possibly saved this woman's life.

As the previous chart indicated, a woman's risk of ovarian cancer increases substantially if a mutation of the BRCA1 or BRCA2 gene exists. Treatment for ovarian cancer is typically removal of the ovaries (oophorectomy). For a woman past her childbearing years, this solution is not as dramatic as a hysterectomy and potentially will prevent the spread of cancer. In the face of a genetic mutation resulting in these dramatically increased odds, an oophorectomy is a very viable alternative. In a recent Mayo Clinic Study where women had an oophorectomy as a preventative measure, 28 percent were found to have cancer that had been undetected prior to the ovaries' removal.[12]

A further benefit to the detection of a genetic predisposition for cancer is that patients who have already had one tumor face a 64 percent recurrence rate if they have an inherited predisposition versus only a 10 percent recurrence rate in the general population.[13] This knowledge will dramatically change the extent and timing of follow-up procedures.

In addition to its existing BRCA1/BRCA2 test, Myriad expects to bring to the market in 1998 a new genetic test known as "CardiaRisk" for hypertension and risk of other cardiovascular disorders. Myriad has identified a single genetic point mutation that exists in individuals who are at risk for "salt-sensitive" hypertension. This same mutation also puts these individuals at a three times greater risk of myocardial infarction before the age of 50 than the general population.[14] Such knowledge allows a change in behavior. Many of us with hypertension discount our physician's advice to reduce our salt intake since it is not clear that our efforts will really have an impact. If individuals know of their predisposition for salt-sensitive hypertension, they can change their diet with full confidence that they should experience a direct benefit. This knowledge will also affect which anti-hypertensive medication the physician prescribes to patients since it is believed that the class of

ACE-inhibitors are most beneficial to salt-sensitive hypertensive patients.[15] The knowledge that this mutation triples the chances of early-age heart attack will also impact the monitoring of cardiac activity earlier in life.[16]

It should also be noted that not only have genetic testing companies developed these extremely beneficial genetic tests; many have done so with conscious thought about the ethical and moral issues surrounding their efforts. Again as an example, Myriad has adopted a philosophy that they will not perform tests on minors (for diseases where there is no treatment) or fetuses.

# Moral Questions

## Prenatal Testing

Much more complex questions are raised by the possibilities of expanding genetic testing of fetuses (as every chapter in this book recognizes). In addition to the common prenatal tests currently performed (triple screen and others), tests for other maladies such as cystic fibrosis are becoming more common. It is likely that virtually all of us would denounce genetic tests of fetuses for physical traits, such as height or eye color, for the purpose of choosing abortion or life. But many tougher choices exist.

If a child has two cystic fibrosis mutations, no good treatments exist currently, but there are some therapeutic possibilities on the horizon. In families with a history of Huntington's disease, some contemplate testing fetuses for the disease even though there is no clear solution in the near future. The family choices based on the results of these tests are agonizingly difficult. None of us can know for certain if we would test or how we would deal with a positive result.

Recently BIO (Biotech Industry Organization) conducted six focus groups of a dozen people each to discuss whether genetic testing on fetuses was appropriate for a range of characteristics ranging from severe physical birth defects to things like physical appearance. These participants, self-described as religious conservatives or fundamentalists, were fairly diverse in other ways (for example, half were republican, half were democrat). Questions focused on the acceptable or unacceptable uses of technology to treat diseases through genetic testing of fetuses. Acceptable applications of *in utero* genetic testing included treatments/cures for all life-threatening diseases, blindness, deafness, asthma, and so forth. Unacceptable applications included adjusting IQ, or such things as height, baldness, hair, or eye color. Participants were united in their views on the ends of the spectrum, but they varied widely in their opinions in the middle of the spectrum. Only after some discussion and occasional dissent were certain other applications determined to be "acceptable," such as alcoholism, depression, diabetes, dyslexia, high blood pressure, and the "violence gene."[17] As people of faith, we need to prepare ourselves for the upcoming debates over these "gray" issues. Pastors and lay persons must become knowledgeable about genetic information and how it will affect people's lives in ways that have never occurred in the past. We must engage people of the biotech industry to influence how this field will evolve.

## Cost Issues

At present, the insurance companies are in the throes of most genetic discrimination issues. As discussed previously, people's greatest fears about genetic testing center around the use of test results by insurers to increase premiums or deny coverage. By law, insurers of group plans cannot use this information in this way, and Congress is considering extending these "anti-discrimination" laws to policies for individuals.

More important, however, is the issue of paying for the genetic tests themselves. If we believe that the knowledge gained from these tests does allow for more effective prevention and treatment, what about those people who cannot afford to be tested? Those 40 million Americans without insurance already deal with the problem of how to pay for treatment. Now they and society must also consider the short- and long-term cost of not being tested.

For those of us with insurance, we must still deal with insurers who will not pay for selected genetic tests. The tests for mutations in the BRCA1 and BRCA2 genes are extremely complex and expensive. For each test, 35,000 base pairs of DNA must be sequenced at a cost of $2,400. The CardiaRisk test is expected to be much cheaper ($300-500) since it tests for only a single point mutation. Jay Moyes at Myriad notes virtually all insurers reimburse at least a portion of the cost of the BRCA1/BRCA2 test. For uninsured individuals or those who are denied full coverage, this high cost is often an insurmountable hurdle. Genetic testing companies hope to reduce costs in the future by providing a whole battery of tests from a single patient sample, but this will not fully alleviate the problem.

In this chapter, I will not address issues of "economic discrimination" that result from the ability of the affluent to test for and attempt to deal with their own genetic predispositions (see Schwandt, p. 47, and Bettenhausen, pp. 97 and 111). The issues around this are no different than those that currently exist around access to high-priced health care options today. As a nation we will continue to contemplate the issues arising from providing fair access to health care.

## Health Care Rationing

In every country, including the United States, health care rationing occurs daily. In the United States, insurers, states, and Medicare/Medicaid exclude medicines and procedures depending on cost and patient status. Transplant recipients are chosen based on such factors as age, need, or cause of need. In Oregon where a state health insurance experiment is underway, nearly 1,000 medical procedures are listed in someone's descending order of importance and an arbitrary line is drawn somewhere between 500 and 600. Procedures above the line would be paid for; below the line, they would not. In countries with a national health care system, the rationing is more extreme. In Canada or the United Kingdom, it is not uncommon for an 80-year-old woman to be told she can get a heart transplant, but she will be put in a priority waiting line that means her transplant will occur in seven years.

Genetic testing has the potential to reduce health care rationing by reducing costs and increasing the effectiveness of health care spending by allowing earlier and more accurate intervention.

# Future Developments

## Genetics and Behavior

While companies in the industry are working to find disease-predisposing genes and drugs to offset them, identifying genes for normal or abnormal behaviors is primarily occurring in academia. To date, biotechnology companies have not ventured into this area because it is controversial, involves a complex interaction among a large number of genes, and presently does not appear profitable.

Researchers predict that in five to six years we will be able to talk about specific examples where genetics affects behavior. We may know that certain groups of people who are "thrill seekers" or "sensation seekers" share the same gene(s).

It is unlikely that the biotechnology industry will venture into this area in the near term. As one individual in this segment of the industry said, "How can you test for a predisposition for honesty?" We see the extreme example of Jim Carrey's role in "Liar Liar," but who can say they have a family history of never being untruthful? To whom would we compare a "dishonest" person's genes in order to identify differences? Companies interested in these types of evaluations will be better served from an information and cost standpoint by using the "psychological" tests that already exist.

In any case, a specific genetic variation will clearly not be a predictor of behavior in the same way a gene for cystic fibrosis predicts disease. Even genes for mental illness are not expected to be precise at predicting disease. Other genes and obviously the environment are clearly factors affecting behavior.

In a paper in the June 1997 issue of the *American Journal of Human Genetics*, leading researchers describe the status of research into genetic links to behavior. The authors ask the question, "Genes must play some role but how much is environment and how much is genetic?" The authors write: "Only a few decades ago, psychologists believed that characteristics of human behavior were almost entirely the result of environmental influences. These characteristics now are known to be genetically influenced, in many cases to a substantial degree. Intelligence and memory, novelty seeking and activity level, and shyness and sociability all show some degree of genetic influence."[18]

While genetics is only one factor in behavior, it should not be completely disregarded. Numerous questions will arise as we learn more about the impact of genetics on behavior; for example:

- Can tobacco companies be held responsible for the addiction or damage caused by cigarettes?
- Should this "genetic predisposition" information be allowed to be used for or against someone accused of a crime?
- How does genetics affect mate selection?
- What is the impact on individual value adoption?

## Pharmacogenomics

What do you do with a drug that virtually cures 40 percent of people suffering from a disease, has no effect on 40 percent, and causes 20 percent to have an adverse reaction? This is the case for a number of therapeutics. Genetic testing allows us to begin to answer this question.

Why do certain people respond to certain drugs and others do not? Scientists from Vanderbilt University reported on this question at the American Chemical Society Conference. They showed that 10 percent of Caucasians and 2 percent of Asians do not respond to codeine due to a genetic mutation; they lack an enzyme. The lack of this enzyme also causes patients to experience exaggerated effects of certain existing drugs for high blood pressure, mental illness, and depression.

Many conventional drugs are marketed to broad populations such as individuals with high blood pressure. They often work in only 30-35 percent of their target populations. If physicians try one blood pressure drug and it does not work, they try another drug. Trial and error takes time and is expensive and essentially turns the patient into a "guinea pig."

Things have begun to change because of a new concept in biotechnology known as "pharmacogenomics." At its simplest, a pharmacogenomic drug would be discovered and developed based on detailed genetic knowledge of the specific segment of a disease population in which it has maximum benefit and minimum side effects. The drug would be tested in and marketed to a specific subset of patients. Pharmacogenomics allows physicians and patients to have a much higher level of confidence in their treatment decisions.

# Summary

Genetic testing is being developed by businesses that are made up of individuals very much like any strata of society, including people of faith. There is no sinister "master plan" behind the overall flow of development. To many of us involved in the industry, genetic tests are viewed as a tool that allows patients and their physicians to make more informed decisions. Genetic test development will occur and at an increasingly rapid pace. I hope that my comments here will aid the kind of conversation that we need to have in the church as these developments increasingly influence our lives. It is crucial that those of us in the church become better educated so that we can enter into and attempt to affect the ongoing debate.

It is also crucial that we participate in the debate in order to witness that while the genes God has given us are a gift, he transcends our genetic make-up. We must affirm that we are more than just the sum of our genes. While genetic testing is a useful tool in helping us make intelligent choices about medical care, we must affirm that there is more to life. We must affirm the importance of God's plan for each of our lives even though we can never fully fathom it.

# SECTION TWO

# ENGAGING WORLDVIEWS AND PROPOSING ALTERNATIVES

# THE GENETIC "FIX": CHALLENGE TO CHRISTIAN FAITH AND COMMUNITY

## *Philip Hefner*

We encounter genetic testing and screening clothed in very specific garments, wrapped in what we might call the habits of our hearts. I have some points to make about these American habits: (1) Genetic testing and genetic medicine in general are governed by a prevailing worldview and also by the possibilities that our technology offers us; (2) the church will interpret its faith, nurture its people, and shape its community life in response to these two factors of worldview and technology; (3) the adequacy of the church's proclamation and spiritual nurturing will be judged by whether they engage the worldview, whether they reflect helpfully on the actual practice of genetic testing and screening, and sustain the men, women, and children who participate in our congregations. These points lead to my main concern: As individual Christians, we must work to make our congregations places where all our people can find a vital community. A vital community is one where people can talk together in Christian freedom and mutual respect, while at the same time acknowledging their differing perspectives, needs, and suffering. In such a community these people can think together within the framework of the Christian faith and minister to each other in Christian friendship. The first half of this chapter focuses on the prevailing American perspectives that condition our thinking about genetic testing and screening; the second half sets forth in detail how we can bring our faith and life to bear upon the quest for vital community in our churches.

In brief, the context in which American society is offered the vast potential of applied genetics is a prevailing worldview that conveys a substantially false understanding of the world and promotes a correspondingly perverse behavioral response to the world, yoked to an economic system that necessarily defines persons in terms of production and consumption. Moreover, this set of forces comes to us in the form of a powerful spirituality that laps at the hearts and minds of every member of our society. What response is available to Christians, and to the church? I believe the church should affirm its character as a microcosm of larger society, a community that represents the individuals and groups that fill the roles that play in the script of the applied genetics drama that presently claims our attention.

# I. Worldview

## 1. Worldview and the Tapestry of Our Lives

We live in an age in the United States marked by what might be called the mentality of the hammer and nail. We like to think that our problems, like nails in a board, are best handled with a little pounding. We devote a lot of time searching for the best hammers available, and we prize very highly men and women who know how to wield those hammers. Much of the approach to medicine today, particularly the genetic aspects of medicine, is presented to us in this manner: Hammers for dealing with the problems that disturb us. Genetic testing, we are told, is one of these tools.

Hammers and nails, however, are never just hammers and nails—as if they were in isolation—waiting on the rack at the local hardware store to be taken wherever they are needed and placed in the most competent hands. They exist rather in a web of relationships that encompasses everything in our lives—including our image of ourselves, our view of the world, the persons and communities that are dear to us, and our Christian faith. I use the term "worldview" to refer to the tapestry of ideas, commitments, hopes, and fears that forms the background for all that we believe, say, and do. "Spirituality" also refers to this tapestry. Spirituality refers to the fact that we not only look at the tapestry and learn about it, but we also try to shape our lives so they will fit into the tapestry.

The threads of this tapestry remain indistinct most of the time, often defying our attempts to bring them out of the shadows of our heart's deepest habits. They do not come easily into the light, where we can examine them and speak clearly about the tapestry that is so important for our lives. Genetic testing is situated in this tapestry; it comes with a worldview and a spirituality. If we recognize this basic fact, then we can understand that our task is to be sure that worldview and the spirituality are genuinely Christian, and that they are appropriate to us as the Christians we are and want to become.

## 2. How Nature Is Imaged in the Prevailing Worldview

Even though it is not monolithic, and has not grasped the hearts and minds of everyone, there is a prevailing worldview powerfully present in our culture, and it seeks to shape us inwardly as we go about living our lives in the everyday world. Since the media of television, radio, and the press are powerful instruments for shaping opinions in our society, we can expect to find the prevailing worldview presented in the media. Let me give two vignettes.

A television commercial comes on the screen, with an appealing scene of a mother tenderly holding an infant. A voiceover says: "Giving birth to a child is one of the great experiences of life." The voice continues as an anguished young couple appears on the screen: "Yet, many couples find themselves unable to have children." A doctor appears, a figure that elicits respect and trust, as the voice continues: "If

*ENGAGING WORLDVIEWS AND PROPOSING ALTERNATIVES*

Mother Nature is not cooperating with your desires, call Dr. Doe at ABC Fertility Clinic." The name and telephone number hold our attention as the commercial fades.

Recently, as I faced myself in the shaving mirror, I heard this commercial on a radio station's morning drive-time show: "You care about yourself. You eat healthy foods, keep your weight down, and you exercise regularly. You take care of your body. When you look in the mirror, do you see that your body needs re-shaping? Are you unhappy with what you see? Perhaps you should consult XYZ cosmetic surgery clinic."

*Nature, body, and medical science*—these are decisive threads in the tapestry of life in which genetic testing becomes a reality for us. Genetic testing, along with every other aspect of genetic medicine, comes into our lives tightly interwoven with these elements as we interconnect them in our real-life, day-to-day worldviews.

Note four things about these two vignettes: (1) They emanate from the medical community, in terms and images that are designed to elicit our trust in physicians and technicians who come across as highly respected persons, who are concerned for us personally and also scientifically competent. (2) These vignettes show the impact of the market economy that is such a significant thread in the tapestry of life today; they appear on the radio and television as commercial advertising, which means that they are couched in terms that are designed to sell services to us. We receive the message about fertility therapy in the medium of a sales pitch—a fact that ought not be overlooked. Medicine is now substantially subsumed within the market economy, and we are told that in the case of medical care, as with other purchases we make, we must now behave as informed and aggressive consumers. (3) The very fact that they occur as commercials in the mass media tells us that they are assumed to be relevant to a large number of persons in the target audience and, therefore, worth the expense of developing and broadcasting. Certain groups of people—marketing specialists, advertising writers, and the client who paid for them—apparently believe that these commercials are worth the money, because they will have the desired results. (4) The commercials play to very basic hopes and fears of everyone. They tug at the heartstrings and also the mind: the joy of having children, the obligation to live healthy lifestyles, the pride and the anxiety that go with body shape. In a few words, these commercials touch our sense of values very deeply, well beyond superficial matters of taste and comfort.

Medical doctors, biotech labs, pharmaceutical companies, hospitals and clinics, and their advertising agencies are all betting considerable amounts of money that certain worldviews do drive our lives and that they can guide the application of those worldviews to accomplish ends that each of these groups believes is worth pursuing.

The worldview expressed in these vignettes includes an idea of nature and how we relate to it. It presents us with normative ideas, and it urges us to develop a spirituality that will fit our lives comfortably into its embrace. In simple terms, this worldview holds to the following:

1. All of nature should finally be re-shaped in the ways that humans deem most desirable.

2. We have the obligation to do this re-shaping. Nature unshaped by human hands, when it is in our advantage to do so, somehow stands as a judgment on us—we have not lived up to our potential and its obligations. This is true of our relations to nature as environment: rivers, mountains, seashores, and mineral ore; it is true of nature as plants and animals—agricultural seed hybrids, and the total control of animal species that we consider important to our well-being. For example, cloning animals for commercial and health benefits is now a prominent choice for us. Finally, this nature that we are to manage includes our very own bodies. There is a sense in which, under the impact of this worldview, we treat all of life, from hybrid seeds to our own bodies, in one consistent manner: manipulating nature to what we consider to be our advantage.

3. All diseases should be eliminated or at least countered. For instance, we assume infertility should be rendered fertile, wherever possible, whereas fertility, when it is deemed necessary and desirable, should be interrupted. We should have a reliable projection of our body's future, whether that involves determining the gender of unborn fetuses, specific genetic tests, or mapping our individual and family genomes.

*This is the major characteristic of the ideological garments in which genetic testing meets us. We approach nature—including our own human nature—in terms of what we can make of it; nature is not something we accept, rather it is the object of our fantastic ability to re-shape our world. Further, this characteristic is not incidental, but it reveals itself as a fundamental American habit of the heart.* When in the course of this essay, I speak of the dominant or prevailing worldview, I refer to this body of ideas.

## 3. The Roots of the Prevailing Worldview in Human Nature

My critique of the prevailing worldview grows out of genuine *ambivalence*, meaning that I hold two opinions of this worldview: positive and negative. The positive response acknowledges that this worldview is deeply rooted in our human psyche; it cannot be dismissed out of hand.

Freedom, for example, is deeply rooted in human nature, even though we are also to a considerable extent creatures of determinism. Our brains both enable us and compel us to create culture. Culture consists of the recipes for living that are not simply written in our genes, but recipes that we learn and teach, the product of our freedom and creativity. Culture is just as essential to human life as the inherited genetic recipes that we hold in common with the rest of the creaturely world. Our human nature includes both genes and cultures, both biology and free choice. Just as surely as our brains are basic features of the natural processes by which God has made us, so, too, the freedom and culture that those brains enable are basic to our human nature.

Biological nature makes babies possible; the culture and freedom of our brains make fertility clinics possible. We may attempt to re-shape our nature when the flow of our lives seems to be uncooperative. What we often overlook is that, as elements of our culture, the fertility clinics are as much the product of our human nature as the infertile biological processes that make babies impossible.

We can go even further to say that we have no choice but to synthesize our freedom and our biological determinedness. If we pretended that newborn babies do not require the nurturing and parenting that we fashion in our freedom and culture, most babies would die. Human births cannot just happen out on the range, as calves' births do. The genes may direct the mother to care for the infant and to nurse it, but they cannot provide cribs and nurseries, nor remedies for mothers who cannot breast feed, nor a thousand other things that newborn infants require in our contemporary society. Parenting does not proceed full-blown from our biology; it is a learned skill that depends on the knowledge that we gain in our creativity and freedom.

In other words, the prevailing worldview is correct in its assumption that there is no nature on planet earth that is exempt from our freedom to define and shape it. There is no forest on the planet, no river or animal species, that does not live its life in the embrace of human freedom and decision—whether we choose to alter them, or whether we choose to leave them alone. There is, in the last analysis, no way to escape the human nature that is innately co-creating and nature-shaping. The prevailing worldview I have described recognizes this aspect of our basic human nature, and has made it the major motif for interpreting human life. I attempt to express this fact by saying that we are *created co-creators*.

## 4. The Dilemmas Inherent to the Prevailing Worldview

My ambivalence toward the prevailing worldview includes not only a positive response to its emphasis on the freedom that is truly an essential feature of human being, but also a negative response to what the prevailing worldview leaves out of consideration. A dilemma emerges, when we recognize that alongside a legitimate concern for freedom an imbalance appears within this worldview that actually falsifies what human life is about. The tapestry of human life that the dominant worldview presents gives virtually no attention to the fact that we are fully as shaped by nature as we are its shapers, as much a part of nature as the creators of nature. This is our creat*ed* aspect, and for this reason it is better to say that we are *created* co-creators, rather than simply *co-creators*. Just as we must not minimize the free, nature-shaping dimension of our nature, so, too, we must not forget that human nature is innately created and shaped by nature that is beyond our control.

We do not choose our genetic make-up, just as we do not choose our parents, our time or place of birth, our race or gender, or the economic and social class location of our birth. We are thoroughly creatures of natural processes, just as surely as are the plants and other animals on our planet. The billions-of-years-long process of nature's evolution has made us what we are—it is the means God has employed to create us.

When we acknowledge that we belong to the whole of nature, we accept our createdness—as the human race and also as the individuals that we are. It is just as important for us to accept who we are as creatures of nature as it is to affirm that we can shape and alter the nature we have been given. The dilemma of the prevailing worldview, its falsification of what it means to be human, lies in its almost complete refusal to acknowledge this *createdness* of human nature. The prevailing worldview offers no support for a wholesome acceptance of our nature, with its limitations. Whether those limitations be natural boundaries of our strength and reason, or what is called physical or emotional "defect," or illness and disease, or the natural propensity to age and to die, the prevailing worldview offers little besides pity or stigmatizing strategies of separation.

A "fix-it" or "repair-it" mentality comes hand-in-hand with this refusal to accept our createdness. There are spokespersons among the so-called "disabled" segments of our society who attack this mentality, because it designates them as persons who "ought to be fixed," rather than accepting them as valuable human beings. Many deaf persons reject out of hand the notion that they are in need of repair due to their lack of hearing. They insist on the recognition of sign language as a valid alternative to speaking. The fix-it perspective tends to segregate and ostracize those whose nature deviates from the norm, rather than receiving the contributions they can make to our common life.

Because it cannot acknowledge that we belong to nature, the prevailing worldview has difficulty admitting that we lack the fundamental wisdom that is necessary if we are to be adequate shapers of nature. We discover more vividly every day that we do not really know what nature is for, or what our proper relationship to it is, whether it be nature as environment, as other animals, or as our own human selves as bodies within nature. Are rivers, canyons, and seashores simply at our disposal, to serve our interests however we determine? Are other species of animals simply resources for us to use for our own benefit, even if it requires total subjugation of the species? Are we in any way obligated to serve the welfare of life-forms other than our own—are chickens put on this earth simply to provide humans with food? Did baboons have no integrity in the creation until it was learned that their bone marrow may be used to enhance the human immunity to HIV? At what point does genetic engineering trespass the boundary of what is genuinely and normatively human? Is there a normative human nature, and, if so, how would it be defined?

The fix-it mentality regards the fully repaired body to be the norm for human nature. The fact that we have no consensus in our society about this norm reveals the basic inadequacy of the worldview that prevails in our culture. One of the most powerful habits of our hearts is the supposition that every woman and every couple has the innate right to give birth to a baby; no medical or technological intervention is too extravagant to fulfill this normative right. There is another habit among us that holds up as normative the freedom to choose not to give birth—whether by practicing abortion or abstinence. These views carry with them latent ideas of what is normative for human nature, and they justify whatever manipulation or intervention is required in order to fulfill their norm. These views presuppose foundational answers to the questions: Who are we? What is the norm for our human nature? Ironically, most of the time our society tries to avoid facing up to these basic questions. The prevailing worldview cannot, in fact, be put into practice except at the cost of bracketing out the larger, ultimate questions concerning nature and human nature, and restricting ourselves to the more immediate definitions of human preference and survival.

One of the most perplexing dilemmas raised by the prevailing worldview is that it blurs the distinction between healing and "fixing." There is a basic human sense that healing disease and disability is a basic good for human existence, and Christian faith reinforces this sense. It is also true that human creativity and ingenuity are basic elements of healing processes. Where does the distinction lie between healing and restoration of a life to healthy and useful existence, on the one hand, and an obsessive intention to eliminate all disease and defect and a compulsion to shape life in ways that conform to our preconceived stereotypes of what is normal, beautiful, and useful, on the other hand? This dilemma is near the top of the agenda of perplexing and urgent issues that genetic testing and engineering present to us. This distinction between healing and fixing must be dealt with, because perverse agendas for engineering life can easily be subsumed within the aura of wholesome healing, in ways that may well prove to be demonic.

We open ourselves to the greatest distortions if we separate genetic testing and screening from this worldview that shapes our lives as Americans. Christians will want to examine the elements of this worldview, to understand what basic issues underlie them, and to relate those issues both to genetic testing and to our Christian faith.

## II. The Actual Use of Genetic Testing

The actual practice of genetic testing is discussed in detail by other authors in this volume. Here I will provide a summary, in briefest terms, that serves the purposes of this essay.

*1. Genetic testing becomes an option for us, first of all, within the practice of medicine.* It shares the psychological predispositions to intimacy and dependency that medical practice awakens in us. We usually go to our physicians for check-ups or because there is something wrong that we want corrected or healed. The very fact that genetic testing is done by physicians and their associated health care workers, and mainly in hospitals, reinforces its association with medicine. Other associations could just as well be made: with the science of genetics and the genetics lab, with the technological means by which testing is carried out, or with the manufacturing and marketing processes of the businesses that provide the wherewithal for genetic testing. Indeed, some persons will make these associations first—scientists, engineers, and business persons—but they are a relatively small group. Furthermore, when these persons face the decision of genetic testing for themselves and their families, it will come to them in the context of medical practice.

*2. Genetic testing will be of two kinds:* screening large populations for certain defects, in which case the testing is a matter of public health; and testing that is occasioned either by the medical judgment that a possible defect may be present or by the request of the person involved, such as Orthodox Jewish couples contemplating marriage, who wish to learn of the risk of Tay-Sachs disease. There are many complex ethical issues arising in both of these testing situations, on which a large literature of discussion exists. Many of these ethical issues are dealt with elsewhere in this book.

*3. The actual practice of genetic testing will be driven by the interests of several different groups in our society.* These groups include those that represent medical and health care delivery, biotechnology companies, insurance companies, various levels of government—including public health departments—the judiciary and legal professions, the communications media, marketing/advertising companies, and the desires of the patient/consumer. All of these groups must figure in our thinking as we consider the issues that pertain to genetic testing. (The chapters in Sections One and Three of this book delineate the views of several of these.) The ways in which these groups express their interests will influence society and its individuals wholistically; it will be difficult to separate the impact of one group from the others. In summary fashion, we might say that the following forces will shape the actual practice of genetics testing in our society: (a) medical and public health judgment, (b) the market economy, (c) the ways in which conflicts are adjudicated legally, (d) government regulation, and (e) the needs and values of consumers, chiefly consumers who are patients, but also physicians and other testing practitioners (since they also function as first level consumers of the products of the biotech, insurance, and marketing companies). When Congress approved the Human Genome Project in 1987, it recognized the scientific and economic dimensions of the project, but its publicly stated motivation for approval was the project's role in the medical processes of healing.

*4. Genetic testing pertains, for the most part, to the unborn, their mothers, and the young and their families.* Most genetic testing now involves—and probably will continue to involve—couples who are contemplating conceiving a child, pregnant women, and infants and children. For the most part, genetic testing is not a medical challenge to middle-aged and elderly adults. Most often, testing challenges adults to make decisions in behalf of those who cannot decide for themselves. A significant percentage (perhaps 75 percent) of such testing involves women's bodies, and therefore also places women at greater risk. In the case of children and adolescents, the testing may provide knowledge that will alter the family life, maturation, and self-understanding of the patients for the rest of their lives. The knowledge may also be a constant threat to the insurability and employability of the young person, which also affects the entire family. One writer has described the results of genetic testing as potentially "toxic knowledge."[1]

5. *Genetic testing is an entree, a passage that leads to further actions.* Genetic testing is not carried out for its own sake, but only because of what may come about as a result of the testing. It provides knowledge, and this knowledge may call for specific action. Persons will not be tested unless there is a sense that something might be amiss that the testing can detect or rule out. If the test is a screening, a good finding will be the end of the matter. If the test is diagnostic in character, its results may well lead to further explorations and therapies; if the condition is untreatable or beyond therapy, the end result will include dismay, frustration, and even depression. We are presently much more successful at diagnosing genetically based disease than we are at treating or curing it. This means that genetic testing for the patient, the family, and the medical professional will—quite regularly—be the prelude both to a decision to re-shape the patient's nature and also to the processes necessary for carrying out that decision. After all, the personal anxiety and public discussion of medical ethics are not occasioned by the fact that the testing may provide proof that no problem exists. The anxiety and discussion center on the possible actions that may result if the tests reveal a problem, results such as abortion or various therapeutic measures, or the dislocation that results when there can be no therapy for a dismaying diagnosis.

6. *The prevailing worldview offers very limited personal and spiritual support.* Persons who avail themselves of genetic testing will find the prevailing worldview to be of no spiritual or emotional support when their lives are caught up in ambiguity as a result of the testing. This is also true if the results require that the patient accept the fact that his or her natural condition is not remediable and that personal meaning must be forged in the face of that bad news. Genetic test findings mean these persons are now placed in the category of those whose bodies are not fixable.

## III. Taking Stock: How Far Have We Come in the Discussion?

How far have we come in our discussion? We can take stock by recalling these points:

1. Genetic testing, as with all of the various aspects of genetic medicine, comes to us within a definite prevailing worldview. Even though this worldview has grasped one important point—that humans are shapers of nature, including the nature of their own bodies and spirits, it has focused so exclusively on this one insight that its overall interpretation of human life is one-sided and defective. It leaves out of consideration the extent to which our human nature belongs to the rest of nature and is called to live as a partner to the whole of the natural world.

2. Due to its placement within medicine, genetic testing becomes a passage for us through which we expect to receive healing and well-being.

3. At the same time, there are many different interests in our society that are brought together in the enterprise of genetic testing, and we cannot ignore the multiple players in the enterprise. Each group of players has its own interest in the genetic testing enterprise, makes its own contribution, and shapes the thinking and behavior of the people who belong to the group. One group, however—patients/consumers—includes potentially all people in our society, and offers a common experience that cuts across and relativizes the perspectives of all of the other groups.

# IV. The Christian Faith:
# A Melody We Bring to the Situation

## 1. Genetic Testing: A Kind of Sacred Space

*The situation we are describing is an actual place where we encounter the challenge of determining what it means for us to be genuinely human; it is a kind of sacred space where we meet God and where we discover the meaning of our Christian faith.* None of these challenges happens in the abstract. Our basic humanity is what we live out in the real world in which we exist; God comes to us nowhere else except in our actual day-to-day existence, and it is in this place that our faith speaks to us. Joseph Sittler spoke of our real-life situation as the counterpoint in which the melody of the Gospel is sung.[2] The counterpoint makes a difference for the melody's meaning. So, too, our faith takes on particular meaning when it is played out in the concrete situation that we have described up to this point in the discussion of genetic testing and the worldview that prevails in our North American society.

## 2. A Sketch of the Christian Faith: Story and Ritual

The Christian faith offers a large narrative or story, which contextualizes all of human experience. It is into this narrative that Christian faith invites us to integrate the experience we bring to all the issues of everyday life, including genetic testing.

The narrative begins with the affirmation that all of nature, the entire universe, is grounded in a creator God whose character is marked by freedom, justice, faithfulness, reliability, and love. The traditional Christian doctrine of creation out of nothing expresses the conviction that there is no source or ground of nature other than this creator God, and the doctrine of continuing creation asserts that God continues to be the source of the natural world in every moment, and not just at the point of origins. God's presence as source and ground of nature is everywhere and always marked by freedom, faithfulness, justice, reliability, and love.

Humans are part of this creation: One of the biblical stories depicts them emerging on the sixth day, following a sequence that is generally evolutionary in its form (Genesis 1:1-27), while another pictures humans as creatures of the earth into whom

God has breathed the divine spirit (Genesis 2:7). This spirit is what makes the earth-creature genuinely human. God's will for human identity is affirmed in the single most important statement that Christian faith makes about humans (and it shares this affirmation with Jewish and Muslim faiths), *that they are created in the image of God*. When it is linked to the two creation doctrines, the image of God symbol forms a strong statement that all of nature is rooted in God and that God's specificity is in some way present in humans.

The narrative also speaks vividly of the dissonance that characterizes human existence. That dissonance, however, is not the first note struck in the narrative's theme, but rather comes after the affirmation that human nature and all of creation are rooted in the goodness of God. The dissonance is not presented as essential or normative nature, but it is rather described as a disruption, a fall from original goodness in God, which is conveyed in the doctrines of fall and sin. Even though there is no single authorized way to talk about sin in the tradition of Christian faith as a whole, the tradition emphasizes that the dissonance touches the fundamental structures of human nature and not just its peripheral aspects. *Original* sin refers to the sin for which humans are not personally responsible, but which they inherit in different ways; *actual* sin describes the dissonance as it finds its home in the actual life of each person, for which each individual and community does share responsibility.

Jesus Christ is central to Christian faith. In Christ, on the one hand, the alienation and guilt that accompany sin are transmuted into reconciliation—oneness with self, others, nature, and God. On the other hand, Jesus is the model of the form that human nature should take. Jesus is the norm of human life. When Christians share in this reconciliation and conform their lives to the life of Christ, they are actualizing what they were created to be. Since Jesus does hold this position as revealer of truth, reconciler, and model of normative humanity, and since union with him is the centerpiece of Christian faith, normative human life takes the shape of self-giving for the benefit of the whole creation and its people that God is said to have embodied in Jesus.

Humans, together with the entire creation, are on a trajectory that is defined by God's will as embodied in Christ, and this trajectory will finally bring the fulfillment or consummation of the created order, including humans as part of that order.

The coherence of this narrative must be linked to the ritual of the Christian faith, which centers in Baptism and Holy Communion. In these two rituals we reenact in symbolic form the reception of God's gifts of grace, and also the behavior that conforms to Christ. The task of the believer is to translate this symbolic action into the actual behavior that takes place in everyday life. The rituals thus serve as a bridge or a sort of "interlude" between life as narrated in the grand Christian story and the "arena of the social world where ethical decision making and character formation count."[3] Baptism is a ritual of regenerative cleansing, entrance into the covenant community with Christ, and incorporation into his life, death, and resurrection. Holy Communion is a ritual of community love and solidarity, remembrance of the pivotal events in Jesus' life, and incorporation into his action of self-giving for the world. We are recipients of Jesus' self-giving and also followers who extend his self-giving into our own worlds.

From this Christian story and ritual, we can draw some links to the situation we have described with respect to genetic testing.

## 3. Christian Theological Perspectives on Humans as Shapers of Nature

**Resources:** Christian faith acknowledges the importance of humans as shapers of nature and relates it to the affirmation that we are created in the image of God. As shapers of nature, we participate in transcendence. Evolution itself is a process of "ecological self-transcendence"[4] that is marked by the presence of God in us, as Spirit. It is the dimension of our potential "mystery, depth, and greatness"[5] and as such is an arena in which we encounter God. By virtue of the capabilities with which our species has been endowed, we can say that we are created, in the image of Christ, to be God's created co-creators.[6] The Christian faith brings two of its most powerful symbols to resource this insight: redemption and future fulfillment (eschatology). Redemption is associated with Christ, and it speaks of the creation being re-created and transformed by God's own work of shaping nature; future fulfillment speaks of the incompleteness of this created natural world. Nature is in need of transformation if it is to realize God's eternal will for it. To say that humans are God's created co-creators is, at one level, simply to say that God has chosen to work through humans.

**Challenges:** Bringing this heavy theological freight to our ability to shape nature, Christian faith also insists that in our co-creating, we are accountable and called to obedience. The image of God brings with it possibilities and responsibilities. Christians insist that Christ is the paradigm of the image of God within us, and this means that relatedness and caring are central. This set of meanings will counterbalance and even call into question any manipulative spirit of genetic testing. As co-creators, we can decide to limit or even prohibit some of the things that we are capable of doing, if they do not conform to the Christ-paradigm.

## 4. Christian Theological Perspectives on Humans as Creatures of Nature

**Resources:** Christian faith speaks of the goodness of creation and its purposiveness. Consequently, there is no need to suppress the fact that we are thoroughly natural creatures. One Old Testament scholar has said, following Genesis, chapter two, that in the ancient Hebrew view, we are "dirtlings" into whom God has breathed the spirit.[7] Another has interpreted the same passage to say that we are creatures of the topsoil who are called to till the rest of the topsoil.[8] The desires and hopes for nature expressed in genetic testing are affirmed to be important, even if fraught with ambiguity and controversy. The Christian conception of nature is such that scientific and technological explorations are not prohibited or minimized, but encouraged and considered to be consistent with human nature—even though they may also be controversial and must be subject to critique and boundaries. Since nature is not sacred or divine, interventions into its processes are not necessarily sinful. However, humans are creatures, "dirtlings," not divine, and they are accountable for their interventions.

This accountability is grounded in the conviction that in the natural world we find ourselves engaged by the action of God. The experience of God in and under natural processes is eloquently reflected in Psalm 139: 1-2, 13-18:

> O Lord, you have searched me and known me.
> You know when I sit down and when I rise up;
> you discern my thoughts from far away. . . .
> Where can I go from your spirit? . . .
> For it was you who formed my inward parts;
> you knit me together in my mother's womb.
> I praise you, for I am fearfully and wonderfully made.
> Wonderful are your works;
> that I know very well.
> My frame was not hidden from you,
> when I was being made in secret,
> intricately woven in the depths of the earth.
> Your eyes beheld my unformed substance.
> In your book were written all the days that were formed for me,
> when none of them as yet existed.
> How weighty to me are your thoughts, O God!
> How vast is the sum of them!
> I try to count them—they are more than the sand;
> I come to the end—I am still with you.

Even though it is not easy to understand, Christian faith insists that the psalmist is describing the nature of that which we test genetically, and our testing must not ignore this fact. Here, too, Christian faith brings some of its most powerful symbols to bear as resource for interpreting our naturalness: the incarnation and sacramental theology. The incarnation of God in Jesus Christ is the strongest possible statement that nature can be affirmed, *as it is,* to be a fit vessel for the presence and redemptive work of God; nature does not have to be "fixed" or "repaired" in order for there to be an incarnation—rather, God's presence in itself repairs nature. Our Lutheran sacramental theology of the real presence has also traditionally affirmed the natural elements—water, bread, wine—to be suitable, *as they are,* to work as the means of God's grace. Lutherans have reflected this affirmation of the natural creation with their strong emphasis on what is technically expressed as "the finite is capable of the infinite" and "nature is capable of God" (*finitum capax infiniti, natura capax dei*). We do not have to demean our naturalness, try to escape it, or fix it, in order for it to serve as the instrument of God's gracious presence. These are among the very strongest elements of the Lutheran tradition.

**Challenges:** Christian faith will not tolerate genetic testing or other interventions that look upon nature as one-dimensional or as infinitely manipulable. The human nature upon which we work our genetic testing and manipulation is not trash needing our technological repair. Nature belongs to something greater than our designs, and we are accountable to that Greatness. Accordingly, Christian faith emphasizes the dignity and even sacrality of life, especially human life. Christian tradition asks whether there is an integrity to nature that humans must respect, and it attempts to describe that integrity. We respect science as a source of knowing nature's integrity, but we subject its specific strategies for manipulating nature to critical questions. To know that nature is capable of God is, therefore, also a resource for critique of any arrogant pride with respect to nature.

## 5. Christian Theological Perspectives on the Purpose of Human Life

**Resources:** Genetic testing and genetic medicine continually raise the questions, "What is the purpose of our interventions?" "How should we carry out our mandate as co-creators?" Christian faith has no specific blueprint for dealing with these questions, but it recognizes that they are important and unavoidable. The narrative of the Christian faith does present the normative resource for our defining what is good and the values to guide our actions. It does offer formal answers: we humans are on earth to glorify God the Creator, and whatever our actions at any given period of history, they should look something like those of Jesus of Nazareth. Our faith emphasizes that lives should be lived responsibly, and that they are to be conducted under the rubric of self-giving for the benefit of the creation and its people. The narrative of Christian faith as I rehearsed it above, including the rituals associated with it, is replete with resources for speaking formally of purpose.

**Challenges:** Christian faith despises the life lived without thought of purpose. It will question any genetic intervention that is simply runaway celebration of human technological prowess. It will not tolerate genetic intervention as an end in itself. It presses for the just distribution of the benefits of genetic testing. At any time it may question the priorities that we choose for our society and the uses we make of our human and nonhuman natural resources.

## 6. Christian Theological Perspectives on Finitude, Ambiguity, and Failure

**Resources:** Christian faith insists that finitude and failure do not negate the worthfulness of human efforts. No matter how fraught with danger and vulnerability, human efforts do make a difference. They are part of God's providence, even if we cannot be sure just what the concrete shapes of that providence are. Christian faith will not avoid the prospect of death and its meaning. Inasmuch as Jesus is the model of the godly life, suffering and death will be accepted as the cost of discipleship that aims at self-giving for the welfare of the creation. Our faith provides resources for overcoming the fear of death, just as it insists that illness and mortality do not finally negate human meaning and worth. The Christian church has powerful rituals for dealing with illness, dying, and death. Rather than perceiving suffering and death as alienating us from God or Christ, we may perceive a dignity and wisdom in suffering that are life-enhancing.[9] Nor does our inherent sinfulness prove to be an obstacle, finally, to our fitness to be disciples of God's work in the world. Specifically, Lutherans have understood that we are all sinners and saints at the same time (*simul justus et peccator*).

**Challenges:** Christian faith asserts that the issues raised by our finitude and ambiguity are at the heart of its belief that humans are weak and sinful. None of our plans, none of our designs for improving upon nature, none of our medical interventions is free from sin. The saints are always sinners at the same time. Christians recognize that "this is the way humans are," and that the greater evil is to ignore that fact. Even as it supports humans in their frailty, Christian faith is also quick to scorn their pride and arrogance. Sin may be unavoidable, but to deny our sin and to be proud in it cannot be tolerated. There are things worse than failure, namely, the debasement of our having been created in the image of God. This creation in God's image is a treasure that we dare not exchange for a mess of pottage. However, even as Christian faith subjects pride to critique, it equally motivates us to live our lives in ways that go beyond passivity and inaction.

## 7. Christian Theological Perspectives on Healing and the Worthfulness of Human Life

**Resources:** Christian faith undergirds attempts at healing. Healing activities are in fact sacramental in character. By sacrament, Christian theology refers to natural objects and actions that not only carry meaningfulness and graciousness in their empirical actuality, but also convey intimations of ultimate meaning and graciousness. In proper theological terms, a sacrament has been described by St. Augustine (354-430) as the "visible form of invisible grace" and "a sign of a sacred thing." *The Catechism of the Book of Common Prayer* uses the terms "an outward and visible sign of an inward and spiritual grace."[10] These descriptions are quite usable for understanding genetic interventions, including testing, if we let our genetic interventions be governed by the sacramental meanings. The normative instances of natural things serving as bearers of grace are the sacraments of Baptism and Holy Communion. These normative sacraments throw light on the other activities of our lives as potentially serving the same presence of God that we encounter in Baptism and Holy Communion. Traditionally, the church has spoken of these other activities that reflect the presence of God as *sacramentals*.[11] A sacramental spirituality helps us to understand that healing somehow points to the essential condition that God intends for the world. Although our attempts at healing are always only partial, and often do fail, they are important because they testify to this intention of God that the entire natural creation be finally in a condition of whole-someness and health.

**Challenges:** Christian faith considers healing to be a God-given mandate and possibility, but it also understands that our healing behaviors are provisional. We know that healing finally fails in this earthly realm, but since Christians recognize also that healing is a harbinger of something larger in the future that God has in mind for the creation, they will both support healing and also relativize it. They view healing as a process that is laden with ultimacy, and this means that even as Christians engage in healing attempts, they will not settle for provisional or cheap substitutes. Healing can be a synonym for the Christian life that flows from the narrative of the faith, and as such it is normed by Jesus' life and shares in God's trajectory of promise at the end of time. Sometimes this value-laden perspective will be universally welcomed (for example, in its concern for persons and wholistic perspectives), while at other times it will be considered obstructionist and ideological (for example, its caution concerning abortion and *in vitro* fertilization).

The Christian community will expect genetic interventions to be carried out with the sensibilities and the subtle recognition that our interventions occur within the web of relationships that make up the ongoing history of human individuals and communities. Christians call for an awareness among the scientific explorers, the engineers, the caregivers, and the healers, that in undertaking their genetic interventions, they are, like the rest of us, working out their own destinies in fear and trembling. The challenge of the faith is nothing less than the recognition that in genetic intervention, we are rehearsing God's will for us within the realm of nature.

# V. The Impact of Genetic Testing

## Summarizing in Advance

We now come to the nub of the discussion, the answer to the "so what?" question: What difference does all we have considered up to this point make to individual Christians and to their church communities, the congregations? The response that follows can be summarized in this way: *The church is a community that embraces individuals representing each of the group interests that I listed above (p.80). All of the members of the church live under the impact of the prevailing worldview and must fashion their own lives in its context. The task of the church/congregation is to welcome all of these members into a community that can engage the prevailing worldview with the Christian faith, so as to enable a more wholesome worldview to emerge and also to support and empower each member of the community to live in ways that are accountable to this more wholesome worldview.* The church thus exists as a richer culture within our American culture, seeking to enable all people to live constructively and wholesomely within a host culture whose worldview is seriously deficient and potentially destructive.

We have proposed an interpretation of the spiritual and social situation in which genetic testing becomes an option in the United States, and we have also summarized elements of the Christian faith that can engage our current situation. It remains for us to consider how genetic testing within the American setting makes an impact on individual Christians and their church communities, and how our faith and church life can respond to that impact.

## Shaping the Congregational Agenda: Seven Things to Consider

*1. The prevailing worldview is in fact a spiritual proposal, and it enters into the psyches and spirits of Christians, even when they find themselves uncomfortable with it.* Worldviews as appealing, as all-encompassing, and as powerfully proclaimed as the prevailing worldview we have been discussing, penetrate the hearts and minds of people in our society, including Christians. This spiritual character of genetic intervention is exemplified in the special issue that *Time* magazine devoted to the Human Genome Project on January 17, 1994. Two photos make our point. In one photo, Francis Collins, director of the Project, is dressed in black leather, astride his motorcycle. The headline for the photo reads: "Francis Collins leads an international drive to track down all the genes and take their measure." A generation that remembers Easy Rider, Hell's Angels, Arlo Guthrie, and the love-hate relationship of Americans to their cycles might ask: Why is the director of the Human Genome Project presented in a major mass-culture news magazine in a way that carries such obvious overtones of myth, romance, and adventure—even if it is not a Harley Davidson, but rather a Honda Nighthawk 750? Perhaps because Collins plays the role of an expedition leader in the great American quest for mastery over nature, in this case our genetic nature. The second photo shows French Anderson, who is credited with doing more than anyone else to make genetic therapy a reality. The caption to this photo says that Anderson, "in his San Marino garage, shows off his black-belt skills in the Korean martial art *Tae Kwon Do* by demolishing a stack of pine boards with a single punch." Esoteric, Asian, martial, with religious and ritual overtones—all of these themes come together in the photo, whose headline reads: "French Anderson's obsession has turned fantasy into reality."

Whatever one thinks about this magazine presentation of the Human Genome Project, and whatever the editor's motivation, it clearly expresses the spiritual and worldview dimension of our view of nature and of its relation to genetic manipulations. Little wonder that its impact on persons is not restricted to that of a science or ethics textbook, nor that of an informative lecture or documentary film. It is spiritual in its impact, and it is closer to the genre of Sunday morning preaching and liturgy than it is to the restrained report in a scientific journal.

The church must recognize, therefore, that in engaging genetic testing, it is encountering science, technology, and commercialism, but also, and perhaps most importantly, a secular spirituality that is rooted in a profound worldview that grasps persons in our society at their deepest levels of being. The fact that this worldview is seriously deficient and even perverse does not gainsay its spiritual and psychological force.

2. *Genetic testing is further woven into the fabric of conditions in which people must live today, due to its being thoroughly integrated within the American market economy.* The ideology of the market economy has also attained the status of worldview in our society today. Politics, foreign policy, education, medicine, public welfare, concern for family and environment—all of these aspects of life today, and more, are fully integrated within the concept and practice of the market economy. Bernardine Healey, then head of the National Institutes of Health, the agency that supervises the Human Genome Project, announced early on that the results of the Project would be placed in the service of the economic competitiveness of the United States. Even though she was forced to retract this statement when our European partners threatened retaliation, her original intention reveals how fully indigenous genetic science and technology are to the American economic system. Since the members of our congregations understand that their personal well-being, as well as the fulfillment of their hopes and dreams, depends on how well they come to terms with the market economy, they will recognize that genetic medicine will also be part of their life within the parameters of that economic system.

3. *The respect that Americans hold for medical practice, as well as the skepticism and anxiety that accompany that respect, will also mark their attitudes toward genetic testing.* Even the recent crisis of health care funding and availability has not erased the basic respect, almost veneration, with which we approach medicine and healing. A woman recently asked me whether the church could find a way to sacralize the "twelve days of amniocentesis." She explained that she and her husband experienced intense anxiety in the days of waiting for the results of her amniocentesis. Anticipating a possibly devastating outcome that might raise the question of abortion weighed upon them traumatically. The medical arts unavoidably carry this weight—they foster hope even as they threaten despair. Genetic testing is not the medical equivalent of the annual service check of our automobiles.

4. *Since the desire for health and physical well-being is so deeply engrained in the human psyche, we are naturally predisposed to confer normative authority upon physicians and other health care givers. This can be productive of both guilt and anger.* This predisposition causes us to internalize the advice of the medical professionals as mandates. An advertising placard in a public bus reads: "If you haven't had a mammogram recently, the problem is not in your breasts, it's in your head." Are we approaching the time when a pregnant woman who does not submit to amniocentesis will be perceived as a "bad mother," perhaps even liable to charges of abuse? The recent moves to categorize patients as consumers intensifies this problem, since consumers are expected to be alert, aggressive, and accountable for their own consumer destiny. It is not surprising, therefore, that guilt may be induced among persons who have either inadvertently or intentionally failed to ex-

# Genetic Testing & Screening
## ERRATA

*Addition to page 91, after item #7:*

*8. The denomination, the synod, and the congregation stand under the challenge to gather all of their members in study and reflection upon a Christian story that criticizes the prevailing American worldview, as well as their particular occupational worldviews.* One of the major tasks of the church, if it is faithful, is to foster the study of the Christian worldview and to reflect upon its meaning. It is not an easy thing to disentangle the church's faith from the constraints that individual taste and experience place upon it. The congregation must find ways to honor the objectivity and the freedom of the faith, so that it can be large enough to include all of the types of persons who are members of its community—and their opinions—for the purpose of mutual challenge, critique, growth, and support. In these days when conflict and dispute are so prominent in our congregations, this challenge will require the utmost skill, patience, and caring. But the challenge cannot and dare not be avoided.

*Addition to page 91, after subtitle, "Summing Up: Christian Friendship":*

*The congregation is called to practice a Christian friendship that enables its members to share their genetic experience and its consequences and to find support and care in the congregation as community.* Genetic testing shares in what might be called the "unmentionable" topics that are difficult to talk about, especially in the church. Can a woman and her partner share their feelings and struggle with their fellow Christians if, after amniocentesis, they decide for an abortion? The discovery of genetic defect in a fetus puts strains on a marriage; some counselors report that very few marriages survive this particular result of genetic testing. Often the mother and father disagree on questions of abortion, continuing the pregnancy, and related issues. Can such struggles be shared in the congregation? Can the congregation be a supportive community to both partners in such a situation? Can a pastor admit from the pulpit that he or she would counsel abortion in some cases? Can the pastor's stance in private counseling sessions be consistent with what the pastor preaches publicly? Will a congregation accept the fact that their pastor may continue to support a woman or a couple, whatever their decision in such matters? Can a woman who has chosen for abortion and a woman who is adamantly pro-life stand together at the altar to receive forgiveness and the bread and wine of Holy Communion? Can the congregation be a supportive community for both the couple that considers their Down Syndrome child to be a great blessing from God and the couple that has chosen abortion in the prospect of such a birth—or even with the couple who has chosen to give the newborn up for adoption?

haust genetic interventions that might be called for in their circumstances. On the other hand, since "consumer" is also a demeaning term that can rob the physician-patient relationship of its intimacy and richness, the consumer ethos can engender anger from those patients who do not wish to be defined as consumers.

5. *We have sharp disagreements within our congregations on the value of many medical interventions, including genetic interventions and their limits.* What are the limits within which abortion is to be condoned on the basis of genetic testing findings in a particular instance? Is it appropriate to test to determine the gender of a fetus? How far should fertility testing and therapy go? Should children be told the results of their genetic tests if the outcome is disturbing? Should their siblings be informed? There is no quick consensus on such questions in any of our congregations, yet in their dissensus, the church members come to Sunday worship, approach the Communion Table together, seek the pastor's advice, and look for a caring community.

6. *Not only do our congregations include the entire range of dissensus on questions of genetic intervention; representatives of all of society's groups that are relevant to these questions are members of our communities.* There is no "us" and "them" possible in the church on the issues we have discussed. The much-maligned insurance managers are *within* the church, as are geneticists, physicians and nurses, biotech workers and managers, lawyers, and government officials—and so are the patients/consumers. Each of these persons is deeply touched by the prevailing American worldview—even if they disagree with it—and also by the particular worldviews of the group to which they belong: business, law, medicine, or whatever.

7. *The church is also called to prepare its members to engage concretely the prevailing worldview and their own occupational worldviews with the Christian worldview.* Lutherans hold to the theology of vocation, which emphasizes that Christian faith is lived out in one's worldly occupation and position in society (parent, citizen, and so forth). This gives us particular motivation to assist our members in engaging their concrete situations with the Christian story and ritual. Genetic testing will take its place in this engagement. Since Lutheran tradition does not allow for the church to dictate ethical decisions for its members, we must provide the best possible nurturing context for individuals to live out their accountability for determining their own conduct in the face of the challenges posed by genetic medicine.

## Summing Up: Christian Friendship

Christian friendship in the congregation is not just a matter of sustaining individuals, for the impact of genetic interventions affects families as well, particularly in the case of genetic testing. "Toxic knowledge," that is, knowledge about negative prospects for the future life of a child, may reverberate on healthy siblings who experience "survivor's guilt" when they learn of a dismal prospect of a brother or sister. Some parents have been known to be overprotective to the child whose life-chances are seriously compromised by genetic defect, while others have shown indifference. The ministry of the pastor and the congregation to such families is certainly very difficult, but also just as certainly of critical importance. Toxic knowledge in the pews will make a difference to the preacher in the pulpit.

I propose the image of "Christian friendship" as a challenge to our congregations as supportive communities. By this "friendship," I refer to the challenge to every Christian to offer respect, care, and support to Christian brothers and sisters who face the difficulties and traumas that come with genetic medicine—even when one disagrees sharply with the brother or sister, or even when the brother or sister has chosen a mistaken path. Lutherans hold themselves accountable to the truth that none of us truly deserves God's grace; that we are justified by God in divine mercy, not on our own merit. We believe firmly that as sinners we are continually making mistakes, following the wrong path, and yet we can repent and find forgiveness at the hands of a loving God. Can this set of beliefs in sin, grace, and forgiveness be translated into our life together in our congregations, as sustaining communities of care for those whose lives have been marked by the ambiguities and disappointments that are revealed in their experience of genetic medicine? This is perhaps the major challenge of genetic testing, alongside the challenge of the church's public social ethics.

Is this form of Christian friendship even a possibility in the situations that I have enumerated? Some limited study has revealed that genetically compromised persons who are active in congregations and synagogues are for the most part reluctant to share their burdens with their local religious communities. The reason: those communities are very important to them, and they fear that their burdens are too great, too ambiguous, for their friends to bear. Fearing that disclosure will weaken their ties with the community that they experience in their congregations, they keep their situations a secret from some of the friends who are most important to them. Lutheran pastors have reported that couples seldom ask for counseling before an abortion, but do sometimes ask for pastoral care afterwards—for example, requesting a simple private confessional or grieving service with the pastor.

There is no greater treasure in the church today, however, than the possibility for Christian friendship, as I have described it here. God has given no greater gift of grace than the love that can sustain such friendship. To affirm this friendship is to declare our willingness to trust that God's grace will support us in the midst of diversity and disagreement. To practice this friendship is to live out our free justification by God. As those who are at one and the same time forgiven and yet sinners, we reach out to our friends who are sinners and yet forgiven. Acknowledging our own sin reveals the bond that we share with all the other children of God that we meet; it breaks down the barriers of pride that can keep us from acknowledging one another. Claiming our own forgiveness, which we have received from Christ, empowers us to help our friends claim their own forgiveness. This is what it means to be Christs to our neighbors, as Martin Luther enjoined us. It is also what it means to understand how deeply we are, in fact, saints and sinners at the same time.

Nothing could be a firmer, more joyous witness to our Christian identity than the possibility of brothers and sisters joining together around the table of Christ's Supper: the mother and father who have had to abort their genetically defective baby next to the mother who has chosen to bear her baby to term, even without a partner, next to the physician, the lawyer, the biotech manager, the insurance executive, and the research geneticist, together with the woman who is still anxious about her twelve days of amniocentesis and the teenager who has just discovered that he is a candidate for an early heart attack when he reaches his thirties—and all of these known to each other, all having shared the mutual study and building up of the saints that have preceded this Eucharistic celebration, all of them having shared the ministry and the preaching of a pastor who is friend to all of them, and all gathering strength from the grace and forgiveness they have found in the Christ who is the real Host of the sacramental meal.

Such a community will not be found in many places in our American society. It is the church's calling to be in fact this community.

# GENES IN SOCIETY: WHOSE BODY?

## Elizabeth Bettenhausen

We are living. All that we do and think, feel and plan, all that we are is embodied. But how we interpret our bodies is a complicated story. Staying in shape, eating right, Viagra, dieting, plastic surgery, cholesterol, skin color, wrinkles, herbs, and prescriptions—the list of "perfect body" concerns could go on for pages. Being a living body means being able to enjoy sensory pleasure; it also means being someone who will die. How are we lively mortals? What is body?

Living as body means living always in a world in which others interpret your body. It also means living your own understanding of what body is. Dancing, hitting a home run, making love, unloading garbage cans, changing a diaper, eating grits, cutting paper intricately into art, listening to high tide together—all this and more show how bodies are in creaturely connections.

We speak of the body politic, body count, corporation, bodyguards, body shop. How we understand ourselves as individual persons who are embodied is connected to how we understand social activity. The political ruling body can define the context for everyone's embodied life. Complex embodiment can be reduced to a narrow, forced meaning, such as "light skin is better than dark skin," or enlarged to a generous, hospitable meaning, such as "plenty of cultures in this classroom!" Legislatures, principals, bishops, advertisers, geneticists—all sorts of persons and institutions do this. How in this country do we interpret body? This chapter is devoted to questions about social policies and practices that affect genetic research and treatment. Whose body?

## Embodied Conscience

*Whose Body?* is the title of a mystery novel written in the early 1920s by Dorothy Sayers, who was also a theologian. Genetics research was already taking place then. Sayers knew that belief systems shape how we interpret ourselves. Each science is a group of such systems. So is each religion. How does a particular science or a particular religion interpret bodies? How do we humans understand our bodies as genetic organisms who feel and think? How do we understand our bodies as

*ENGAGING WORLDVIEWS AND PROPOSING ALTERNATIVES*

worshipping persons? Do we believe that our bodies affect how we make choices as social creatures, how we exercise conscience?

Dorothy Sayers' novels raise complex questions in fascinating ways. In the story line of *Whose Body?* Lord Peter Wimsey, the detective, meets Sir Julian Freke, a famous research neurologist. Dr. Freke thinks that biology alone creates what some call emotion and moral judgment. He does not like to be bound by conscience. Conscience depends on norms and rules that count because society, rather than only the individual, says they do. He does not want to be responsible for or accountable to others. So, surgery is the solution! In his view, "The knowledge of good and evil is an observed phenomenon, attendant upon a certain condition of the brain-cells, which is removable." Conscience is a biological mistake, according to him, and brain surgery would "free" us from it.[1]

Novels are fiction, but many deal with actual and urgent questions. How do we interpret our bodies? Does the fact that each person is embodied prove that each person is responsible only to oneself? Some say, as Dr. Freke did, that since the body is unique and separate, so is the person. A social sense is then an evolutionary left-over, like an appendix, and increasingly dysfunctional.[2] For him, emotional and moral states such as "horror, fear, sense of responsibility" are "changes of brain tissue" caused by sensory data.[3] The perfect person is rational without conscience or emotions. Do you agree? Or do you connect your body with reason, emotions, and conscience? Do you connect them only with your own body or also with others'?

The church confesses something quite different from Dr. Freke's disgust with being held accountable, his disgust with conscience and social responsibility. How do you in your religious faith or understanding of religion connect body with reason, emotions, and conscience? How does this affect your interpretation of social responsibility? Does the resurrection of the body (believed in a variety of religious traditions) or the church as the body of Christ (in Christian tradition) lure you into creative moral possibilities? Do they affect how you interpret human bodies?

Daily dramatic developments in genetic research and practical applications raise the same basic questions. How do we interpret the body we are investigating? Is scientific knowledge about the body sufficient in itself for informed decisions? What type of information lures the scientist or the user of scientific research into creative moral possibilities? How can conscience attend to rational and emotional components of social issues in genetics research and policies?

Our society often pictures humans as a collection of independent, autonomous individuals determined by certain body characteristics and the willingness to pull oneself up by the straps on one's own boots. Confidence in institutionally formed social policy is low. Where in our society is public conversation taking place about issues of social policy over which there is significant disagreement and conflict? Can churches, for example, be a location of such conversation, or is the tendency there to talk of the body only a means to some spiritual end? Can schools be a location, or is the tendency to talk of the body only as a means to some scientific end? In the United States is public policy in genetic testing and screening being shaped largely by a combination of scientific curiosity and economic gain? Whose body?

I do not agree with Dr. Freke. Humans have evolved as complex social creatures, not as individuals who think in isolation and grow increasingly free of moral sensibility. Truth is not obtained by imagining that we can "think clearly" only if each of us puts emotion, body, and conscience on a back burner. Rather, truth is obtained as a goal of a cooperative process in community—family, friends, coworkers, colleagues, members of worshipping congregations, groups focusing on civic questions, representatives of corporations with economic interests, and more. In this process, many perspectives are represented by many persons, groups, and organizations. Participants need to recognize the conflict and competing interests that exist in the process, not ignore or suppress them. Whether we call each perspective a distinctive view or a bias, the scientist, the citizen, the patient, the worshipper, the baby, and the doctor—everyone has it. Every one of them is embodied reason and emotion in community, daily confronted with society's expectations and distinctive personal possibility. Whose body? The answer is always in the plural.

I interpret conscience as the capacity to discern how life expresses personal integrity and social dignity. This capacity is always being shaped by the specific context in which it is exercised. How widely or narrowly that context is posed affects what challenges and opportunities conscience encounters. Conscience is also the capacity to judge the metaphors we use to understand ourselves and how these metaphors affect the multitude of creatures on the planet. That includes the metaphorical systems of science and religion.

## Questions for Conscience

How can genetic testing and screening express personal integrity and social dignity? This question is important but general. Specifically, how do different persons and groups discern what integrity and dignity should involve, individually and corporately, in genetic activities?

As we will see, the identity of each person is a central focus of genetic testing and screening. Integrity means to be in touch with one's entire self and not to be invaded (attacked) by others' touch. Privacy, for example, is a major issue in genetic testing. If your genetic identity is placed on a computer chip, how can this identity be disclosed only by you when you choose? Should it be? Or should insurance companies and employers and criminal justice systems have legal access to it when they believe that they need it? (see Varian, p. 62, and Peters, p. 120).

Social dignity refers to the worth of all persons in society. This has always been and is an area of great controversy. In the United States, for example, whole nations have been considered less worthy of citizenship than others. In the first decades of the twentieth century, early research on genetics was used very dangerously. In her *Does It Run in the Family? A Consumer's Guide to DNA Testing for Genetic Disor-*

*ders*, Doris Teichler Zallen writes, "In the United States, eugenic ideas grew into efforts to restrict immigration from southern and central Europe in order to keep out people, especially Italians and Jews, considered genetically inferior."[4] This was one purpose of the Immigration Act of 1924.

Assumptions today about varying levels of worth to society affect how we live our social lives, whether in science or religion or elsewhere. Looking to find "solutions" to conditions defined as "problems," even science—while claiming to be totally objective and neutral—will reflect dominant values in society. For example, the controversy over the drug fen-phen is wider than initially reported. In April 1998 an article in *The Boston Globe* begins with this paragraph: "A government-funded research project that gave children a component of the diet drug fen-phen to test for violent tendencies is being criticized as risky and racist. The boys were all from poor black or Hispanic families."[5] Who defines human worth here?

Whose embodied conscience? Does each answer build sharp social boundaries or honor distinctiveness? To whose advantage is each problem and solution defined? The following questions raise the issues of interest (including basic human needs), resources, norms, and benefits and burdens. These issues are central in forming social policy on particular actions such as genetic testing and screening.

1. What are the *interests*, including basic human needs, of the persons (as individuals and groups) and institutions involved now and in the foreseeable future in genetic testing and screening?

2. What *resources* does each person, group, and institution have to use to gain these interests, to meet the needs?

3. Whose interests are *excluded* or ignored in current genetic research, medical genetic testing, and public policy? What prevents these persons from getting access to resources needed to make their interests play a role in scientific research, medical practice, and public policy decisions?

4. Who has had and now has the resources *to define and to exercise norms* in such a way as to meet their interests? How is "normal" defined genetically?

5. Who receives the *benefits and burdens* from this exercising of specific norms in genetic research and practice?

6. Whose *traditions* are the contexts for the norms, and whose are excluded?

7. Who will be *participants to pose and answer* these and other questions and in what process?

In deliberating in society (the body politic), we are called to be cooperatively and politically sagacious, that is, corporately to make evaluations that discern acutely and are practically wise for the well-being of the whole society. This deliberation both honors the value of curiosity and locates it in a context of basic human needs and resources. The ethics of genetic testing and screening is a matter of public policy, as well as of decisions facing individual persons.

I cannot consider all possible issues of public policy in light of all these questions. So first I will describe six purposes of genetic testing and screening. Then I will look at how cultural traditions in the United States with regard to ethnicity and nationality affect how research is defined and the consequences of it. Especially significant is how research often construes cultural definitions of personal identity as biological givens. Finally, I will draw on an element of Martin Luther's christology that is helpful in overcoming an individualistic morality and look at some possible courses of action for the church to deal with genetic testing and screening as a growing matter of social policy.

# Whose Body? Genetic Testing, Screening, and Identity

Genetic research, testing, and screening take place in labs and offices located on particular streets. Some people think that the lab is free from the cultural biases of life outside. Scientific research is "objective" and "neutral." Other people think that the cultures in which the research takes places shape how the scientific questions are formed and thus the language of the results.

One approach holds that objectivity and neutrality are possible and necessary for persons doing research or giving genetic information to patients or consumers. One purpose of objectivity may indeed protect against imposed biases. The need for repeating scientific tests to check whether a hypothesis can be falsified sees objectivity as a cooperative process, rather than as solitary thinking. Actively making sure cultural prejudices are not in the forming and testing of the hypothesis is also a task requiring many participants.

Another approach holds that it is impossible to transmit such information apart from the traditions and worldviews that give it particular meaning. For example, to claim that someone should know whether she or he is a carrier of a genetic disease so that the individual can make an informed decision about reproduction is not neutral. The world view represented interprets genetic information exclusively as a matter of reason, and deciding is understood as a solely cognitive process. Not to know genetic information is to be uninformed in a negative way, and certain kinds of reproducing are preferable to other kinds. This is not a neutral position.

Cultural expectations, fears, interests, and habit do not conveniently disappear upon request. Attending to the patterns that shape how different persons, groups, and institutions interpret the world is difficult and necessary: difficult, because taking a critical look at our presuppositions is tough; necessary, because the same pattern often pleases the eye of some but drives others to protest or even despair.

Cultural biases—often at the same time life-giving and life-endangering—are evident in the most common function of genetic testing and screening today: describing personal identity. Six purposes of this identification are discussed here: managing inheritance, predicting physical illness, establishing paternity, identifying in forensic contexts, discovering the sexual identity of a fetus, and explaining certain personal characteristics as biologically determined.

## 1. "Life will be better in the next generation."

As Kevin Powell's and Robert Lebel's chapters demonstrate (p. 26 and p. 157), humans have been trying to control biological inheritance for thousands of years. We have tried to get better plants, better animals, and—through intricate rules for marriage and human reproduction—"just the right children." Genetic testing is another step in this attempt.

Biological parents transmit two chromosomal traditions to form one new one in the child conceived. One purpose of genetic testing is to find genetic characteristics that may show how likely a person is to transmit a particular genetic disposition to offspring. In this there may be single gene traits and single gene disorders, and genetic tests are being developed to find both. Huntington's disease, sickle cell anemia, and hemophilia are examples.[6]

I emphasize three aspects of this. First, to have the trait does not mean to have the disease or disorder. Trait and disease are not the same. In the early 1970s, sickle cell trait and sickle cell disease were publicly portrayed as the same. This misinformation led to claims that two million African-Americans had sickle cell disease.[7] But to carry a recessive allele does not mean to have the disease. Discrimination in educational, insurance, and military arenas was pervasive against blacks, who were mistakenly thought to have the disease. Many people, not only whites, urged that genetic testing be done. Until the difference between trait and disease and the existence of the trait in many other ethnic groups were made clear, "black community organizations . . . raise[d] accusations of genocide." Many wanted much more widespread testing.[8] (See Schwandt on this as well, p. 49.)

The second aspect is that having a suspect gene does not predict anything absolutely. Genetic testing cannot reveal how a trait will be expressed. "Even diseases or traits that are due to a single gene vary widely in severity, depending on environmental factors and other genes; the extent to which patients have signs and symptoms of a genetic disease is called 'expressivity.'"[9] Further, the issue of penetrance may come into play. In genetic testing, the term "penetrance" refers to the percentage of persons in a population carrying the gene who are affected at all by the disease. A person may test positive for having the genetic trait for a disease and never get it. The environment and sequences of genes interact in ways we simply do not understand.

The third aspect is the social definition of disease. A biological characteristic, including genetic identity, is not in itself a disease. How does a society define what is a disease or a disability in need of cure or improvement? Our society has been less restrictive of genetic research and technology than European countries who form social genetic policy collectively. In the European Parliamentary Assembly's action in 1982 concerning genetic engineering, the social context was crucial, for "the memory of Nazis' discriminatory and murderous eugenics programs [was] still fresh in their minds."[10] History is a major element of contemporary deliberations about social justice, and that should be the case in the United States as well.

If "being a certain type of person" has been construed as a disease, an imperfection, what types of persons are thought to be imperfect? Who defines what constitutes a birth defect? Is the defining of disease the responsibility primarily of scientists and medical professionals? Or should there be extensive public discussion about this matter of personal well-being and social policy? I will return to this in the discussion of the sixth purpose.

## 2. "Perfectly healthy!"

A second purpose of genetic testing is to test persons for likelihood of a particular condition. At present, no genetic testing can disclose with absolute certainty the health or illness of the born child. Neither is it possible to achieve this in testing adults. (See Powell and Schwandt on these procedures.)

At present no genetic therapy exists for any genetic trait that may cause a disease. Research is underway to discover specific genetic therapies, especially regarding immunology and cancer.[11] Since only experimental genetic therapy exists today, if genetic testing discloses a condition for which other therapy is available, this diagnostic information may be helpful in making moral choices. To know *in genetic terms* that you have an illness for which there is *no* treatment is a mixed blessing. Would this knowing be helpful for family members who may have the trait, for the care of the person, or for the community in which the person lives? While knowing the genetic trait exists may be justified in a context of scientific curiosity, the meaning of the trait cannot be determined simply in genetic terms.

Genetic information is only a part of the needed knowledge. When a person has a genetic trait that is defined as a problem in scientific terms and is untreatable because genetic therapy is not available, informing the person is not a neutral act. Perhaps only when genetic therapy does become available should having the trait be offered as useful knowledge. Public discussion should address this question of personal and social well-being. Until then, if knowing is believing, knowing may be only more sickening.

The headline of an article in *The New York Times* in 1998 is: "Genetic Testing Falls Short of Public Embrace." Wall Street analysts and biotechnology companies that produce the tests expected thousands of people each month to choose to be tested, but only hundreds have done so. Fear of discrimination in insurance or employment and suspicion about the usefulness of genetic information reportedly affect many persons' choices. Recent studies of genetic mutations and breast cancer with population-based samples that are case-controlled studies have also revealed much lower risks for the general population than were reported before.[12] Since we have only barely begun to understand single genes and genetic sequences and how they and many environments interact, caution and humility should be the bottom line of genetic wisdom.

### 3. "Who's the father?"

In a bagel shop, I asked the young clerk what she thought might be good or bad about genetic testing. She hesitated for awhile and said, "Gee, I don't know." After cutting the poppy bagel, she said, "How about to find out who the father of the child really is?" That sounded like a longer story than she was going to tell.

Identifying the biological father of a child by testing DNA serves the purpose of establishing public paternity. One function of this purpose is to determine who must provide legally mandated child support.

Some assumptions are also involved here. First, the sperm's chromosomes, a biological category, and paternity, a cultural category, are believed to be synonyms. Why? Surrogate motherhood has raised plenty of questions about what constitutes a mother.[13] Why should biological paternity be any more than one possible factor in defining fatherhood? Second, legal accountability and responsibility are derived from biological identity in this understanding of parenthood. But a California court recently ruled that the intention to raise the child, not contributing egg or sperm, is what makes someone held legally responsible as a parent. Buying *in vitro* fertilization is one sign of intent. But how is intention to reproduce judged in the millions of more usual instances of heterosexual coitus?

The third assumption is that the legal obligation of child support rests solely on the moral responsibility of both biological parents, rather than also or instead on the community. The social decisions made here affect the well-being of millions of children. Worlds of difference lie between "It takes a village to raise a child" and "Biology is the only cause of parental obligation." Some say that genetic testing is simply providing biological information about parenthood, but the meaning is not so straightforward.

### 4. "Who committed the crime?"

A fourth purpose of genetic testing has two uses: to provide evidence of legal agency in criminal cases and genetically to identify persons convicted of crimes. The first practice began in Great Britain in the mid-1980s. DNA testing has a popular image of being much more reliable than fingerprints as court evidence. However, DNA has to be read and interpreted by human beings, and everything—from good intentions to overwork to special interests—affects this process.

Dorothy Nelkin and M. Susan Lindee, in *The DNA Mystique: The Gene as a Cultural Icon*, report that in "the commonly used DQ Alpha method of testing DNA...the odds that two people will have the same combination of markers are currently estimated as ranging from one to 20 percent—quite different from the figure of 4 or 5 trillion to one commonly cited in the popular literature."[14] Wanting proof, many in this society often trust empirical evidence as if it could be read without interpretation or ambiguity.

Analysis of DNA is done in government and private laboratories. Some states have accreditation processes, and some have not. The analysis varies in quality, both from lab to lab and within the same lab. Since the process is not even two decades old, final judgments about the reliability of identification by DNA sample are premature. Using longer sequences of DNA and more locations of samples for each person would increase the reliability of the material sample.

At the same time, forensic DNA testing is a way to prove that a particular person was not the one who left the hair or semen or other biological sign at the scene. If the evidence is definitely from the person who committed the crime, proving the innocence of the convicted is a very important event in the justice system. If even a short sequence of DNA does not match, it provides defense evidence not available before.

CODIS (combined DNA index system) is the Federal Bureau of Investigation's national DNA identification index system.[15] State and local criminal justice and law enforcement agencies send in DNA records from the DNA analysis of persons convicted on crimes. One of three states that had not been participating, Massachusetts established a state DNA database in 1997, thus receiving $172,000 in federal start-up money for laboratories to do the genetic analytic work. Persons who are "convicts in prison, on probation, or on parole for any of 33 types of crimes, ranging from burglary to murder" are required to give a sample of blood for genetic identification.[16] However, prisoners in state prisons filed legal protests against having to submit blood samples after they have already been convicted on other evidence. Unfortunately, very little public discussion has taken place regarding genetic identification of individuals, whether criminals or others, for governmental purposes.

## 5. "It's a girl?"

A fifth purpose of genetic testing is to determine the sexual identity of a fetus. Sex selection can be done before implanting an embryo developed *in vitro*, and genetic testing can also disclose the sex of the fetus conceived in the usual way. This can be more than fulfillment of a parental wish for a daughter or a son. Some inherited diseases are X-linked disorders and affect boys more than girls, such as hemophilia and Duchenne muscular dystrophy.[17] Disclosing the sex of the developing fetus can be an element in the parental decision whether to continue the pregnancy, given this possibility of genetic disease.

When "female" is seen as a problem in the fetus, in some countries abortion or infanticide is a way to solve what genetic testing discerns as a "biological" fact. However, here again, for problems created within very complex cultural and social systems of values, a biological solution is a way of hiding how biology is defined culturally, including in religion. Who benefits and who is harmed, now and in the future, when parents know the sex of their offspring before birth and interpret it in a certain way?

### 6. "They are born that way."

A sixth purpose of genetic testing and screening studies a characteristic of personality to see if it is genetically based and perhaps for that reason inevitable. The phrase, "biology is destiny," expresses this belief in biological determinism. Biology is thought to be acting quite apart from cultures, society, willpower, and other strands of human life. Finding a gene that "causes" criminal violence or hyperactivity or certain expressions of sexuality is the goal of some research.

Yet every personal characteristic is meaningful only in relation to the way a group or society defines it and never exists as a self-explanatory, solely physiological aspect of a person. The "biology is destiny" belief often draws popular attention. Stereotyping and designating certain groups as the source of all problems are easier if a biological, measurable, unchangeable feature can be called the cause of the problem. But patterns of behavior and institutions are created through social traditions and innovations that interpret biological and other factors of life, not by biology alone.

Evelyn Fox Keller traces the history from the eugenics movement early in the twentieth century, through Nazi genocide, to the current idea of genetic disease by looking at how each period understands nature and nurture, biology and culture. Today, she notes, distinctions are "made by a demarcation between the normal and the abnormal; the force of destiny is no longer attached to culture, or even to biology in general, but rather more specifically to the biology (or genetics) of disease."[18] The "new eugenics" is portrayed as culturally detached, concerned only with biological health, and not in danger, therefore, of the problems of the "old eugenics." In this view, individual choice is "free" if it conforms to the genetic definitions of "normal." The situation today would sound quite comfortable to Sir Freke.

Each of these six purposes is considered by some to be a great benefit and by others to involve serious burdens. Whose interests are served by each; and when there is a serious conflict of interests, in whose favor will the conflict be resolved? Managing inheritance, predicting physical illness, establishing paternity, identifying in forensic contexts, discovering the sexual identity of a fetus, and explaining certain personal characteristics as biologically determined—all these purposes are ways that focus on an aspect of body as the location of personal identity. But biological body is meaningful body only culturally. Genes do not disclose meaning: the meaning attributed to genes discloses culture.

## Whose Body? Cultural Answers and Public Policies

What is normal? How do we decide what is genetically normal? How do we decide what is a genetic abnormality? Is difference always abnormal? What makes a genetic trait a problem? Who is doing the defining? For what purposes? The list of questions could go on forever, sparing us from recognizing that answers are already operating and always being given by someone, somewhere. The social policies and moral options that are thus being created will affect us all. How do we regularly evaluate and change these policies? How do we create new cultural interpretations of body that are genetically and socially wise? As I said earlier, how can we be corporately, politically sagacious, discerning acutely and with practical wisdom the well-being of the whole society?

## Inheritance, Culture, and Race

A long tradition in the United States of racial and sexual ideas is a large section of the context for interpreting the meaning of physical and cultural identity. In *Intimate Matters: A History of Sexuality in America*, John D'Emilio and Estelle B. Freedman describe its beginning this way:

> Ever since the seventeenth century, European migrants to America had merged racial and sexual ideology in order to differentiate themselves from Indians and blacks, to strengthen the mechanisms of social control over slaves, and to justify the appropriation of Indian and Mexican lands through the destruction of native peoples and their cultures.[19]

For centuries marriage has been construed by many European American groups as the major way to ensure that the inheriting generation is "normal"—and that the next generation of a "different" group does not inherit the benefits of the "normal" group.

Biological determinism or biological essentialism claims that biology (or nature or genes) causes identity. In the United States, race and sex are categories often used to express this essentialism. In their book, Nelkin and Lindee have an aptly named chapter, "Creating Natural Distinctions." They introduce the section, "Genes and Race," by pointing out that "genes have become a way to establish the legitimacy of social groupings" in the United States.[20] When we create something and then call it a matter of "nature," we are trying to avoid responsibility for what we do. Humans' social definitions are attributed to imagined genetic determination.

When Tiger Woods called himself "Cablinasian: *Ca*-Caucasian; *bl*-Black; *in*-Indian; *asian*," the unity of multiple cultural traditions challenged the biological definition of race in white culture. In the July 1997 issue of *Ebony*, statements from nine African-American leaders point to race as a political category about cultures, not a biological category of blood or genes. I agree that race is a socially constructed category of power used to create a hierarchy of social relationships that serves the interests of white people, who create and maintain the hierarchy from century to century.

Dorothy Roberts, a law professor, rightly points out that this dominant culture in the United States makes race correlate with a degree of privilege. "Blacks have understandably resisted defining personal identity in biological terms. In America, whites have historically valued genetic linkages and controlled their official meaning. As the powerful class, they are the guardians of the privileges accorded to biology and they have a greater stake in maintaining the importance of genetics."[21] Roberts analyzes the distribution of resources among different cultural groups in the United States in regard to reproduction. "This reliance on high-tech intervention rather than improving basic health and workplace conditions hurts not only Black women but all women and, ultimately, all of our society."[22] How finite resources are allocated is a major element of social well-being.

Much genetic testing and screening focuses on inheritance. Cultural standards for sexual reproduction and inheritance already form part of the context for deciding the meaning of the scientific problems and solutions. A nationwide public opinion poll of blacks and whites in 1997 showed differences and similarities regarding the meaning of integration.[23] Eighty-six percent of whites and 87 percent of blacks have "developed friendships with people of another race." But then the questions turned to dating and marriage. Thirty-nine percent of blacks and 24 percent of whites had "ever dated a person of another race." The next question was more future oriented: "Can you see yourself living in an interracial marriage?" Again, 39 percent of blacks said yes, while only 26 percent of whites did.

What in the history of the United States leads to this view of interracial marriage? Dorothy Roberts writes, "As early as 1662, Virginia amended its law prohibiting fornication to impose heavier penalties if the guilty parties were from different races. By being faithful to their husbands, white women were also faithful to their race."[24] White women who bore mulatto children were viewed by whites as corrupting the white race.

In the United States, laws against interracial marriage have been unconstitutional only since 1967. Even today, Roberts says, "one's social status in America is determined by the presence or absence of a genetic tie to a Black parent. Conversely, the white genetic tie—if free from any trace of blackness—is an extremely valuable attribute entitling a child to a privileged status, what legal scholar Cheryl Harris calls the 'property interest in whiteness.'" Ensuring genetic relatedness may be important for many reasons, but in America one of the most important reasons *for whites* has been to preserve what is thought to be white racial purity.[25]

In the United States, the phrase "blood relative" is common. Jefferson M. Fish compares how different societies, the United States and Brazil, describe variations within the human species. He writes, "Americans believe in 'blood,' a folk term for the quality presumed to be carried by members of so-called races. And the way offspring—regardless of their physical appearance—always inherit the less prestigious racial category of mixed parentage is called 'hypo-descent' by anthropologists." [26] In hypo-descent in the United States, "the various purported racial categories are arranged in a hierarchy along a single dimension, from the most prestigious ('white'), through intermediary forms ('Asian'), to the least prestigious ('black')."[27]

While this hierarchy of values is attributed to "nature," to biological identity transmitted in reproduction, the descriptions are all cultural. Scientific research takes place in the cultural context. As Fish points out, studies that limit causes of difference to biology are making mistakes in logical thinking, as well as hiding their social judgments. "This can easily be demonstrated by asking researchers how they know that the white subjects are really white and the black subjects are really black. There is no biological answer to this question, because race as a biological category does not exist."[28] While the "blood" metaphor is much older than the genetic metaphor, the racism of the hierarchy of imagined biological distinctions continues, now infused by so-called "objective" genetic discoveries.

## When Is Different Abnormal?

In the 1990s in the United States an intense scientific and legal fight has been underway. Should information about genetic identity be admitted as evidence in the courts and, if so, how should it be interpreted? Unfortunately, it is not surprising that race and ethnicity are at the center of the debate.

How reliable is a match of DNA in forensic use in the United States? A match based on statistical chance is thought to be solid evidence. How is statistical chance determined? In particular, what is the genetic norm by which this judgment will be made? "What constitute[s] a genetically 'random' population?"[29] The answer to this question affects the usefulness and significance of statistical information.

Steve Jones, a British geneticist, points out that the FBI in the initial use of DNA fingerprinting "set up a reference group of innocent DNA donors made up of white police officers."[30] Since race is a cultural, not biological category, this would seem to be fine. On the other hand, a white norm means that any departure from it signifies a difference synonymous, in this context, with guilt.

The FBI now uses a different interpretation of norm. Ruth Hubbard, professor *emerita* of biology at Harvard University, has written *Exploding the Gene Myth*. In a chapter on "DNA-Based Identification Systems," she describes this. "For identification purposes, the FBI has established reference populations, which they call 'Caucasian,' 'Black,' or 'Hispanic.' Each group is assumed to be homogeneous and people are assumed always to select their mates at random from within their own group."[31]

The FBI categories assume, for example, that intermarriage among many European ethnic groups has been common in the United States. The multitude of jokes about a Swede marrying a Norwegian or a Dane marrying an Italian are evidence of a more complicated situation. Hubbard argues that this gross homogeneity assumption "may be convenient, but it has no genealogical or biological meaning." Regarding the statistical usefulness of data based on it, she says, "[T]he statement that the odds are less than one in a hundred million that two individuals have the same pattern of VNTRs [variable number of tandem repeats on base sequence of chromosome] is based on the assumption of random sampling from a fictitious, homogeneous, and randomly interbreeding 'Caucasian' [or 'Black' or 'Hispanic'] community."[32]

In *And the Blood Cried Out: A Prosecutor's Spellbinding Account of the Power of DNA*, Harlan Levy devotes a revealing chapter to the FBI's role in the struggle over admissibility and interpretation of DNA in forensics. He describes the intense arguments between researchers in genetics working for the FBI and others. The debates have expanded from the Office of Technological Assessment of the United

States Congress[33] into *Science* magazine, reports from the National Academy of Sciences, and the Supreme Court of the United States.

While the details of the struggle are well worth reading, I want to draw attention to the concluding point of Levy's chapter. The struggle has been over admissibility of DNA evidence. This seems at the moment to be resolved in the criminal justice system in favor of admitting DNA data as evidence. "Still," Jones writes, "the weight that a jury may choose to give a DNA match is another matter. Defense lawyers and scientists remain free to question and criticize DNA evidence in court. Race and ethnicity remain an issue for trial."[34]

Nelkin and Lindee also discuss the popular assumption in our society that some groups may be biologically prone to violence. "[G]rowing concerns about domestic problems—the cost of welfare programs, the changing ethnic composition of major cities, and the growing 'underclass'—encouraged speculation about the role of genetics in perpetuating poverty and violence."[35] The FBI categories are part of a program to prevent violence that entails implicit decisions about biological identity. "Natural" often has the ring of "not subject to change" or "given." Biological interpretation of so-called race tries to obtain this sanction of inevitability for the hierarchy with "white" at the top.

Hubbard makes a hard statement: "DNA-based identification, though highly questionable in its present form, is being sold to a terrified public as a way to solve the heinous crimes we hear about every day."[36] Earlier I referred to the scientific research project that investigated the effect of fenfluramine on the brain chemistry of boys, 6 to 10 years old, from poor black or Hispanic families in New York City. The purpose of the study, which was government approved, was to try "to identify factors that could trigger aggression 'in a population at risk for the development of antisocial behavior.'"[37] Scientific objectivity is not immune to racism.

## The Human Genome Project

The federal government of the United States is spending $200 million every year for at least fifteen years on the Human Genome Project. The central purpose is to create a map showing the location of every gene in the human body. Hank Greely, a law professor, addresses one aspect of this project: "So far, most work on the human genome has involved Europeans or North Americans of European descent, largely because that is where the research has been done."[38] Of course, Europe and North America have people of many cultures, which he ignores here. But something else is also at issue.

The use of "white" bodies in the genome project reflects the dominant society's assumption that research needs "normal" bodies for the results to be "undarkened," pure. Here again cultural values are defining biological research. In the September 1997 issue of *Emerge*, Harriet A. Washington wrote "Piece of the Genetic Puzzle is Left Out." After introducing a common justification of the Project—that it "will illuminate genes' relationship to disease risk"—Washington writes, "To study as many human genes as possible, the genes of 67 extended families worldwide are being analyzed." While agreeing that mapping more than 3 billion base pairs is a great amount of work, Washington names another problem. "The technological achievements, however, pale before a serious scientific misstep: All 67 families studied are Caucasian, which means project scientists have severed the African branch of the human family tree."[39]

The tree has many more branches too. But all the branches other than "Caucasian" are defined as "non-White" by the Human Genome Project participants who actually have the power to define the norm: white. Geographical location, cultural identity, biological identity, disease, risks, and distribution of resources—how are they interacting? Do different environments around the planet interact in a scientifically interesting way only with the genes of Caucasian extended families? How is difference understood in the basic hierarchy of privilege created by and most favoring European cultures in the United States?

The limits of the Human Genome Project have been noted by some who want a global Human Genome *Diversity* Project (emphasis added). However, here too, the resources available to western scientists and others in defining this project are much greater than the resources available to populations around the world who are proposed as providers of samples of their genes for the research.

Further, some scientists are arguing that the diversity of the human genome is such that samples are needed from around the world and from many ethnic groups and cultures. Testifying in a congressional hearing, a professor of genetics, Dr. Cavalli-Sforza, said that limiting the genetic testing to Caucasians provides misleading results. "There is considerable ethnic variation in genetic disease and predisposition to disease, which is important in planning health surveys, providing dietary advice, searching for donors for transplants, and so on."[40] He referred to the "substantial question" of whether "this study of intergroup genetic difference might foster racism. I am persuaded that it will have the opposite effect." Expressing a particular belief, he continued, "Knowledge about our real, and very limited genetic differences can only help to defuse the 'race bomb.' It is, however, obvious that any data can be misused and abused. The best protection is education based on solid facts and research."[41] I think, however, the solidity of the facts and research is variously defined, depending on the ethical elements of the culture in which the research takes place.

In the same hearing, Dr. Robyn Nishimi, a Senior Associate in the Biological and Behavioral Sciences Program of the federal government's Office of Technology Assessment, said, in a prepared statement:

> [M]any of the populations proposed for sample collection are in developing nations. What if certain data gathered under the Human Genome Diversity Project prove commercially valuable? The United States must be sensitive to the concerns of developing nations, while simultaneously preserving legitimate interests of U.S. companies to pursue commercial development and intellectual property protection of "biotechnological" products.[42]

At the Rio de Janeiro summit in 1992, developing nations protested this use of resources for the scientific research and corporate financial interests in Europe and the United States. Nishimi said that their concerns included questions of "intellectual property" and the Biodiversity Treaty. But their concerns "are heightened by the prospect that the substance now in question is human biological material from vulnerable populations. As Chaim Sheba of Israel has put it, 'You have taken our gold and diamonds; now you are taking our genes.'"[43]

Very different interpretations of the significance and impact of the Human Genome Diversity Project are alive today. Andrew Kimbrell indicates clearly one end of the spectrum in his closing comment on "High Tech Piracy": "Until a sophisticated means of predicting the effects of gene alterations on the environment is established and adequate regulations are enacted, the genetic engineering must stop. Collection of cells and blood from indigenous people through projects that violate all legal principles of informed consent and represent a threat to their dignity and survival must end."[44]

On the other end of the spectrum, Hank Greely described the purpose of the Diversity Project as follows: "The project hopes to collect, preserve, and analyze DNA samples from about 500 populations around the world . . . that have not been extensively studied. The resulting data should be an invaluable resource for studying how closely different people are related and, therefore, the history of our species."[45]

Who is the human genome? Given our history of conflict as cultural and national groups, it is unlikely that we can accumulate scientific data in a context abstracted from the burdens and benefits that racism distributes to different groups. At the same time, we are not readily able in the United States to treat difference from the dominant norms as worthy. Difference is a way to find the "guilty" or the "abnormal" or the "dangerous." This is a sobering element of the social interpretation of genes.

## Global Well-Being

The distribution of resources for and from scientific research affects the basic quality of life across the planet. How is that quality determined? The answers are innumerable, their effects global. But in a fascinating study, Christopher J. L. Murray and Alan D. Lopez developed the Global Burden of Disease Study (GBD). It "provides a standardized approach to epidemiological assessment and uses a standard unit, the disability-adjusted life year (DALY), to aid comparisons."[46]

Murray and Lopez begin the Background paragraph with this: "Prevention and control of disease and injury require information about the leading medical causes of illness and exposure or risk factors." They begin the paragraph on findings this way: "Developed regions account for 11.6 percent of the worldwide burden from all causes of death and disability, and account for 90.2 percent of health expenditure worldwide." They begin the paragraph on Interpretation this way: "The three leading contributors to the burden of disease are communicable and perinatal disorders affecting children." At the beginning of the Discussion of their findings, the authors write:

> [D]espite dramatic improvements in child health conditions in the developing world, the three leading contributors to the burden of disease are lower respiratory infections, diarrhoeal diseases, and perinatal disorders. Together with measles, [they] account for 25 percent of the whole burden of premature mortality and disability in developing regions. Two important risk factors that contribute to a large share of this burden are paediatric malnutrition (16 percent of the worldwide burden), and poor water, sanitation, and hygiene (7 percent).[47]

Are these genetic problems? Hardly. Disability and early death may have genetic effects of some kind. But the major cause of the problem is the distribution of economic and political resources across the globe in a way that furthers the interests of the most powerful—resource-full—persons and institutions, primarily in the developed nations (also called "established market economies" and "formerly socialist economies of Europe" in the study). In these societies, of course, 80 percent of the burden is in the disorders of noncommunicable diseases, with malignant neoplasms (13.7 percent), neuropsychiatric disorders (22 percent), and cardiovascular disorders (20.4 percent) the three most prevalent elements in the disability-adjusted life year figures.[48] How an affluent culture defines well-being is a contributing factor to behavior that may not be conducive to physiological health. Economic definitions of abundant life, consumerism, toxic consequences for the environment, competition as prerequisite for success—these and other basic social structures steadily compete with the icon of healthy body.

Economic resources are one significant means of power in defining what constitutes health and illness. Since genetic research is a comparatively new dimension of science, its economic support strongly affects its influence. One aspect of this appears in "Academic-industry research relationships [AIRRs] in genetics: A field apart," the results of a survey of "life-science faculty in the 50 universities that received the most funding from the National Institutes of Health in 1993."[49] Three men analyzed these relationships in the United States and found that "Significantly more genetics than non-genetics firms funded AIRRs, and genetics firms' AIRRs were larger and longer. Genetics faculty with AIRRs were significantly more likely that non-genetics faculty to report that patents, licenses, new companies and trade secrets had resulted from their university research; and that they had refused to share research results or biomaterials with colleagues."[50]

How should we relate ideas of private property and human biological resources? How can the costs of the research, the benefits and burdens to various groups, the accessibility of genetic testing and future therapies, and economic profits be related? (See Varian, p. 64, for one viewpoint.) Belief in the objectivity of empirical research is always located in a particular context and a particular time. The ideal of a "disinterested" perspective is sometimes a rhetorical cover used by privileged persons to deny that every person, group, or corporation interprets life from a distinctive angle and for certain interests.

DNA identification systems are also economic realities. Emerging possible uses of genetic testing and screening have not only purported effects on illness and health; they also are to the economic advantage of certain persons and companies, often including the researchers investigating new approaches. For example, one of the many promises of revolutionizing medicine is in a field called pharmacogenomics (see Varian, p. 71). The belief that genetic differences among individuals are so great that they affect how a prescribed drug will work on each person is another impetus to identify every person by "genetic profile." This would provide a different population sample for drug testing. "Costly clinical trials of new medications could be smaller, quicker, and far cheaper if researchers knew which drug-response genetic variations the trial volunteers carried, say proponents."[51]

New companies in this biotechnology often have interesting names, such as Millennium Predictive Medicine, Inc. Another is Variagenics, a company involved in pharmacogenomics research. What variation might be at issue here? "While pharmacogenomic drug-tailoring would presumably improve the public's health, that's not the only motive at work. Variagenics' promotional material asserts that pharmacogenomics will increase the profits of both pharmaceutical companies and health care providers."[52] New medicines are hardly ever cheaper medicines, whether they are genetically individualized or not. Who benefits the most from this profit-making aspect of medical care, and who bears the burdens? How are individually unique genetic identification and social well-being and justice related?

## Personal and Social Well-being

Within so-called developed nations, disorders vary among groups from different economic classes due to the resources available to them. In terms of prenatal care in the United States, a disproportionate amount of economic resources of the country goes to high-technology intervention in reproduction rather than to public health concerns. Hubbard points out that "among affluent women in the United States, predictive tests are becoming part of routine prenatal care. Such tests are a source of regular income for drug companies, hospitals, and private physicians."[53]

Hubbard highlights the competition between an individualistic model of the genetic person and the focus on public health.[54] Philip Kitcher describes this in the following way:

> The ideology of individualism is a powerful friend to genetic determinism. Genetic solutions reassure the successful: The rich man in his castle, the poor man at his gate (or, perhaps, in the dungeon), genes made them high or humble and governed their estate. Aspects of society that trouble us need not be traced to the breakdown of community, to the failure of affluent classes to find ways of alleviating the environmental desolation that callouses the spirit. There is ample motive for thinking that our temperament and our actions lie in our genes.[55]

Defining the genetic future's norms by attending primarily to the interests of those affluent individual women and men in the United States and other "developed" nations raises the question again: How and by whom and for what purposes are these interests defined and at what cost to others?

In articles on surrogate motherhood and postmenopausal motherhood, I argued that technological developments were being done so that the maternal agency in reproduction would be increasingly placed in the hands of the researchers and others who financially profit from this shift.[56] The resources, norms governing them, and the purposes to which they are used are most likely to be defined by the persons who have the largest composite of education, professional standing, and research money to realize their self-interest. In the United States this is defined in a highly competitive way. The interests of affluent people, women and men, get more attention than the interests of poor people. This can mean, for example, that a mother who wants income above minimum wage in order to feed her children gets subjected to "welfare reform" and less than minimum wage work by the same Congress that approves scientific research on her children for genetic disposition toward violence.

At the same time, genetic testing and screening of affluent women today also entails some risks. Why are most genetics patients women? Because generally conditions are determined to be "genetic" problems in prenatal diagnosis, and pregnancy is impossible for men. Thus, therapy for any "genetic problems" of the next generation is today largely a matter of trying to obtain a "satisfactory" conception and pregnancy. "Prenatal diagnosis followed by abortion is already a widely used method of preventing genetic disease. Preimplantation selection is an option offered at a growing number of fertility centers."[57]

Several concerns arise. First, who has determined that a genetic problem exists and on what criteria? The earlier discussions about defining genetic function and the dimensions of person are relevant here. If a person wants to produce a "perfect child," by what standards is the genetic information interpreted? What standards are used to interpret the society in which the child will live? If a society holds sons in higher privilege than daughters, does aborting the female embryo solve a "genetic" problem, or is the problem rather a social problem that requires other types of solutions?

Second, in the United States "handicapped" replaced "defective" as a descriptive term, and now "disability" has joined "handicapped" in daily use. Ability means to have the resources necessary to meet a need. Ability refers to access to resources that are available in a society and to how they are distributed. Too often the model of private property of individuals or single corporations is used to describe this distribution. Disability then refers to an individual person but not to the decisions of public policy that affect the standards by which the resources are distributed. Treating a person's body, rather than the body politic, as the location of the problem may leave many people *and justice* disabled.

A key question is how care-giving is construed and exercised. If both adults work full-time and must do so in order to buy sufficient food and pay the rent, is caregiving of a disabled newborn possible with their resources of time, energy, and so forth? If the culture into which the child would come is based on extended families with mutual responsibility for care, does this make a difference in the defining of disability? Defining "normal" serves the interests of particular persons or institutions and affects how ability is understood and treated. Genetic testing to make sure everything is "normal" is a highly controversial matter. As I wrote in regard to postmenopausal pregnancy technology, "The motivations and needs of some individuals do not necessarily constitute a sufficient basis for public policy and moral direction."[58]

In the introduction, I said that conscience is the capacity to discern how life expresses personal integrity and social dignity. The position I have taken here emphasizes the need for conscience to look at the way specific characteristics of our culture provide the context that shapes genetic testing and screening. Conscience is embodied in the interacting of unique person and distinctive culture. We are not genetically programmed to discern certain norms by which public policy should be judged. Embodied life daily requires resources to live. How are they distributed, and whose interests does this serve?

## Whose Body? Christians in Public Conversation

In *The DNA Mystique: The Gene as a Cultural Icon*, Nelkin and Lindee point out that some geneticists describe the human genome "as the 'Bible,' the 'Book of Man,' and the 'Holy Grail,'" thereby conveying "an image of this molecular structure not only as a powerful biological entity but also as a sacred text that can explain the natural and moral order."[59] Nelkin and Lindee claim that just as Christian theological stories have talked "about the boundaries of personhood, the nature of immortality, and the sacred meaning of life," so too does current popular talk about DNA. The question is not only "Whose body?" but "Who is a person?" For many people, "DNA has taken on the social and cultural functions of the soul. It is the essential entity—the location of the true self—in the narratives of biological determinism."[60] Perfect DNA is salvation.

Locating the "true self" in only one part of a person reduces divine and human creativity. This is true whether that part is conscience, skin color, genital activity, genes, spirit, or any other single aspect turned into the whole. When individuals or research programs or institutions isolate and interpret an aspect of the whole person, they endanger integrity and social dignity. A mistaken meaning is achieved. In focusing a research experiment on a single aspect, such as a single gene, we may well help to understand a particular question about that aspect, but we make the scope too narrow for interpreting its significance adequately.

Remembering Luther's insistence that a person is best understood as life in interacting relationships can help us in the church. "Personhood" is a matter of living reciprocally in the presence of God, of oneself, of other persons, and of all creation. Luther believed that conscience has to do primarily with our relationship with God. Christologically grace-filled, we are free to live in this world in joyful service of others and ourselves. The right moral decisions do not get us into a better relationship with God. Keeping the Ten Commandments is not done to get on the good side of God but rather, as Luther puts it, "[T]hese works should be done freely and for no reward, to the benefit and advantage of our neighbor, just as the works of Christ were done freely for us and for no reward."[61] When conscience is lived in this freedom, it is a free conscience. Freely exercised conscience is justice oriented, not individually autonomous.

When Luther discusses the interdependence of faith and actions in the world, he emphasizes that boundaries that protect one's own interests at the expense of others' interests are false. The boundary between God and human beings is transformed when God becomes a human being, and we too are empowered to live this new reality. Slogans like "too different" or "mutually exclusive opposites" or "they aren't like us" are now just bad excuses for not wanting to take action in the world. Writing about the Eucharist, Luther said,

> You must take to heart the infirmities and needs of others, as if they were your own. Then offer to others your strength, as if it were their own, just as Christ does for you in the sacrament. This is what is means to be changed into one another through love, out of many particles to become one bread and drink, to lose one's form and take on that which is common to all.[62]

I think that God's power is such that we can even keep our distinctive forms at the same time that we take on the distinctive characteristics of the other and "that which is common to all." We do not have to lose ourselves completely in order to live in grace. But living in grace definitely does not mean living as unique, separate individuals with no responsibility and accountability for and with each other, whether as individuals, groups, institutions, or civil communities.

But what does this have to do with genetic testing? How can we determine "the benefit and advantage of the neighbor"? What are the needs of the neighbor and of ourselves in genetic testing and screening?

The need within the church is not for increased specialization in conversations on genetic testing and screening. Rather, the church can be precisely a corporate communion in which attention is always given to the specifics of a particular science or profession but explicitly in the larger context of human society. The church as embodied communion can regularly ask what assumptions about body and health have to do with moral responsibility for each other. How do we understand differences among human beings in light of our confession that we are all created by one God?

In terms of genetic testing and screening, how we analyze interests, resources, benefits, and burdens will be affected from the beginning by a strong bias in favor of "the least of these," meaning persons with the fewest benefits and most burdens in the society. If these people are less likely to be able to participate equally in the creating of public policy because of existing norms and unfair distribution of resources, the church can point this out and propose ways to overcome the imbalance. This may at times include proposing public policy that causes certain interests of one's own congregation to be set aside so that other, more basic human interests can be met for others.

While such conversations in the church are obvious expressions of a free conscience, carrying them on with persons from very different religious traditions and from none at all is equally important. The use of wise reason to figure out what is necessary for the well-being of all of society is possible not only for Christians. The confession is not that God in Jesus became Christian but that God became human. Erecting religious boundaries that exclude millions from engaging in the conversation about justice is like attributing redemption to genetic patterns: both hold back divine and human creativity.

Because life in the world has to do with this constant attention to the needs of all people and other creatures, ethics must include attention to questions of fair, equal participating in this deliberation. Luther emphasized this when he insisted on the need for public education for all children, girls and boys. "A city's best and greatest welfare, safety, and strength consist rather in its having many able, learned, wise, honorable, and well-educated citizens." The city needs "good schools and educated persons."[63] In a democratic system such as ours, no one is to be excluded from this.

Certain questions can help us to analyze a new technology and its social effects or an old social practice and its effects on individual choices and social policies. The answers do not exist somewhere just waiting to be discovered. Rather, we use all the dimensions of our embodied lives—including reason, emotion, and community—to discern what is helpful for the well-being of creation, including us. The participants in the conversation must be representative not of one community or congregation or denomination but rather of the city of creation.[64]

Conversation in society is an opportunity for the church to engage many more cultures and perspectives than exist within a particular denomination or congregation. Divine power in the Eucharist moves us to engage persons and situations and institutions that we thought so different from ourselves as to be outside our responsibility. In the process we may well discover others more than willing to distribute powerful resources to us too: more information on genetic research and therapy, new approaches to distribution of food globally, vital compassion, and much more. May the conversation always include all the very different perspectives and struggle to answer the question in united agreement: Whose body? Ours.

# LOVE AND DIGNITY: AGAINST CHILDREN BECOMING COMMODITIES

## Ted Peters

Weather forecasters feel good about themselves when they can tell their audience that sunshine with recreational warm weather is coming. No one wants to predict gray clouds and rain on our parades. Yet we ask our meteorologists to be conscientious—that is, to be honest about the facts and predictions as they see them. We want this even when the future looks gray and dismal.

As a social forecaster regarding the likely impact of genetic research on our way of life, I would like to promise fair weather. Yet honesty requires identifying storm clouds on the horizon and warning that we need to put up our ethical umbrellas.[1]

What I forecast is *free market eugenics*. The first quarter of the twentieth century witnessed political activity in England and the United States that included eugenics advocacy. Eugenics was a movement to use family planning to improve the health and intelligence and productivity of the human race. By encouraging the proper people to breed and by discouraging the wrong people from making babies, eugenicists sought to prepare the way for future generations of superior people. Positive eugenics encouraged intelligent men and women to meet, marry, and propagate in order to provide civic leaders for the future. The negative eugenics platform lobbied for legislation to discourage baby making among the mentally retarded, feebleminded, physically disabled, alcoholics, and petty thieves. This led to the forced sterilization of thousands of inmates in America's prisons, on the grounds that convicted felons should not propagate children who might also become felons and cost the state corrections system further expenses.[2]

Support for eugenics in America and England dried up in the 1930s because it was based on faulty genetic theory. When it became clear that two mentally retarded persons could give birth to a child with normal intelligence, the assumptions on which eugenics was based dissolved.[3]

The situation was more ominous in Germany. By the mid 1920s the National Socialist Party in Germany had brought together eugenics with anti-Semitism; and "racial hygiene" became party policy. Nazis sought and received advice from California officials as to how to implement eugenics measures in state-run institutions. Eugenics became the means for enhancing the interests of the so-called Aryan race. This led to the Nazi version of the Superman (*Übermensch*). Adolf Hitler's SS was charged with the mission of racial hygiene that led to the gas chambers and other extermination procedures used on children who were physically disabled or mentally handicapped. Eventually the gas chambers were used on political dissidents and Jews.

Am I forecasting a revival of Nazi eugenics? No. Nazi Germany was a fascist dictatorship. Eugenics was imposed from the top down. This top down approach is not likely to repeat itself in the near or medium range future. The political climate has changed. However, the idea of neo-eugenics may sweep over us quite soon; if it comes, it will blow in on the winds of a free market economy.[4]

For a barometric reading, take a look at the Herman J. Muller Repository for Germinal Choice. This sperm bank, established by Robert K. Graham in the late 1970s, collects sperm from Nobel prize winners and offers insemination to women under thirty-five with high IQs. The goal: to help guide nature into producing more intelligent children. This overt eugenic program is singular and small, hardly worth including in a weather report about things to come.

Yet I forecast that a new form of eugenics may eventually come upon us at gale speed. Like moving air that is invisible to the eye, at first we will feel but not see eugenic winds blowing from two directions: first, discrimination in health insurance and employment; then, secondly, personal tastes for designer children accompanied by the rise of the *perfect child syndrome*. I forecast that these winds will advance to gale or hurricane force, and future children will walk in the debris of the coming storm over selective abortion.[5]

In what follows, I will report on the coming controversy over possible discrimination in employment and insurance due to presymptomatic and predisposition genetic testing and screening.[6] I will then forecast that prenatal testing combined with the opportunity for designer genes may lead to a downpour of selective abortions and the treating of children as commodities.

My theological and ethical concern is that free market eugenics will set us up economically and culturally to view future children as commodities, as merchandise. Genetic discrimination in insurance and employment will bring economic pressures upon families to eliminate future children with undesirable—read expensive—genes. In turn, the power to discriminate between future children with desirable genes and those with undesirable genes may lead to applying quality control measures; those children who do not measure up genetically may suffer loss of respect, loss of dignity, and perhaps even loss of the opportunity to be born.

Martin Luther once said: "Even if a child is unattractive when it is born, we nevertheless love it."[7] With this in mind I offer a paraphrase of 1 John 4:19: *God loves each human being regardless of genetic make-up, and we should do likewise.* This will be the umbrella I suggest we open up during the genetic storm coming our way.

# Genetic Information Without Discrimination, Please

Discoveries in genetic research are leading to the advance of medical diagnosis, and genetically-based diagnosis in turn is leading toward possible discrimination against people with bad genes. Why? Because bad genes are thought to be expensive, and private insurance carriers would like to save the money. Or, to put it more broadly, as financial resources fall behind the rise in medical costs, health care delivery systems of all types are looking for cost-cutting opportunities. Will genetic discrimination provide such an opportunity?

Obvious to any observer is that the frontier of genetic research is sweeping across the medical landscape like a prairie fire. The swift movement can be measured in part by the discoveries of disease-related genes. By summer 1997 the underlying cause of 674 single-gene diseases had been discovered. A single gene variant, called an allele, has been found that confers susceptibility for cystic fibrosis on chromosome 7. Huntington's chorea was discovered lurking on the end of chromosome 4. In 1994 inherited breast cancer was traced to a defective gene on chromosome 17, now called BRCA1; a year later a second breast cancer gene was found on chromosome 13, BRCA2. Alleles of four genes are responsible for nonpolyposis colon cancer. In 1993 scientists found that in some families late-onset Alzheimer's disease is associated with high concentrations of apolipoprotein (Apo E4) coming from an identifiable gene; a person with two copies of the Apo E4 gene is likely to contract Alzheimer's at about age 68 but with only one copy not until age 76. Muscular dystrophy, sickle-cell anemia, and Tay-Sachs genes have been isolated. Predisposition to diabetes and numerous other multifactorial conditions is being tracked to locatable genetic origins. The search goes on for disease-causing alleles leading to 4,000 or more genetically based diseases. The search goes on as well to find the DNA switches that turn such genes on and off. The search includes the creation of genetic therapies to turn the bad genes off and keep the good genes on.

Ordinarily, discoveries such as these would fill us with cheer and hope because this new knowledge could be used in medical care for diagnosis, prevention, and therapy. It could mean advancing the quality of health for everyone. However, this apparent good news comes as bad news to people born with genetic susceptibilities to disease when medical care is funded by private insurance companies, and when medical insurance is tied to employment. An identifiable genetic predisposition to disease counts as an existing condition, and the pressure is on to deny coverage to people with existing conditions. Just as new techniques for prevention and therapy become available, the very people who could benefit may be denied access to these medical services.

Here is the logic of the emerging situation, at least as it is discerned by the American Association for the Advancement of Science (AAAS) in Washington, D.C. The AAAS convened the Dialogue Group on Genetic Discrimination and Health Insurance that began work in 1996, a group that includes scientists, ethicists, theologians and other religious leaders of different faiths, plus representatives from consumer advocacy groups, government, and the pharmaceutical and biotechnology industries. As the AAAS sees it, the new genetic knowledge is "a double-edged sword." On the one hand, gaining knowledge of our predisposition to a genetic disorder opens up the possibility of prevention or effective treatment of the disease. On the other hand, this same genetic information could be used to classify us according to immutable characteristics—genetic characteristics are immutable—that may lead to discrimination and stigmatization. As health care costs rise, people found to be genetically at risk for disease may be denied insurance or forced to pay exorbitant premiums to obtain it based on the results of genetic tests. Out of fear of loss of coverage, some of us may choose not to avail ourselves of such tests, thereby denying ourselves the advantage of potentially helpful therapies. This would be a tragedy. We need to avoid this tragedy, if we can. Even basic research could jeopardize participants, the AAAS dialogue group fears. "Neither threats of, nor actual, discrimination based on genetic information should be allowed to impede access to the discoveries of such research or the ability and willingness of persons to participate in critical studies."[8]

This is a public policy issue. Public policy requires governmental involvement. The United States Congress has listened to testimony regarding genetic discrimination. Testifying before Congress, geneticist and bioethicist Paul Billings said he encountered one woman who, during a routine gynecological check, spoke to her physician about the possibility of her mother having Huntington's disease. She subsequently lost all insurance when she applied for life insurance and her medical records were reviewed. Billings also reported on an eight-year-old girl who had been diagnosed with phenylketonuria (PKU) fourteen days after her birth through a newborn screening program. A low phenylalanine diet was prescribed at the time, and her parents effectively followed the diet rules. The child has grown to be a normal and healthy person. Her health care at birth was covered by her father's group insurance policy associated with his employment. When he changed jobs, however, the carrier associated with his new employer declared her ineligible for coverage.[9] Once a genetic predisposition for an expensive disease becomes part of one's medical record, insurance carriers and employers connected to them will find it in their best financial interest to minimize or outrightly deny health care coverage.

Here is the threat we face: loss of health care and perhaps loss of employment opportunities may, if left unchecked, create a whole new underclass. After hearing from Paul Billings and others, Congressman John Conyers said,

> Like discrimination based on race, genetic discrimination is wrong because it is based on hereditary characteristics we are powerless to change. The fear in the minds of many people is that genetic information will be used to identify those with "weak" or "inferior" genes, who will then be treated as a "biological underclass."[10]

As of this writing twelve states have adopted laws prohibiting discrimination in health insurance on the basis of any genetic characteristic, and seven prohibit discrimination in employment. At the federal level the Kennedy-Kassebaum bill includes genetic provisions regarding use of genetic information for determining preexisting conditions, and the Americans with Disabilities Act (ADA) offers limited protection in employment. These laws are inadequate, however. They prohibit only direct forms of discrimination—that is, they prohibit insurance carriers from denying enrollment or charging higher premium rates on the basis of an individual's genetic make-up. What they do not prohibit is the option on the part of the health care insurers simply to exclude specified genetic disorders from coverage. With the exception of New Jersey, the laws do not require insurance plans to enroll persons with expressed genetic disorders. By avoiding the targeting of individuals, the insurers could eliminate an entire genetic class of persons from coverage.[11]

Researchers in the Working Group on Ethical, Legal, and Social Implications of the Human Genome Project at the National Institutes of Health and at the Department of Energy created a task force and produced a 1993 report calling for action. The task force included geneticists, ethicists, and representatives from the insurance industry. The central message of the report is this: information about past, present, or future health status—especially health status due to genetic predispositions—should not be used to deny health care coverage or services to anyone.[12]

The AAAS dialogue group supports such a position, and it proceeds to offer five guiding principles: (1) all individuals are born with equal rights and protections; (2) no one in our society is "genetically perfect;" (3) society will benefit by providing protections against the misuse of genetic information; (4) individuals should be able to control the disclosure of personally identifiable genetic information; and (5) we should support research studies aimed at alleviating suffering associated with illness.

The AAAS fourth principle is known more widely as the privacy principle, sometimes called "confidentiality." Among the strategies most frequently proposed by ethicists and legal theorists, the privacy principle recommends legislation to protect genetic privacy—that is, to protect an individual's right to control information regarding his or her genome. According to this strategy, an individual would not be required to share private genetic information with an employer or insurance carrier. Elsewhere in this volume, John Varian details the position taken by the Biotechnology Industry Organization (BIO) in arguing for federal legislation that would protect the privacy of an individual's medical information, including the results of genetic testing (p.62).

However, a policy of genetic privacy would not be adequate to the challenge, in my judgment. Even though laws to protect genetic privacy would appeal to our sense of autonomy, to our desire to take control of what appears to be our own possession, our genome, by themselves these laws could not combat the threat of genetic discrimination. I offer two reasons.

First, protecting genetic privacy probably will not work. Genetic information as well as medical records are computerized. Computers are linked. In the world of computech someone who really wants to penetrate the system to gain information will eventually find a way to do so. An attempt to maintain control over genetic information is likely to fail.[13]

Second, privacy regarding one's genome is undesirable. Knowledge of one's genome could be of enormous value to preventative health care. The more our physician knows about our genetic predispositions the more she or he can plan to head off difficulties before they arise. Rather than privacy, it seems to me that we want *genetic information without discrimination.*

The problem is genetic discrimination. One proposed solution is genetic privacy. I believe this proposal is inadequate. The better solution would be legislation that prohibits the use of genetic information, regardless of how it is gathered, for the purposes of denying or restricting access to adequate health care. Because of the competitive nature of providing health care in the United States—competition in the insurance industry, managed care programs, and HMOs—it may be difficult to put teeth into a policy of *genetic information without discrimination.* Yet it must be done. This may require a single-payer program for basic health care, or some other form of legislated right to health care access that would place all competitors on an even playing field and eliminate the cost advantage in denying coverage to those of us with expensive genes.

## Should We Abort Children With Expensive Genes?

I am using the term "genetic discrimination" here to cover more than one phase in the scenario. First, the term refers to the threat that some persons will be denied equal access to employment and health care due to a genetic condition with which they were born. Second, the term can apply to the process of discriminating between fetuses to see which will be allowed to be born. Prenatal testing for genetic defects has already begun, and with the discovery of each new genetic predisposition to a disease new tests will be devised. One can imagine three hundred or four hundred genetic tests to be routinely run during pregnancy. Which tests and how many tests must the child-to-be pass in order actually to be a child?

Even if four hundred such genetic tests would be developed, practical considerations might limit the number of actual tests given to a particular child in the womb. At present tests are expensive and complicated, so unless a test seems warranted by the family history, it may not be administered. For example, screening for sickle cell anemia might not be ordered for a Norwegian family, because the incidence of the sickle cell trait is so minimal in that population. Screening for cystic fibrosis might be called for, however, knowing that one in twenty-five of this population carries the cystic fibrosis allele. Screening for sickle cell anemia might be warranted for a family of Nigerian descent, however, because it is known that in this population the incidence of the sickle cell allele is high. The actual number of such tests warranted and given to a particular child in the womb is less important than the significance such tests will have for health care providers and for prospective parents. The question is: Which tests will a potential child have to pass in order to become an actual child?

Here is a weather vane case. A couple living in Louisiana had a child with cystic fibrosis, a genetic disorder leading to chronic lung infections. When the wife became pregnant with the second child, a prenatal genetic test revealed that the fetus carried the mutant gene for cystic fibrosis. The couple's health maintenance organization demanded that they abort. If they refused to abort, the HMO threatened to withdraw coverage from the newborn and to withdraw coverage from the first child as well. The couple threatened to sue. Only then did the HMO back down and grant coverage for the child coming to birth.[14]

On the basis of this case, what can we forecast? With the advance of prenatal genetic testing, both parents and insurance carriers can tell in advance that a given child might be prone to having a debilitating and expensive disease. Pressure to abort may emerge from the financial interests of the institutions paying for health care: HMOs, the insurance industry, Uncle Sam, and so forth. It would be easy to imagine a decade from now a published list of genetic predispositions that, if found in a fetus, would mandate an abortion under penalty of loss of coverage. This would outrage pro-life parents. Even those who may have taken a pro-choice position on abortion would find this financial pressure to be the equivalent of a compromise on choice.

The economic pressure systematically to abort fetuses with expensive genes may be augmented with a growing cultural pressure to bring only healthy children into the world. The desire to give birth to only healthy children could soon yield to an additional cultural influence, namely, preference for children who are genetically designed to meet parental desires.

In addition to formulae dictated by cost-conscious health care providers, parents themselves will likely develop criteria for deciding which fetuses will be brought to term and which will be aborted. All this will begin quite innocently with what most parents-to-be want, namely, health and wellbeing for their future children. To want to bring a child into the world with the best possible chance of avoiding debilitating disease and accompanying suffering is an expression of genuine parental love. To want to bring a child into the world who "looks like" one or both of the parents is quite common, and usually not thought to be morally objectionable. The advance of genetic technology in general, and genetic testing in particular, will seem to offer aids in fulfilling these wants. Genetic testing combined with selective abortion may become the means to achieve these ends.

Parents wanting what they believe to be a perfectly healthy child may abort repeatedly at each hint of a genetic disorder. Parents willing to accept some degree of malady may abort only the most ominous cases. Aborting to eliminate defective or expensive genes will constitute negative eugenics. This may be combined a short time later with positive eugenics—that is, with actually seeking a certain genetic make-up for future children and terminating all those that fail to test positively for that make-up. What we can fully expect is that choice and selection will enter the enterprise of baby making at a magnitude unheard of in previous history.

The ethical dimensions of this scenario will first arise at the point when parents-to-be find themselves in a clinic office talking with a genetic counselor. Routinely before pregnancy or even before marriage, genetic services involving analysis of heritable family traits will be offered to help in planning for future children. Currently, however, talking with the genetic counselor typically begins with a pregnancy already in progress. The task of the genetic counselor is quite specific: to provide information regarding the degree of risk that a given child might be born with a genetic disorder, and to impart this information objectively, impartially, and confidentially (when possible) so that the autonomy of the parents is protected. (See Kirstin Schwandt's chapter for further detail on genetic counseling.) As an aside, we should note that it is frequently surprising and disconcerting to mothers or couples in this situation to learn that genetic risk is usually given statistically, in percentages. The assumption that medical science is an exact science is immediately challenged, and the parents find themselves confronted with difficult-to-interpret information while facing an unknown future. Conflicting values between marital partners or even within each of them increase the difficulty. Anxiety can rise.

These statistical unknowns come in two forms. First, for an autosomal recessive defective gene such as that for cystic fibrosis, when both parents are carriers, the risk is 50 percent that their child will also be a carrier and 25 percent that the child will actually inherit the disease. Upon receiving information regarding this risk, the parents decide to proceed toward birth or terminate the pregnancy. Second, via amniocentesis and other testing procedures being developed, the specific genetic make-up of a fetus can be discerned. In cases of Down's syndrome, for example, which is associated with trisomy (three copies) of chromosome 21, we know from experience that eight out of every ten positive tests leading to a negative prenatal diagnosis lead to the decision to abort. Even though the genetic disorder can be clearly identified in this way, what remains unknown is the degree of mental retardation that will result. Mild cases mean near-normal intelligence, and such individuals are pleasant members of families. Yet the choice to abort has become the virtual norm. The population of Down's syndrome people in our society is dropping, making this a form of eugenics by popular choice.

By this time the reader should recognize that I do not favor the unreflective and wholesale use of genetic testing for the purposes of family eugenics. But, one might ask, just how should we evaluate this forecast when drawing upon theological resources? How should we think about genetic testing and selective abortion in light of Christian commitments? Scott Rae offers the following: "Prenatal testing *per se* does not appear to be wrong—though couples are not morally obligated to use it. Rather, it is important that couples acknowledge that the womb is still the 'secret place' over which God alone ultimately has control (Psalm 139:15)."[15] I affirm with Rae that prenatal genetic testing provides a medical opportunity; and I affirm that couples need not feel obligated to employ it. However, I am less sanguine about restricting the womb to a "secret place" if this means that we should restrict medical investigation and shut off potentially valuable genetic knowledge. If genetic testing can help us to plan the medical future of both child and mother, then the principles of stewardship may encourage such testing. And, yes, such testing may in rare instances raise for the conscientious Christian the specter of abortion.

Neonatologists judge that in 3 percent to 5 percent of cases with abnormalities the prenatal diagnosis reveals the presence of a genetic disorder so severe—so lethal or so horrific in prospective pain—that the probable level of suffering on the part of the child warrants consideration of abortion. This judgment raises the solemn and difficult question: Might genetic knowledge foretell a life of such suffering or loss of life-chances that it might not be worth living? It invokes a principle of compassion, what bioethicists dub the principle of *beneficence* aimed at reducing human suffering whenever possible. We are talking about the small percentage of cases wherein medical science at its best cannot make life worth living for the newborn child, that the suffering is unbearable. In these extreme situations the principle of beneficence weighs life with unbearable suffering against the absence of life with its absence of suffering.

To render the judgment that a future life might not be worth living lays a moral yoke of enormous weight on the clinical geneticist and the potential parents. There is no clear technical calculus we can turn to when confronted with such a decision. Scott Rae wrestles with this by saying, "Even if the degree of deformity to be experienced could be predicted with certainty, it is presumptuous to suggest that the lives of genetically or otherwise disabled persons are not worth living. . . . Not even parents should have the right to set the standard of a 'life worth living' for their child. . . . The notion of a life not worth living should not be used to disguise the wish of the parents to avoid a great burden themselves . . . the hardship on the parents does not justify ending the pregnancy. . . ."[16] This helps in the abstract (see Tiefel also on this, p. 146). In the concrete situation, things are quite messy. Even in the messiness, however, we find room for compassion.

In situations where an extreme diagnosis is rendered prenatally and where the prospective parents strongly desire to bring a child into the world as an expression of their love, a number of things happen. First, without thinking about it, the parents refer to the child as a "baby," never a "fetus."[17] They clearly think of the life growing in the womb as a person. Second, when confronted with the bad news, they experience turmoil. The turmoil leads more often than not to a decision to terminate the pregnancy, but certainly not always.[18] It is not the job of the genetic counselor to encourage abortion; and advocates of procreative liberty stand firm in protecting the right of parents to decide to bring such a child to birth. Third, even when the decision to terminate is made, these grieving parents see their decision as an expression of their love, not a denial of love. It may be an act of compassion.

Significant as an ethical consideration here is the distinction between convenience and compassion.[19] Although the term "convenience" may tend to trivialize what the potential parents are experiencing, the distinction between the child's burden and the parents' burden needs to be kept in mind. Only a thin line separates burden from preference or taste, and when we place the responsibility of choice on the parental doorstep, the line is virtually erased.

As the practice of prenatal genetic testing expands and the principle of autonomy—that is, the responsibility for choice—is applied to the parents and not to the unborn child, we can forecast that the number of selective abortions will increase, perhaps increase dramatically.[20] Each pregnancy will be thought to be tentative until the fetus has taken and passed dozens, perhaps hundreds, of genetic tests. A culturally reinforced image of the desirable child—*the perfect child syndrome*—may eventually lead couples to try repeated pregnancies, terminating the undesirables and giving birth to only the best test passers.[21] Those finally born in this fashion risk being commodified by their parents. In addition, those who might be born with a disability but still with the potential for leading a productive and fulfilling life might never see the light of day.

The practice of selective abortion may produce an unintended social byproduct, namely, increased discrimination against living people with disabilities. The assumption could grow that to live with a disability is to have a life not worth living. Persons with disabilities find this fearsome. They fear that the medical establishment and its supportive social policies will seek to prevent "future people like me" from ever being born. This translates: "I am worth less to society." The imputation of dignity to handicapped persons may be quietly withdrawn as they are increasingly viewed as unnecessary and perhaps expensive appendages to an otherwise healthy society. This would be a tragedy of the first order.

Disabled persons are persons who deserve dignity and, furthermore, deserve encouragement. Marsha Saxton, a disabled rights advocate who herself suffers from spina bifida, reports that such people can gain victory in their difficult life struggles. "Most disabled people have told me with no uncertainty that the disability, the pain, the need for compensatory devices and assistance can produce considerable inconvenience, but that very often these become minimal or are forgotten once individuals make the transition to living their everyday lives."[22]

Given the precedent set by Jesus who spent so much of his time with the disabled—whether born blind or having contracted diseases such as leprosy—it seems that no disciple of Jesus could lightly acquiesce to the wholesale aborting of this group of people. One could easily imagine Jesus' disciples today organizing social services and advertising: "Don't abort! Send us your genetically defective babies."[23]

## Should Parents Play God?

Let us ask two quick theological questions. First, is God responsible for genetic defects that cause suffering, and, if so, should we try to improve the human situation through genetic planning? Second, if we try to improve the situation, would we be *playing God* and, if so, would we be committing idolatry?[24]

Regarding the first question, many hold that the Christian doctrine of creation requires us to believe that God creates our individual genome and that, for good or ill, we must fatalistically live with it. Michael S. Beates provides a contemporary example: "God creates some people with genetic anomalies for the sake of his glory . . . also to show us our own brokenness and our need of his grace."[25] According to this view, we need to submit totally to our Lord and our God, even to the point of accepting the evil that befalls ourselves or our loved ones. This total submission will allow us to trust that divine providence will bring a higher good out of the present evil. "When we grasp the truth of God's sovereignty, we begin to understand that pain and suffering are never wasted in God's plan."[26]

Beates is certainly right in inviting us to trust totally in God and to await divine glory to sort out the meaning of today's pain and suffering. Yet I would not like to interpret such trust in creation and providence to mean that we should sit on our hands rather than lifting them to help alleviate human suffering. Genetic science and genetic therapy and even genetic planning have as their aim *beneficence*—that is, they aim to improve human health and wellbeing. Regardless of the source of our genetic anomalies—whether it be divine creation or an accident of evolutionary history—we still have a divine mandate to be stewards of our science and stewards of our medical technology.

This brings us to our second question: Would aggressive genetic intervention constitute playing God? In today's controversies regarding genetics, the phrase "playing God" can be used negatively or positively. Negatively it refers to human pride or *hubris* that leads to an ethical form of idolatry. Allen D. Verhey reports that "The phrase 'playing God' . . . invokes a perspective . . . in which God is superfluous, in which humanity is maker and designer, in which knowledge is power, and in which nature must be mastered to maximize human well-being."[27] To assume that the God of creation is superfluous so that we the creatures take God's place would be a form of idolatry. Truly a negative assessment. Yet Verhey suggests another way to look at it. Rather than dub ourselves substitutes for God, we could imitate God. We could follow God like a child follows a parent. Specifically, we could imitate God's care and grace. Verhey invites us to play God "in imitation of God's care and grace."[28] Playing God "means to promote life and its flourishing, not death or human suffering. Therefore, genetic therapy like other therapeutic interventions which aim at health, may be celebrated."[29]

Significant for our discussion here is the implication Verhey draws for genetic intervention and selective abortion. "If God's purpose is life rather than death, then those who would 'play God' in imitation of God will not be disposed to abort; they will not celebrate abortion as a 'therapeutic option.'"[30] Having made this strong statement, Verhey still grants reluctant approval to abortion under unusual or tragic conditions. This is a concession to avoid intolerable suffering. Abortion, maybe yes. Celebration, certainly no.

Such a concession to selective abortion under unusual or tragic conditions presupposes beneficence—that is, it seeks to reduce suffering and promote well-being. The genuine concern on the part of parents-to-be for the well-being of their future children can certainly take the form of genetic planning, of genetic selection,

*ENGAGING WORLDVIEWS AND PROPOSING ALTERNATIVES*

or even engineering to increase the likelihood of good health. Such planning at the pre-pregnancy stage of gamete selection prior to conception could be considered good stewardship; it could be considered an ethically sound principle for conceiving only children more likely to flourish and find fulfillment in life.

The *Chevre Dor Yeshorim*—meaning "generation of the righteous"— programme created by The Committee for the Prevention of Jewish Genetic Diseases is instructive here. Among the concerns of especially Ashkenazi Jews are Tay-Sachs disease and cystic fibrosis, both autosomal recessive traits that appear in one of every twenty-five persons of this population. To avoid giving birth to children with two copies of either of these genes is the aim of this program. Young men and women of marital age take blood tests to see if they carry the problematic alleles. They are assigned numbers. The test results are filed according to numbers—so the persons remain anonymous—with the Committee. When a proposal for marriage is made, the couple telephones in their numbers. If this particular couple would put a future child at risk, they are told. Formulae determine permissible and nonpermissible marital couplings. This entire enterprise is aimed at avoiding genetic tragedy. This is high tech communal ethics at work.

Not all Jewish ethicists are sanguine about this. Laurie Zoloth-Dorfman writes, "But if the concept of prenuptial and prenatal screening is *halakically* acceptable for Tay-Sachs, and the technology exists to uncover more and more diseases, then the process shifts perilously close to the eugenic imperative."[31]

I do not wish to debate the wisdom of such testing and ethical thinking at this point. Rather, when looking at the wider culture, I want to raise the prospect that this primitive desire for the wellbeing of one's children could become shaped in its expression by market forces that could in turn commodify children born through genetic high tech. The science of genetics will lead to advances in the technology of reproduction—not *procreation* but *reproduction* in the sense that a baby will become a high tech *product*—and our otherwise deeply personal images of what it means to become a father or a mother could be affected.

## Marketing Babies

Market forces will be both negative and positive. The negative market forces placing constraints on our freedom to bring children into the world as we wish will come from the insurance industry and its influence on employment and health care. We will feel constraints on our freedom of choice in this quarter. However, we will gain a sense of increased choice from another quarter, namely, the predictable rise in the marketing of reproductive services. We can forecast that, as genetic science advances our knowledge, reproductive clinics will open and advertise services to facilitate making designer babies. These scientific and economic forces will influence the rise of a new cultural force: the *perfect child syndrome*. Parents-to-be will naturally want to avail themselves of the latest science to bring into the world the genetically perfect child. What will happen if the technology fails and the child is born less than perfect? What will happen in a neighborhood where genetically perfect children grow up with other children born the ol' fashioned way with the good or bad luck of the genetic draw?

My concern is this: under such market conditions, will babies become commodities? The issue is less that they might be bought and sold, in my judgment; rather, what is at stake is the *value* children will have for us when they are the result of engineering or selection in order to manufacture a superior product. Of course parents want their children to enjoy good health. But choice at the level of reproductive technology means selecting the healthy baby and discarding the unhealthy. Of course parents may yearn for a child with certain genetic traits or talents or abilities. But choice at the level of genetic testing for acceptable embryos or engineering for superior genetic configurations will likely lead to the perfect child syndrome, wherein the neighborhood children born the ol' fashioned way may be led to feel inferior. Or, worse, something might go wrong—technology is seldom perfect—and something less than the perfect child will be produced, causing the parents to deprive the child of unconditional affection.

The possibility of treating children as commodities raises the specter that human dignity will be threatened. So, based upon observations of how Jesus behaved with poor and diseased outcasts, and also upon the theology of the incarnation wherein God loves the imperfect world enough to become a part of it, I reiterate the following as a fundamental principle: *God loves each human being regardless of genetic make-up, and we should do likewise.* Scott Rae might draw a corollary: "The entity in the womb, however genetically deformed, is still a person."[32]

Those less interested than I in basing an ethic upon Jesus might hold some reverence for the Enlightenment commitment to human dignity, to Immanuel Kant's dictum that we treat each person as an end and not merely as a means. My central concern here is that children—perfect or imperfect, by choice or by destiny—receive unconditional love from their parents and equal opportunities in society. I cede a certain *presumptive primacy* to the babies being made by reproductive technology, so that they are treated as ends in themselves and not merely as means for attaining some other social or parental values. I want an ethic that successfully places the love of children first and foremost and that orients all secondary concerns for parental fulfillment and technological means toward this end.

## Conferring Dignity On Future Children

Love and dignity go together. In fact, love creates dignity in the beloved. To be the object of someone's love is to be made to feel valuable, to feel worth. Once you or I feel this sense of worth imputed to us by the one who loves us, we may then begin to own it. We may begin to claim self-worth. Worth is first imputed, then it is claimed.

Most of us assume that human dignity is innate, that it is inborn. Legally, of course, this makes sense. To assume that dignity is innate permits us in court to defend the rights of every individual regardless of how humble he or she might be.

Yet I offer another way to look at it. Dignity—at least the sense of dignity understood as self-worth—is not simply inborn. Rather it is the fruit of a relationship, an ongoing loving relationship. A newborn welcomed into the world by a mother and father who provide attention and affection develops a self-consciousness that incorporates this attention and affection as evidence of self-worth. As consciousness becomes constituted, this sense of worth can be claimed for oneself, and individual dignity develops.

Dignity also has a proleptic structure—that is, it is fundamentally future oriented. The conferring of dignity on someone who does not yet, in fact, experience or claim it is a gesture of hope, an act that anticipates what we hope will be a future actuality. Our final dignity, from the point of view of the Christian faith, is eschatological; it accompanies our fulfillment of the image of God. Rather than something with which we are born that may or may not become socially manifest, dignity is the future end product of God's saving activity which we anticipate socially when we confer dignity on those who do not yet claim it. The ethics of God's kingdom in our time and in our place consists of conferring dignity and inviting persons to claim dignity as a prolepsis of its future fulfillment.

Here and now the ethic of dignity makes a strong claim: There is nothing in this world we may value more highly than the existence and welfare of a human person. Yet, as we make social forecasts based upon the advance of genetic science, we perceive a possible threat in the form of free market eugenics. The threat arises from the commodification of children due to the commodification of so many things surrounding the making of children. As the industry of reproductive technology expands in the free market, are we likely to treat the products—the babies being born—like other products we purchase, namely, as commodities we choose by taste and then consume if they please us? Or, will we be able to differentiate between products and persons, consuming the former and loving the latter?

Science impacts technology. Technology impacts business. Business impacts culture. And culture provides the ethical framework within which we make important decisions. Because we can foresee how scientific advances in genetic knowledge may lead to a chain of impacts leading to the possible commodification of future children, we need to ask: What can we do to encourage unconditional love of children and to protect their dignity? I urge that we in the church vigorously engage our society at the cultural level, calling all of us to a high level of commitment toward the welfare of children brought into the world through genetic high tech. We have a biblical mandate of sorts: *God loves each human being regardless of genetic make-up, and we should do likewise.*

# INDIVIDUALISM VS. FAITH: GENETIC ETHICS IN CONTRASTING PERSPECTIVES

## Hans O. Tiefel

Moral issues in bioethics cannot be adequately understood or resolved immediately by searching for moral principles or norms or by asking what is morally right or wrong. Such direct focusing on what to do proves premature. We must first probe the meaning of the problem. Problems in bioethics, like those of genetic testing and screening, come wrapped in diverse beliefs about the meaning of life. Diverse visions flow from different beliefs and yield alternative readings of facts and issues. As with those Rorschach ink blots, what we bring to it proves more decisive than what might be there. We must begin, then, with the way we think and see rather than with what to do. Here, at the deepest level of our convictions of who we are and how life makes sense, we find and begin to understand the root of our disagreements over issues in bioethics.

Abortion, the most controversial bioethics problem in the land, and one directly relevant to our genetic topic, proves that point. Opposing camps actually do not disagree about principles or norms. For we all believe that we should respect both life and choice. No one advocates either killing human beings or depriving persons of liberty or autonomy. Where we persistently differ is on basic convictions about who we are, wherein human dignity and worth lie, and what we owe each other and our offspring. If we understand ourselves primarily as rational beings, if our dignity lies in the capacity to think and decide, then our earliest bodily form—tiny, embryonic, mindless—cannot be important enough to restrict our freedoms. By contrast, if we understand ourselves to be embodied beings that count simply because we exist regardless of developing or losing our thinking capacities—or because this is where the image of God is first formed—then the earliest versions of ourselves count and are protectable. We differ on what it means to be human and on what gives humans status and worth. In short, we disagree on the meaning and purpose of human life.

The way to understand and to decide bioethics issues, then, is indirect. It leads through what Philip Hefner elsewhere in this book calls prevailing worldviews (p. 74), expressions of which he discovers in our popular media. While popular culture does indeed reflect our deepest assumptions about what is real and important, the initial focus in this essay is on language, on key words that both express and shape the meaning of reality. My goals in this paper are twofold. I attempt first the analytic-critical task of understanding the ethics of genetic testing within our contemporary culture, which I label loosely as American individualism. As a part of this initial goal I shall probe the affinity of our prevalent cultural mainstream with biological sciences. My second and constructive task is to place several specific questions of genetic testing into the context of our communal biblical and liturgical faith. The method in both tasks is to concentrate on key words, for how we speak is how we see, think, and decide.

# Genetic Ethics in the Context of Contemporary Culture

We tend to remain unaware that we move and think in the secular mainstream of our culture. In the study of history we see readily enough that the times, the places, and the cultures shaped Christian thinking all too readily. But we resist the unnerving thought that we, too, are creatures of our time and place. Yet Paul's warning to believers in Rome ("do not be conformed to this world," Romans 12:2) remains perennially relevant. Without that critical awareness, we cannot "discern what is the will of God." The real starting point for religious ethics, therefore, is to note where we are culturally located before we can think of where we should be.

## American Individualism

Individualism constitutes a major stream in American culture in which we all move. Certainly it constitutes the predominant influence in current bioethics and therefore also shapes the literature of genetic ethics. With its roots in the Enlightenment, individualism with its claims to autonomy and control branches into all dimensions of our public and private lives. At its heart stands the dignity and worth of the *individual*, grounding claims to privacy and liberty. In deliberate reaction against bloody religious wars, the Enlightenment, of which we are all inheritors, looked elsewhere than to God for bestowing dignity on individuals. It believed that what makes persons unique and different from animals is not our kinship with God, but rather our capacity to think and decide. Each person counts—not for any religious reason and not for any contribution one might make to the common good—but because persons can think and decide rationally. I think, therefore I count. This worth of the individual is to be protected with rights. We are so convinced of this that "we hold these truths to be self-evident." But not so self-evident that it did not take a couple of centuries to liberate Jews, blacks, and women—western individualism's great historic contributions. American individualism continues to champion equal rights of all persons and fairness in public policy.

Such individualism regards communal bonds as something deliberately created by individual choice, such as a social contract, rather than envisioning social ties as the presupposition and nurturing network in which individuals emerge. This, in turn, influences views of generational links and loyalty. If it takes a contract or consent to create bonds between individuals as the Enlightenment believed, then the given links with parents, the ties of being kindred, and one's identity as a member of communities all become less important to one's identity. This, too, will have bearing on genetic inheritance, on how one regards adoption, and on the need for having children of one's own.

Individualism is protected with the right to *privacy*. Of late this right has taken on greater importance in both American law and ethics. In abortion law the right to privacy and the liberty it assures trump any state interest or communal responsibility prior to fetal viability. In genetic screening and testing as well, very personal matters are at stake. Invocations of "the most private and self-defining personal decisions" often work like magic incantations in our culture. They isolate genetic and procreative decisions from public scrutiny and keep us from "imposing" moral judgment on anyone.

Since respect for inviolable privacy pervades the minds of believers like everyone else, it is not at all self-evident that bringing this topic of genetic screening and testing into a communal religious context will be welcomed. This book assumes that the church might have something important and worthwhile to say here. Indeed, the contributors to this study believe that the church has the responsibility to reflect on these issues in the context of faith. But that may ignore the value we all place on privacy. Even if clergy or congregations deemed themselves to be qualified to address these issues, they may still fear to intrude into a personal space where God may enter but even angels fear to tread. It is not self-evident that what we have regarded as private medical problems should now be seen as religious and communal. American individualism's respect for privacy may thus obstruct the main goal intended by this anthology. The early chapters here may serve as a genetics primer, but cultural individualism may prevent any other uses of this book. (I give fuller consideration to this topic in the section on genetic and pastoral counseling, p. 139.)

What I am calling American individualism not only looks to the self for the meaning of life but also for life's *virtues*. Self-realization constitutes an ideal in education, the arts, and personal relationships. "Be all that you can be" becomes the motto to attract a generation to what used to be called "serving your country." Our moral virtues focus on the self: We recommend self-reliance, self-awareness, self-knowledge, and self-respect. We admire the proverbial self-made man. Words with the prefix "self" must be among the longest listings in American dictionaries. Our vices may also find their rationale here, for the one unforgivable sin in a pluralistic and tolerant culture is for the self to become seriously dependent: to "impose" in the sense of becoming burdensome to others. Aging and ailing parents are often terribly embarrassed to impose on their children. Caring for children with genetic diseases that make them dependent on sustained medical and parental care is also affected by the bane of becoming burdensome. When more and more genetic diseases become predictable, testable, and avoidable through abortion, not only our insurers but we ourselves may find little virtue in offering such care (see Peters, p. 127).

Our virtues focus on the self and recommend self-reliance, and our *popular heroes* manifest such excellences in pure form. Our heroes in film and comic books tend to be super-individuals doing their own thing. Their feats may offer benefits for the common good but never because they *owe* such contributions. Their deeds arise from *noblesse oblige* or mere coincidence. Nor will the Marlboro Man need the community; a good horse and a smoke will do. If he contracts lung cancer, he will. . . . Well, at least the ideal type will disappear into the woods and die like a man rather than sue the tobacco company. Litigation, of course, has its own individualistic appeal.

Acclaiming individuals and their rights to privacy and self-affirmation means acknowledging mental capacities. Only *rational agents* have a role to play on the stage of the Enlightenment. Non-rational creatures, whether human or animal, remain mere props. That is the main reason that the cry for animal rights fails; no serious environmental ethics can be built on this rationalist foundation. More relevant to genetic ethics, our future children have as yet no mental or other capacities and therefore can claim no rights. They have no status as persons and also lack all hope if they prove positive in genetic screening and testing. For whether in law or culture, they lack standing and may be jettisoned by quality control. If genetic counseling and genetic responsibility are to consider future generations who will be affected by our procreative choices, the language of rights does not look promising. This need not imply a rejection of rights-language. It merely notes that if we wish to take the rights of future generations seriously, it will take a richer language than rights. (Since rights constitute the main concept in which our society discusses ethical, political, and legal issues, the term will reappear repeatedly in this essay.)

This American individualism envisions a secular universe of persons protected by self-evident rights of privacy, liberty, and autonomy. The ideal is to be unencumbered by natural communities; to be obligated only by fairness and contracts; and to be virtuous in self-reliance and self-realization. Such individualism seems ominous for those of us who become sick and therefore dependent, whose privacy offers no protection against hereditary disease, who need communal support in our incapacities, who have no contractual claims for anything more than what we can pay for, and who are subjected to the indignity of flawed genes. Moreover, these effects of our cultural individualism are reinforced by the very language of genetics and the life sciences.

## The Language of the Biological Sciences

Issues in bioethics emerge in the language of empirical science. Not that physicians speak only as scientists—the language of their training—since they offer care and take care not to speak with patients as they talk with colleagues. Yet, genetic information, as found in this book, will be presented in the language of the biological sciences. The authority of science, its objectivity, its antiseptic no-nonsense expertise, and its clinical white are mirrored in scientific language. Failing to speak scientifically when talking about genetic ethics suggests ignorance and proves more serious than a mere awkward blunder: Linguistically one is not dressed for the occasion and therefore feels embarrassingly out of place. Nevertheless scientific language resists humanistic coloration and, when it becomes exclusive, subverts moral and religious concerns.

There is of course nothing wrong with scientific language in its own context. One could hardly be scientific without it. Its troubling and troublesome uses arise from making this language definitive, from using it in such settings as law, ethics, public policy, and religion. In those contexts scientific descriptions turn out to be not value-neutral but can lead and mislead. For example, issues of genetic screening and testing include choices about human "*reproduction*." In the world of medical science and technology, "reproduction" addresses both animal husbandry and human fertility. While human organisms may prove more complex and technically challenging, no qualitative distinction can exist between reproducing mice, sheep, race horses, or human embryos. There is no room for a divine or a human image that might make a difference in the status of such an incipient life. Moreover "production," as the main ingredient of "reproduction," hints of manufacture (*manus*: hand)—not altogether misleading in reproductive technology where the human hand plays a vital part. This offers a quite different perspective than humans as the handiwork of God. Finally, the manufacturing and economic flavor of human "reproduction" may also fittingly express commercial reproductive services that will be closely linked with quality control. But the term "reproduction" will not do beyond the scientific and commercial context: We would worry about a couple that ponders having a child with the question, "Should we reproduce?" Ethical, legal, social, or public policy contexts require more humanizing words, such as "procreating," "begetting," or simply, "having children."

Screening and testing seek out the "*abnormal*." While the scientific meanings of "normal" may be simply statistical, the common use of the word implies a standard or norm. The scientific uses of abnormal do not imply a negative value judgment, but common usage does. To call a newborn child "abnormal" distances us from that child. When we have become sensitized to the harm that word can do and, if we care for the child, we prefer the euphemistic "special" instead. What we call the condition discovered by a positive result of screening and testing or the human life so marked is not neutral. Our choice of words has value implications. In prenatal screening and testing, medical technology presents us with a "*defective pregnancy*," a condition easily ended, or a "*diseased fetus*," that sounds more like an underdeveloped mammal than an early human being and implies its own solution. By contrast, we might prove hospitable to "a handicapped unborn child."

If ethical and religious reflection were to adopt such scientific language or were to use it uncritically, it would violate its own beliefs. One cannot think morally or religiously without a language that unlocks the dimensions of caring and believing. A human being described by the biologist lacks the precious sanctity conveyed by humanistic and religious visions. No science may acknowledge that life itself is good and that we should care for it—or that genetic diseases should call for therapeutic responses. "Good" and "bad" have no moral meaning in the sciences. Where scientists must remain strictly descriptive, legal, moral, and religious dimensions acknowledge values. Where science notices only what can be empirically detected or sensed, believers acknowledge a human spirit and a divine image that transcends our senses, elicits respect, and grounds our morality.

Lest this contrast echo popular conflicts between religion and science, the warning here is not against science or its language but against using that terminology beyond the scientific context as if it were the only way to speak. Scientific words do not remain value-neutral when transplanted into bioethics and biolaw or Christian educational literature. Scientific words invoke the assumptions of their origin. The scientific method is deterministic and empirical. Religion and ethics assume freedom and transcendence. Science seeks general principles in investigating "*a case*" of cystic fibrosis. The community of faith speaks the name of that person so afflicted. Science groups such a case in statistics of disease. Faith encloses that individual in a caring community whose responsibility is not to understand how and why but to be there for that sufferer. Science must remain objective, and its language may never be personal. The Christian weeps with those who weep and speaks a language of solidarity.

## A Marriage Not Made in Heaven

The language of prenatal genetic testing proves to be a godsend to the sort of American individualism that locates human worth only in mental capacities. The language of such individualism at its best has nothing to do with the sciences: human dignity, respect, freedom, equality, and rights cannot appear in biological contexts. But American individualism refuses to extend these honoring and protective words to human lives not yet or no longer rational. Such lives remain outside any protectable humanity and only count insofar as a person might want or protect them. The technical nomenclature of prenatal testing that excludes all personalizing, humanizing, and valuing qualities, proves remarkably useful for individualism's political, legal, and public policy agenda: We owe nothing to these incipient organisms and everything to individual persons. Here American individualism, the mainstream of our culture, allies itself with the prestige of biological science—a formidable alliance indeed.

If believers were to be swept along by this unholy union and adopt this biological vocabulary or the individualistic language of rights, privacy, and autonomy in prenatal screening, they would not be able to illumine these issues with the light of biblical traditions or of faith. God plays no role in an a-religious scientific cosmos. And American individualism restricts religion to the private or inner self, insisting on religious anonymity in discussions of medical policy. To speak as believers—in genetics or anywhere—believers must be able to speak a language of faith. The church cannot be itself unless it finds words that emerge out of and resonate with biblical traditions, faithful communities, creeds, liturgies, hymns, and prayers.

# Genetic Ethics in the Communal Context of Faith

The Christian church has two identities: What it is in practice, the community of sinners saved by grace, and what it is called to be by God, the body of Christ. The moral imperative results from that dual identity and from our calling to be more of what we should be. Surely that is not unlike the human condition generally. Thus we become parents by the creative gift of God. Yet learning to be a parent is an endless process—that we get halfway right about the time our grown children leave home. It makes perfect sense to say both: you are a parent, so be a parent! It makes sense as well to confess, we are the body of Christ, therefore let us be the body of Christ! Yet as Lutherans we remain very much realists, aware of the pervasiveness of sin and skeptical of all self-transformations not to mention the world. We write Sin large in a culture in which that word has died. If grace be larger than sin, we hesitate to press such grace much beyond forgiveness into the shaping of a transformed life. Nevertheless, what follows here takes its cue from the prayer in our Brief Order for Confession and Forgiveness that begins, "We confess that we are in bondage to sin" but ends with the petition, "that we may delight in your will and walk in your ways, to the glory of your holy name." The sequence and logic of that prayer sets the tone for what follows. The reaches of that logic will appear unfamiliar and extreme. Indeed I ask myself whether we can demand so much of our church. But perhaps even immodest implications of who we are might be affirmed with that liturgical, "Yes, by the help of God."

Over against the individualistic self-understanding of the mainstream of our culture, the common theme in what follows is that of community, of solidarity both within the church as the body of Christ and between generations as parents and children linked with bonds of kinship and love. The resources for this task lie in our scriptural and liturgical traditions. A few such examples will characterize how we might speak with God and with one another as members of the body of Christ in the context of genetic testing. The themes of the rest of this chapter follow a sequence that first considers truthfulness in carrier testing. When we do discover the truth of genetic abnormalities, guilt and despair—the topics of the second theme—are likely reactions. Genetic and pastoral counseling, the third issue, offer different approaches to painful genetic dilemmas. The fourth focus describes diverging attempts to resolve or at least confront dilemmas of genetic risk to offspring: appeals to rights or to love. A last segment considers prenatal testing, again from diverging perspectives of individualism and faith.

## Carrier Testing: Knowing and Telling the Truth

If ignorance is bliss, knowledge may multiply misery. The ever-expanding information about our genetic identity confronts us with disconcerting options. If marriage partners suspect that they may be carriers of serious genetic abnormalities because of disease patterns in their families or because a child has been so afflicted, they face the question of whether to be tested. If it is a grave prospect, such as Huntington's disease, in which the symptoms are progressive, and fatal neurological deterioration may not appear until after childbearing years, it may make sense not to know. If given the choice of knowing the prospect of our years and the way in which we shall die, who would inquire? If our genetic inheritance might forebode a death sentence, looking into that future may seem masochistic. The shadow of the inevitable would loom over the present and darken our days even before any symptoms manifest themselves. Here genetic testing seems a sure-fire prescription for misery. Since facts never speak for themselves, however, one could invert the results of such knowing: Being aware of the coming end can result in treasuring the little time left and making every minute quality time. Such existential resolve to salvage every moment would welcome the chance to know one's genetic destiny.

But whether or not one *wants to know*, whether the prospect of death is seen as a specter or spur, the focus in the preceding paragraph is on the self. Do I want to live with knowing what will happen to me? How natural that question is in our individualistic culture! This self-focusing tendency offers an opportunity to learn to think like believers. Who then are we as believers? If Christians are stewards rather than owners of their own lives, accountable to God, it seems reasonable to know how much time there is left to do God's will. To be sure Jesus warns everyone to be ready to meet God, since no one knows the day or time of the end of this age (Mark 13:35-37). But some of us now have a chance to find out when our time is up. If there be wisdom in numbering our days, we should want to know. While such news may plunge us into enervating despair, stewards who will be held to account will want to know how much time is left for doing what needs to be done.

If wary Lutherans detect a whiff of works righteousness here, the issue is not one of salvation but of being accountable to use our talents responsibly. To do whatever proves useful with the rest of one's life makes sense for trustees who hope to point to something over which the Giver of Life, the angelic host, and the communion of saints might rejoice—in this life and the next. Therefore, yes, we should ask how it stands with us in genetic screening and testing. And while not all truth need be told, we must share this truth with our children to warn and to enable them to make their own answerable decisions. Here there is no difference between the secular and the religious: We need to know and to tell—as well as to share the burdens that such knowing and telling brings.

## Discovering Genetic Abnormalities: Guilt and Despair

Genetic testing and screening seek and discover abnormalities. Reflective Christian faith needs to confront the shock that genetic bad news inflicts on its hearers. How could the life we engendered and intended as a blessing turn into a curse? Discovering something seriously wrong in one's own or one's children's genetic make-up can elicit a search for explanations. Scientific answers of chromosomal combinations or of mutations will not do. Job's question, "Why me?" becomes ours. No pastoral care and no Christian community may ignore that. The question may be timeless, but it is never more pertinent than in our individualistic times. We also share that ageless need for a morally balanced universe. Suffering interpreted as punishment worked well enough for Job's friends but was hard on Job, who shared the logic but could not make it work for himself. But Job was not a Lutheran. He knew himself to be innocent. We Lutherans, by contrast, acknowledge sinfulness as a radical reality and might think that we really deserve it—the sins of parents visited upon their children.

A New Testament response to such tempting but unacceptable logic must insist first that it belies what we truly believe about God. This God creates us; and we are grateful. But lives entrusted to us do not come with a lifetime warranty. Indeed some wretched people experience such grief that they envy the dead (Ecclesiastes 4:2-3). As thinking and believing beings, we inevitably try to make sense of life by relating all things to God. And since we find it reassuring that God is generally in charge of things—at least of the really important events—we may want to name God as the cause of genetic diseases and look for divine but concealed purpose. A generous God who sends rain on the just and the unjust might have some divine design when genetic illness strikes with similar lack of discrimination. Disastrous genetic mutations, accidents, illness, and untimely death throw our sense of God's created world out of moral balance. Further, giving God credit for the good but not for the bad proves awkward, since we have no understudy waiting in the wings to play the villain.

We look to God for all that is good and that includes religious answers to our desperate questions. We probably cannot help but insist: "For surely God knows." While that pious phrase actually means that we do not know, we insist that God must. And such insisting not only may make God accountable to us but may turn our Lord into "the heavy." As Job, we may unintentionally malign God: "Will you condemn me that you may be justified?" (Job 40:8) Both frustrating and possibly inevitable, our human story keeps having loose ends, and we want to tie them up. But our theology does not tie up such ends by ascribing the origin of evil to God.

To be sure, in retrospect we may discern that God has worked with and for us even in the terrifying times. Terrors can take on new meaning as we look back. But when we face them we lack such assurances. Just as Job found no answer and withdrew his question, the best we can hope for is friends who will sit with us for days in sympathetic silence (Job 2:13) and a Lord who becomes present without answering our questions (Job 38-39). In the face of incomprehensible misery, Job's silence remains the best we can do. We must live with what we get without answers. Our loyalty to each other and to God does not depend on or presuppose good explanations. While never relinquishing the quest to understand, biblical faith remains unconditional. We are bound to each other and God for better and—as in these questions of theodicy—for worse. Faith-informed theological language speaks of "mystery" here, seemingly rescuing a touch of profundity where answers fail us. A sobering and plainer admission, though not normally cited in theological reflections, is the feisty bumper sticker, "Shit happens!"

But what Christians do claim with assurance is that this God seeks our good both here and in the life to come. This Lord stands with us—not against us—in our illnesses, despair, and dying. If Job's balanced theology of merit leading to blessings and sin to suffering were to be true, there could be no Gospel. Then God would not be seeking the good of sinners but giving them what they deserve. The merciful and forgiving love of God, just as undeserved suffering, destroys a morally balanced universe, but in a gracious direction.

## Genetic and Pastoral Counseling

As Kirstin Schwandt's chapter clearly describes, genetic counseling informs persons of their genetic condition, of possible risks to children or to themselves, and of therapeutic options where they exist. The point is to inform so that a rational and responsible decision can be made by the affected individual. "The primary emphasis on information-giving is based on an ideal of 'nondirectiveness,' a goal that attempts to recognize the person counseled as an autonomous decision maker."[1] While such nondirective counseling is controversial and may be impossible to achieve completely, "making recommendations to clients could amount to an imposition of [the counselor's] own opinions or values and has underscored the importance of [basing the discussion] on the beliefs of the person being counseled."[2] To "impose" is, of course, bad by definition. The patients' rights movement has only recently vanquished what it denounced as medical paternalism, in which the expert in the white coat made decisions for the patient. Moreover, since the patient will bear the consequences of any decision, it should be the patient's call.

Consistent with my earlier reflections, I will argue that this value-neutral role of genetic counseling mirrors the poverty of our pluralistic culture. Minimally we can agree on the dignity of persons, on their autonomy of free self-directed choice, on their privacy, liberty, and rights. But such choosing occurs in a value vacuum where nothing else is objectively true. We seem collectively stumped about what values to pursue with that liberty and choice. The "opinions" in the last quote are all that is left from what used to be called convictions. And "feelings" prove perennially popular. Opinions and feelings express something about the person: they are individual and personal; their truth is limited strictly to "true for me;" they will not be held accountable to reasons and therefore remain exempt from moral justification. Philosophers note that we as a society merely share a "thin" notion of the good. As a society we have lost the confidence to rank values—such as what importance to grant to our children as we make procreative choices. Values and choices become subjective and "personal" (read: individualistic, beyond scrutiny or judgment by others). Since we lack shared convictions of what is good and true, the patient's own values and preferences become king. That solves the problem of what values to acknowledge. But it must trouble medical professionals who dedicate themselves to the patient's welfare when patients' decisions are short-sighted, selfish, or harmful. And it should unsettle a community of believers pledged to seek God's will and glorify the divine name.

When it comes to human illness, we as believers have made a strange peace with our culture of privacy and personal preference. To be seriously sick constitutes a communal matter for the church. We pray for the sick by name. That constitutes a certain invasion of privacy, even when we omit last names. Of late we have even rediscovered a healing ministry in which individuals come forward to be anointed. It takes courage to get up, walk to the altar, kneel, and confess to all one's need for healing. No privacy there! And no doubt about what good to pray for. Yet, when it comes to decisions about health care in general or genetic problems in particular, we withdraw from each other behind a curtain of privacy. In genetic problems, as in so many aspects of life, we see nothing religious. Such matters remain "intensely personal," and therefore private. We also identify such problems as medical so that only medical professionals have something to say that is worth hearing. The only exception may be when we have tried everything and all else has failed. Such troubles take on religious meaning only when we run out of every other resource in dealing with them. Shades of American self-reliance? Must we not trouble God or the congregation unless it is really bad? Or is it simply the ancient inclination to divorce important segments of life from religious transformation because it proves so costly to be faithful in all aspects of life?

Clergy may accept and endorse such preference for privacy, conceiving their own role in a religious parallel to genetic counseling: providing a sympathetic hearing and enabling parishioners to make their own informed and religious decisions. In this view the pastor listens, reassures, reminds, and comforts—but does not guide—the afflicted. "Your will be done" constitutes no reference to God. Such pastoral nondirectiveness parallels nondirective counseling. But there is a value-added element; for whatever the individual's decision, it will be pastorally blessed. After all, these problems are complex, involve inevitable compromise, and will not endanger our salvation. Nondirective pastoral counseling is at best religious agnosticism in the face of unnerving dilemmas, at worst ethical relativism in a religious collar.

When the community of faith remembers who it is, it draws on stronger stuff than the thin concepts of our individualistic culture. The church is sustained by a "thick" biblical tradition; it is fed by rich liturgies, hymns, creeds, and prayers. Believers may disagree theologically, hermeneutically, exegetically, and ethically, but we remain a community as we seek to discern a will other than our own. We may argue, but we remain one body that seeks not its own truth but the way, the truth, and the life. Our individual preferences, therefore, cannot have the last word.

Pastoral counselors and other qualified members of the family of faith are therefore called to a quite different role than genetic counselors (see Holst for his discussion of a pastor's role). Church members are bound to those in trouble differently, for they are members of one another. Only Christians (and Jews and Muslims) are obligated to hallow the divine name in this context of genetic decision making and to discern what that might mean in practice. This does not imply that they pursue some esoteric mysteries. Rather, they seek God's will for all—a will that aims at human flourishing for all God's children. The point is not to recommend a Christian version of the traditional halakic Jewish practice of asking the rabbi, the authority and expert in probing texts and precedents, for a clear solution. The aim rather is to draw this so very modern and increasingly important aspect of our lives (genetic decision making) into the orbit of faith. The process of bringing these bioethics issues before God and the community of believers seems more important than the results of that process or any consensus about the results. Our very flesh, animated by God's life-giving breath, now has genetic labels. Even as we are individually diagnosed genetically with awesome and troubling scientific symbols, we already bear God's indelible mark. God already has "dibs" on us through baptism into a great body of believers. We cannot then be private and autonomous decision makers—our own and on our own. We are so joined to one another that the whole body hurts when one member suffers (1 Corinthians 12:26). We are so bound to God that our genetic decisions must also bear witness to whom we belong.

If we be true to that identity, then we seek to be informed in our decisions by what we know of God in our traditions and practice in our worship. Then we implore and seek to honor the divine name not just when all else fails but as we face all else. Getting clear answers about what to do becomes secondary to learning to ask genetic-ethical questions as believers. We need not be discouraged by the frustrating fact that "for now we see in a mirror, dimly . . . [that we] know only in part . . ." (1 Corinthians 13:12). No doubt we, too, shall continue to behold our own cultural reflections. But that did not keep Paul from offering some rather specific advice in the name of Christ. And it need not keep us from struggling to discern collectively the will of God in this new dimension of our shared lives, even if ours shall not be the last word.

## Genetic Risk to Offspring: Invoking Rights or Love

Carrier testing of persons of reproductive age can identify individuals with a gene or chromosome abnormality that, if passed on, may be seriously harmful for their children (see Schwandt for examples). Whether it is morally right to attempt to beget children when one knows oneself and one's partner to be carriers of serious genetic disease *depends in part* on *how* one asks the question. "Is it morally right to play genetic roulette with the health and lives of prospective children?" answers itself. So does the question, "May we interfere with the reproductive right of persons who want to conceive, knowing the risks involved?" Each question leads, but in antithetical ways.

The second version of the question relies on *rights, the* linguistic trump and dominant word in bioethics. In our individualistic culture many assume in practice and defend in theory this rights-centered approach as the moral formula for decision making in all procreative issues, including those that threaten harm to offspring. But with the focus on genetic risk, let us look closely at the strengths and ultimate inadequacies of such a rights-approach before we consider a faith-informed perspective.

In our society, rights constitute our strongest legitimate claims. Negative rights, the sort meant in "reproductive rights," function like protective fences around individuals. Appealing to reproductive rights is a defensive move, warding off eugenic and utilitarian interference of government or even of prudential policies of health maintenance organizations. While no right is absolute, rights form our most powerful claim as individuals against hindrance by others. Using rights in this context is almost culturally fail-safe, for what could be more American than individual rights? We may have no other word as powerful in our public policy polemics. "Rights" is the language of justifying claims, whether one argues for adults procreating at risk to their offspring, for condemned prisoners engendering offspring, or, of late, for cloning oneself. When values are relative, nothing proves powerful enough to contradict reproductive rights, no matter how bizarre their content.

Rights might be countered by other rights. Future children now conceived at risk will have rights against being harmed once they are born. But, as noted earlier, these children do not yet exist to protest risky procreation on the part of their progenitors. Once they do exist, it will be too late. For they cannot press legal rights, since the courts have dismissed wrongful life suits on grounds that the only alternative for such a child would be nonexistence. Retrospectively it is this life or nothing, and the courts deem not existing to be worse than being subjected to genetically inherited disease. One might invoke future children's moral rights, but that requires advocates to stand up for them. In our individualistic culture, however, we lack any sense of solidarity with future generations. In short, not just legal but moral rights prove notoriously difficult to apply prospectively. Actually such rights are never even considered when it comes to reproduction. Since procreative rights are self- and not other-referring, since they focus exclusively on progenitors, the interests or protection of future children remains irrelevant.

Placing prospective parents and children-to-be into such an adversarial setting as genetic risk illustrates the insufficiency of rights for resolving their moral problems. This is not to say that rights are dispensable. They constitute our last line of defense for protecting individuals and, as safety nets, keep the worst from happening. When we are forced to resort to these emergency measures, however, we already have failed each other. To insist on the right of child support, for example, implies that something has gone seriously wrong. It should never come to that, since parents owe each other and their children so much more. The problem is that when rights becomes the dominant word, we narrow the generous scope of human relationships into an adversarial confrontation. Such linguistic, conceptual, and therefore moral poverty will not do for perceiving and constructing the width or depth of our moral responsibilities.

Sole reliance on rights as the major word for ethics endangers and impoverishes how we understand ourselves and what we owe each other. Certainly it will not do for the church, which must look to the richer heritage of its scriptures and liturgies. "Rights" will not accommodate all or even most of what believers owe one another and God. Biblical ethics finds its norm not in rights but in *love*. Love will affirm rights when all else fails but seeks never to let it come to invoking them.

What then might love counsel when a couple, knowing themselves to be carriers of serious genetic disease, begets offspring and thereby risks the welfare of their child? Do we owe anything to our prospective children? Traditionally we believe that we do, anticipating the needs of children even if we cannot promise them all they will need or will want. We can and do look ahead, and anticipating the foreseen consequences of our actions is an indispensable ingredient of being responsible. Can we then love our children-to-be even as we bring them into life, knowing that our doing so as carriers of serious genetic disease puts them at serious risk?

It is tempting to evade that question by pointing to God as our Creator. We could say that God gives us not only the perfect child we all seek but also all those "defective neonates" whose congenital afflictions fill genetic texts and whose depictions make us shudder. So it is God's or nature's doing when children suffer from genetic illnesses, and both parents and children must take what they get. Such reasoning proves unsuitable, however. To be sure, we are tested by life's threatening surprises. Our loyalty in such crises to each other and to God tries our character and our faith. But through genetic knowledge God is now giving us the opportunity to prevent some of those terrible surprises. God creates us through human bodies and human decisions, placing the creation (and often the death) of human life into human hands. While it might sound Promethean here and can be cruelly misused, we are, to use Philip Hefner's words, created co-creators with God.[3] That role expands as we know more and can do more. It is literally we who hold more and more of the world in our hands—whether we refer to the environment, to nuclear weapons, to sustaining human life at its limits, to physician-assisted dying, procreation, or genetic manipulations. That makes our responsibility for human and other life unavoidable, including our responsibility in begetting children known to be at risk.

The question of whether we can love our children even while placing them at genetic risk might be evaded as well by noting that being at risk constitutes the human condition. We are at risk from the invariable genetic abnormalities and mutations that we all embody, at risk from genetic inheritance that leaves many less intelligent, less strong, less healthy, and shorter lived than others. We face risks from others and from a nature rather indifferent to us as its supposed crown. And we cannot protect our children from most of life's harms. Such a litany promises to minimize and perhaps absorb the risk we take when we procreate under serious genetic hazard. But while it is true that we cannot be responsible for what we could not prevent, we protect our offspring as best we can. Now we can keep them out of harm's way even before we initiate their lives. New occasions—the age of the human genome project—teach new duties. Genetics offers us new self-understanding and with it comes new responsibility to our offspring and our God. It will not do to leave it to God as the giver of life, for God has placed these decisions into our hands, for better or for worse.

Again, can we then love our children-to-be even as we bring them into life knowing that our doing so puts them at serious genetic risk? If the sort of loving we mean as Christians is a caring that seeks the good of others more than one's own and that imitates a divine care especially for the defenseless and vulnerable, then the answer is No! *No*, we may not beget or engender children knowing that we may burden them with a genetic inheritance we merely carried but under which they will suffer and die.

That illiberal and novel conclusion may offend not only readers pledged to procreative rights but conservatives for whom tradition forms a safe guide for present and future. That conclusion may strike pastoral counselors as reversing the whole enterprise of bringing genetic issues into the orbit of faith, recommended in this chapter. For even if parishioners were willing to think of genetic risks in the presence of God and congregation, such a No may slam shut doors that were just tentatively opened. Moreover, such a No does not offer precise guidelines and leaves moral decisions in shades of grey rather than black and white. The crucial points of the argument remain vague and complex: assessing serious risk of harm to a future child, reconsidering what is morally required of potential parents, applying the biblical command to love in a new context, and seeking new insights into our bodily selves and bodily links to our offspring. We must grant that all of that requires interpretive judgment and risk and offers less-than-firm criteria for a firm No. But the firm No remains.

This No can be easily misunderstood. All that has been said here concerns our offspring *before* they are conceived. The hard recommended choice is about the prospect of conceiving children. We should not call offspring into existence when doing so may seriously harm them. Not to procreate under such conditions does not harm any child, since one cannot harm what does not exist. But once their lives have begun, once they are on the way even in their earliest forms, we owe them loyalty, respect, and care. Since these claims may appear inconsistent, they bear repeating: If a couple knows that they are at risk of engendering a child with serious genetic disease, then that couple should refrain from conceiving. Once that child is conceived and now exists, however—no matter how early or how small—that new human life must not be killed. In the body of Christ, love is not governed by quality control, as I shall argue in regard to prenatal testing.

## Prenatal Testing and Tentative Pregnancy

The advent of genetic testing of the human unborn through such procedures as amniocentesis, chorionic villi sampling, and ultrasound offers prospective parents the opportunity to test the health of their unborn child. This opportunity is especially important for couples who know themselves to be at some risk either because patterns of illness have appeared in their families or because of their own relatively advanced age. Since currently very few therapies are available for any anomalies that might be discovered, the common assumption in testing is that any abnormal pregnancy should be interrupted or ended. Such termination does not refer to birth, of course, but to abortion. Referring here to "abnormal pregnancy" or to the condition of the woman diverts attention from what else is to be terminated and makes the decision easier. Genetic testing, therefore, may imply that pregnancies become tentative. And that makes prenatal testing into poor preparation for becoming a mother or father.[4]

The practice of such prenatal testing is now well established and may have almost achieved the status of good prenatal care. To classify this procedure under "care" may not be wholly ironic either, since most of these tests prove negative, relieve the prospective parents of worry, or prepare parents for what is to come. Knowing that one's unborn child is afflicted by a genetic disease might also enable one to marshall communal resources to help the child when he or she arrives. Not recommending such testing would expose physicians to the risk of subsequent litigation. Most importantly, both our laws and our culture endorse such prenatal caution as the only way to prevent the birth of an abnormal or defective neonate. Who would not want to avoid that?

"Birth prevention" turns out to be a particular useful phrase here, since it includes not becoming pregnant in the first place. If that reference is dominant, then choosing to end the life of this unborn child is no more problematic than avoiding conception. Aborting genetically diseased fetuses might even be called "medically indicated." But if one does not hide the meaning of this choice behind verbal camouflage, aborting the unborn child kills that child (at least as long as medical technology lacks an artificial womb). Doing so will be classified under health care, and insurance will pay for it. In fact, eventually for-profit insurers may insist on aborting genetically compromised fetuses, since it is always much cheaper to end such lives than to sustain them. Ted Peters makes this point with an actual case elsewhere in this anthology under the theme, "Should we abort children with expensive genes?" (p. 122). If such unborn children are not identified and "prevented," social attitudes in an individualistic culture may well find parents of children born with prenatally detectable genetic diseases to be blameworthy and regard the children themselves as pitiful, preventable, and prodigal. No doubt rights language will adapt itself to these measures under the motto that "every child has the right to enter the world free of genetic disease." Of course advocates of prenatal testing can defend against its fatal implications by noting that since most tests turn out negative, such assurance prevents abortions. But that already assumes that pregnancy is tentative and conditional.

This bleak assessment of prenatal testing may change in time, if and insofar as the capacity to perform prenatal therapy expands. Then such testing may dedicate itself to the good of the afflicted unborn rather than to assailing disease by eliminating its bearer. Prenatal testing thus lands us in the abortion controversy, where our country as well as the Christian Church remains divided. We in the Evangelical Lutheran Church in America affirm the church as a community supportive of life.[5] But we can also affirm both—continuing and ending a pregnancy. When it comes to the latter, we cannot bring ourselves to speak of killing an unborn child for good reasons but find that "a pregnancy needs to be interrupted."[6] We Lutherans cover the spectrum of disagreement, rely on the individual Christian conscience, and support both those who do resort to abortion and those who do not. What follows below argues for a smaller range of our options.

To achieve a clearer vision for Christians facing prenatal genetic testing and subsequent abortion, consider a reversal of perspectives: Ordinarily in genetically based abortion decisions, we use scientific language to focus on the pregnancy or "fetus." Is it healthy enough or too physically compromised to keep? The pregnancy or fetus constitutes the problem. Yet we ask the question. We make the decision. We become the masters over life or death. Could *we* be the problem instead? If we be judged by how we judge those who would join us, can we live with the roles of gatekeepers to the land of the living? Or are we called to a different identity, as is implied in the leading question of a Christian theologian: "What kind of people should we be to welcome [these] children into the world?"[7]

That returns us to the initial question of the identity of the church. Who are we as we guard the gates to the human community and also stand within the church and before God (*coram deo*)? Do these offspring-on-the-way only belong to the body of Christ at baptism and therefore remain merely one's own? Claiming rights to privacy and autonomy will not do before One who searches the human heart, whom we confess as Lord, and to whose law we commit ourselves with every "your will be done." If we are tested even as we test prenatally, if we stand answerable to God even as we make our unborn children answerable to us, what shall be the measure? If it be love, even a minimal love must mean, "It's good that you exist; it's good that you are in this world!"[8] If love be intercessory care, especially toward those despised and rejected or, to the "least of these," if our Lord identifying with strangers urges welcoming them (Matthew 25:35), may we turn away our own? That brings clarity to genetic testing of our unborns: If it is not loving toward them, we may not—in the name of God and as members of the body of Christ—end their existence when the tests result in bad news.

But could aborting seriously ill pre-borns ever be loving toward them? I find this the most troubling of all problems in this essay. Certain genetic diseases may be so severe as to be declared "incompatible with life." Lesch-Nyhan syndrome, anencephaly, and Trisomy 18 come to mind. Geneticists will add others. If such bleak prospects be genuinely incompatible with life, as medical professionals assert, abortion would merely hasten the inevitable. It would forestall the agony of bonding with children whose fate is sealed. It would prevent the excruciating suffering by parents who, if they could, would give their life in exchange for that of their children. There is, after all, nothing we can do for these unborn children. Their diseases remove them beyond our caring reach. Moreover, not to end their lives early by abortion might protract their pain and prolong the process of perishing. It would not sound absurd to invoke God's mercy in ending these doomed lives. And abortion allows grieving and healing to take place sooner.

And yet. . . . And yet this brief life is all that these children have. Our killing them before their disease will do them in shortens their existence even more. The wisdom of biblical communities has always claimed that we may permit death. We need not fight it to the bitter end. But we must not hasten or cause it. For human life and the divine image in human flesh, that special kinship with God, prove too precious. Such patience and loyalty to the dying have been understood to resonate with divine compassion.

Moreover these brief afflicted lives are all that we as parents will ever have of them. It will not be the child we expected and wanted, but it remains ours, and we belong to it. The promises of the marriage covenant must now include these unborn children. What we promised in marrying but always hoped to avoid—faithfulness even "for worse" and "till death does us part"—now faces parents of these children living in the shadow of death. Such faithfulness never meant inducing or hastening death.

The latest Lutheran social statement on abortion concludes that in "circumstances of extreme fetal abnormality, which will result in severe suffering and very early death of an infant . . . the parent(s) may responsibly choose to terminate the pregnancy."[9] The alternative suggested here instead is that we might at least ask whether Paul's convincing words about love—it bears all things, endures all things (1 Corinthians 13:7)—apply in this context. That question cannot be asked without trepidation. But does such anxiety arise from faith or from individualism?

I conclude that our faith may require more of us in the context of genetic testing than we are inclined to believe or accept. Our traditional responsibilities to the dying, our including the afflicted unborn in the community of faith, our remembering what we promised when we married, our commitment to God's will over our own (a God who does not explain our misery but shares it), our Christian definitions of love—all seem to point us toward keeping company with the dying until *their* disease rather than *our* choice takes them from us.

This conclusion is hard and possibly cruel for prospective and actual parents of genetically diseased children. Medical costs for serious genetic disorders can be astronomical. The emotional burdens will be abysmal, and the endurance such care requires may be more than flesh and blood can bear. Invoking the help of God is a desperate necessity. Not only God but the body of Christ becomes indispensable. Here the Christian church must again learn what it means to be members of one another and to bear each others' burdens. Focusing on the Christian rite of baptism may help us to do both.

Our merely ceremonial speaking of "the family of faith" and "the body of Christ" requires reform along moral and practical lines in the context of children born with fatal diseases. If we are the family of faith, then let us be the family that proves unconditionally loyal to its children. Caring for handicapped and dying children is so demanding that it probably can be sustained only by the closest of family relationships. What we as congregations pledge in a child's baptism—"We welcome you into the Lord's family"—is that this child is one of ours! We belong to each other in a family way and this child can count on us. The needs of genetically ill and dying children and of their families may teach us that those baptismal congregational promises actually claim us. New ways of being the family of faith—trained lay ministers, groups of friends—attest our willingness and ability to be that family.

When we let the unborn genetically afflicted and even terminally ill child live to be baptized and to join the body of Christ, the very opening words of our baptism ritual take on a surprisingly new literal meaning: "In Holy Baptism our gracious heavenly Father liberates us from sin and death. . . ."

# Summary

I have reflected on questions of genetic ethics from two perspectives: that of contemporary culture and that of biblical-liturgical faith. These perspectives constitute deeply and coherently held beliefs about values, human identity, and the meaning of life that generate and direct moral conclusions. Such beliefs express themselves in characteristic words, words that unlock the respective visions and shape their ethical judgments. American individualism as our cultural mainstream focuses on the intrinsic worth of persons in terms of their rational capacities, protects them with such inalienable rights as autonomy and privacy, emphasizes the self, and classifies and thereby exposes incipient and nonrational human lives with the language of the biological sciences. Biblical and liturgical traditions ascribe human dignity to a transcendent source, envision relationships of solidarity between members of the body of Christ and between generations, and speak a language of love understood as care. While both a secular individualism and Christian faith welcome knowing what genetic testing reveals, faith confronts such knowing in the presence of God and of the community, places these dilemmas into the orbit of religious commitment, and bears its burdens as shared responsibilities. Such faith acknowledges but does not explain the suffering caused by genetic disease and knowledge. It affirms knowing and telling the truth in carrier testing and does not initiate bringing children into the world when doing so places them at serious risk. Finally, it refuses to reject genetically threatened children-on-the-way with prenatal testing since they can still be reached by care, and it calls upon the church to be an embracing family of faith for all human life.

# SECTION THREE

# CONFRONTING PROFESSIONAL CHALLENGES

# A GENETICIST'S SYNTHESIS: EVOLUTION, FAITH AND DECISION MAKING

## Robert Roger Lebel

The notion that all things are in constant motion, that one cannot step into the same river twice, has been attributed to Heraklitus, ca. 500 B.C.E.[1] In various guises, this ancient idea has taken root in both scientific and religious forms of thought. All of evolutionary thinking rests on it. One religious expression of this perspective is in the writings of Martin Luther: [God] "does not stand still . . . the life of faith implies progress."[2] Luther might well object to his being quoted here since his notions of scientific progress are not those followed in the present essay. The point remains that progress, in various guises, underlies both scientific and religious life and thought.

To make progress, a person of faith sometimes confronts deeply personal decisions related to the fundamental biological drive to reproduce. Making such decisions in view of complex technological input and moral challenge requires a perspective enlightened by both faith in the risen Christ and appreciation of the advanced scientific milieu (shaped by advances with computers and genetics, etc.) of the twenty-first century. It demands evolutionary thinking (awareness that all things move, and that God's work in our lives implies progress).

How does one understand the demands that sometimes seem to compete in regard to: (1) fidelity to the Gospel, (2) the desire to bear children, (3) the imperative to give those children an opportunity for productive and creative living, (4) the availability of preconceptional, preimplantation, and prenatal testing to discover significant abnormalities in the reproductive effort, and (5) the expectation that a modern person should not submit blindly or without proportionate purpose to preventable suffering?

To put it more simply, how does one follow the lead of St. Paul while also giving serious attention to the insights of Charles Darwin and Gregor Mendel and their intellectual descendants? Many people have thought that evolutionary insights are at odds with a divine Creator, or that genetics has inserted into moral discussion reasons to suspect determinism (even predeterminism?), or that the appreciation of relativity demands abandonment of any moral imperative. I disagree.

I believe that Christians ought to reject fragmentation of the intellectual, mystical, and corporal elements of human existence, and seek a theological formula (a heuristic) by which these might be integrated, radically and progressively, to form a seamless attitude of mind and spirit. This would be a stance in awe of the beauty of creation, reflecting deeply on the notion that God calls us to accept an active role in its emerging complexity—to be "created co-creators" (see Hefner, p. 77). It is essential that we understand the notions of autonomy, responsibility, justice, beneficence, creativity, and love in a way that unites our conviction that we are caught up into salvation by an undeserved radical gift of love, and with a sense of being placed at the cutting edge of evolution and presented with the power and challenge to direct its course.

This chapter is an attempt to explain my perspective as a Christian geneticist, a perspective which I believe offers such a synthesis since it supports these apparently diverse elements and unifies the competing notions of faith and science. I devote the first section to sketching this synthesis which depends on the kind of evolutionary thinking I think we need. The second and third sections deal with the moral content of genetic decisions. Then follows application to a case study taken from the chapter by Kirstin Schwandt (p. 41). The final section comments on the problem of evil in this evolutionary perspective.

In the event that the reader finds the philosophical and theological explorations to be somewhat cumbersome, it may be helpful to skip ahead to the case discussion and return to the evolutionary process later.

# A. Fundamentals of a Christian-Scientific Worldview

Any Christian and scientific analysis that would support a decision on reproductive choices confronting families who face genetic disease requires a faith that is not naive. This faith, rather, takes into account what is now known about the complexities of the evolutionary process by which we came to exist in our present form in the universe—individually and corporately—not just as a species, but as the Body of Christ. Further, it must attend to the process that sets the directions open to us for further development.

The insights of evolution need not be threatening. In fact, they are fundamental. Each individual goes through an evolutionary process whereby genetic potential posited in a gamete is useless until it is combined with that of another complementary gamete (egg and sperm). Approximately 200,000 genetic elements require the support of a hospitable maternal environment (womb) to produce a child, who in turn depends on those entrusted with care for many years before being capable of acting as a moral agent.

If we extend the evolutionary perspective to personal maturation, moral agency may be seen as a highly advanced personal development. Proper moral action, then, involves choices that express creativity, love, generosity, and dedication to justice (as opposed to indifference and selfishness). Such agency contributes positively to the process of creating the whole world. From a Christian viewpoint, submitting to incorporation into the Body of Christ is an active process requiring expenditure of considerable energy to build it up and make a personal contribution to it.

I believe we operate on a series of planes of reality, each successive one built and dependent on those preceding it, both temporally and logically. Our existence requires operation on all planes simultaneously. The evolutionary process that brought us to our present condition can be discerned as having taken place in a series of events, each a breakthrough to a new higher plane. Any attempt to unify science and faith depends on a clear notion of the nature, importance, and roles of these levels in the process of evolution.

## 1. The Laws of Physics

The laws of physics require certain patterns of behavior of subatomic particles and atoms, which must relate to each other in prescribed patterns that are, as far as we know, immutable. Microscopes, telescopes, accelerators, and other investigational instruments are dedicated to deeper understanding of those laws.

Insights into the physical laws were expressed in the works of Nicolaus Copernicus (1473-1543), Galileo Galilei (1564-1642), Johann Kepler (1571-1630), Isaac Newton (1642-1727) and Albert Einstein (1879-1955). Revolutionary and controversial at the time of their first articulation, these ideas are now part of the consciousness of intellectuals from every specialty (social and natural sciences, philosophy, theology, etc.); every school child is taught them.

## 2. The Laws of Chemistry

Atoms may establish relationships with other atoms, whether of the same atomic structure or of a different species. The periodic table of Dmitri Mendeleev (1834-1907) affords a way of organizing for study the physical properties of different types of atoms, according to the laws of chemistry whereby they interact with each other to form compounds of greater complexity. A sugar molecule is made up of oxygen, carbon, and hydrogen atoms; each of the many sugars has characteristics established by the exact way in which these elemental subunits are arranged. Yet the chemical properties of any sugar molecule are thoroughly different from those of the elemental building blocks. Thus the laws of chemistry are built upon, supported by, and supersede those of physics.

A chemical entity may lose its chemical integrity without ceasing to obey all the laws of physics. Subjected to digestive enzymes, the sugar molecule may cease to be sugar without change of the elemental subunits. But subjected to bombardment by radiation, disintegration of one of its carbon or oxygen atoms into elements of lower molecular weight may occur, radically altering the physical reality at the same time as changing its chemical nature.

# 3. The Laws of Biology

The idea that living things may spring up independently (e.g., maggots from meat) was widely held as true until the advent of the microscope. William Harvey (1578-1657) had already contemplated the essential role of the ovum before Anton Leeuwenhoek (1632-1723) used a microscope to study spermatozoa. Now it is commonplace to appreciate that a living being only exists as the direct product of previously living things, and that the web of life is a single unbreakable fabric evolving (probably) from a single breakthrough.

*Biogenesis* expresses the notion that life appears or emerges in a place where it had not been present previously; it implies the notion of a process of appearance, with a certain logic and appropriateness of the event. Most biologists believe today that a kind of primordial "soup" existed on the surface of this planet some 3.8 billion years ago. Processes involving water, simple chemicals, and electrical energy brought about ever-more-complex molecules until the capability of self-replication emerged. Biogenesis, the emergence of the first living being, began the flow of life from which all known living things have descended.

The insights of Charles Darwin (1809-1882) and Gregor Mendel (1822-1884) paved the way for us to discover much about the ways in which living things function and evolution occurs. Neither of those great contributors lived to hear of chromosomes or DNA. Nor does either today enjoy the unencumbered acceptance by all thinking persons that is offered to Copernicus, Galileo and the others whose contributions are more remote in time and deal with the physical rather than the biological (and thus more complex) aspects of our being.

Yet today, as many people are still struggling with the basic ideas of evolution as God's way of writing a marvelous story with creation, thousands of geneticists worldwide are laboring to map the entire human genome. Our current knowledge of genetic traits in humans has grown rapidly but constitutes only about 10 percent of what we believe must be present in the DNA of our cells.[3]

Considering the mystery of biogenesis, we encounter a great paradox: life as a plane of reality, emerging from the chemical plane only once on any given celestial body, is at once both beautifully fragile and astoundingly hardy. Uniqueness of the event is one of the expressions of fragility, but its hardiness is expressed in the commonplace "life goes on," which may be uttered in cynicism or in resignation, but is true nonetheless. The life of the individual may be snuffed out in a moment with the eruption of a volcano or a bullet released by the twitch of a finger (physical events), the effects of cyanide which disrupt processes in the cell (chemical event), or the effects of a tumor (biological event). Yet we have all known individuals whose continued living astounds us due to the obstacles they overcame against terrible challenges.

Life also goes on in evolutionary time, with increasing diversity and complexity as new species emerge while others fall away from the project because of exploring avenues that reach dead ends rather than participating in the upward and onward process by which life tends toward a yet higher plane of existence. Extinction of species always has been part of the overall process of life on the planet. This idea does not justify acceptance of human practices that erase from the diversity of our world those delicate species whose habitat is destroyed by greed or indifference. On the contrary, diversity is essential to success in the whole fabric of life; we depend on it for *speciation* (the emergence of new forms) as much as an individual body requires a complex variety of cells functioning in specialized ways.

The exuberant energy driving evolution produces a startling diversity of forms. One thinks of the proliferation of trilobites during pre-Cambrian time, to become the dominant life form of the Cambrian period (500-570 million years ago), all traces of which vanished at the end of the Permian period 225 million years ago.[4] The dinosaurs of fabled size and ferocity were gone without a survivor at the end of the Cretaceous period (65 million years ago). These made their contribution not by leaving descendants but by helping drive diversification, essential to the forward progress of evolution.

Aesop (620-560 B.C.E.) spun a fable about the parts of the body at odds with one another over which organ had the greater dignity and honor, which was more essential than the others to the ongoing success and health of the whole. Half a millennium later, St. Paul borrowed the simile to describe the Body of Christ (1 Corinthians 12:14-31). The resolution of the debate was, of course, that removal of any part impoverishes the whole even if it does not bring an end to life entirely. A human being needs a working heart and brain in order to carry on at all; it is far better to have two hands, two eyes, two lungs than only one. Blindness or deafness is tolerable for ongoing life only if the individual enjoys the support of others who supply those functions, directly or indirectly; in primitive settings, loss of these senses leads quickly to death.

## 4. The Laws of Spirit

At the next level of emergence, *homogenesis* refers to the appearance of thinking humanity among the array of biological forms. The implication is that this event brings about a qualitatively new plane of being. This plane exhibits reflective thought capable of abstraction, planning, contemplation of the future and creative organization of experience to posit new formulations, and these activities all require abilities not found in other living things.

The current theory of homogenesis has it that all members of our species probably descended from a single female—Nicknamed "Eve" by anthropologists (in honor of the biblical character)—born in southern Africa approximately 50,000 years ago. The biblical account of human creation from one individual might seem naive and simplistic, but the delicate experiment in evolution which gave rise to our species is more likely to trace to a single small community or family of primates than to any large sweeping mass of organisms, perhaps a single female.[5]

In our emergent model of being, we see that humans must obey the laws of thought and creativity along with those of biology, chemistry, and physics, since none of those at "lower" planes have been repealed. The process of emergence to "higher" planes entails ongoing increase in complexity ("complexification"), but remains dependent on the "lower" plane's continuation.

Pierre Teilhard de Chardin (1881-1955) expressed a sense of awe and wonder in contemplating that the human organism appears to be poised at the midpoint between the immensely small (subatomic particles) and the immensely large[6] (the cosmos of innumerable galaxies). Since his time, scientists have pushed these limits further back in both directions. We at the midpoint continue to represent the deepening of complexity in an immensely complex project of rational and emotive energy that is humanity. Now at last the players in evolutionary progress are no longer only passive, but may undertake to plan and execute portions of the project. We are active participants, created co-creators. This brings heady opportunities but also awesome responsibilities.

Some two thousand generations would follow from "Eve" before consciousness achieved such milestones as written language. Ever higher and more complex expressions of technology would follow, until in our present century the rate of progress in new achievements has accelerated. Today we are awestruck on a regular basis by the discoveries of the Hubble space telescope and the Human Genome Project. Yet the most profound import of this homogenesis that we have been describing is that our creative effort is no longer bound by the demands of biologic imperative to reproduce. We can recognize the single schoolteacher who leaves no children as making an immeasurable contribution to the human project in the hundreds of lives she has improved by training young minds. Nor are we concerned that Abraham Lincoln (1809-1865) has no living descendants today, or that we can identify few socially prominent descendants of Johann Sebastian Bach (1685-1750); their contributions to culture (the higher reality) are more important than contributions to the gene pool.

## 5. The Law of Christ

Somewhere someone awoke one day to a sense of being invited to live generously rather than according to the "law of the jungle" (strictly selfish survival). She or he must have found this awakening both confusing and exciting; it is not surprising that this person opted to continue living on the lower plane of self-preservation rather than respond to the invitation to love. However much this choice might have tarnished the emergence of humanity with "original sin," it did not leave us devoid of all opportunity for, and interest in, creative and generous living; these burgeoning possibilities would find various expressions in the millennia to follow.

The notion of self-gift, of generous (sacrificial) living, represented a new evolutionary breakthrough possible only when superimposed on the substrate of creative thought. The entry of Christ into history would have been meaningless if living things had not yet achieved self-consciousness; he invites us higher, deeper, further into the evolutionary project. We speak of his chief mandate being to love one another as he has loved us (John 13:34). Not simply appreciating one another, respecting one another, helping one another, but giving ourselves over in the love of self-sacrifice, even unto death (*agape*). Thus Christ represents the next (and final?) layer of reality, emergence of the ultimate unitive force, bringing to tangible, visible form a new notion that revolutionizes the process.

Luther would write: "Rather than seeking its own good, the love of God flows forth and bestows good. . . . Sinners are attractive because they are loved; they are not loved because they are attractive. . . . This is the love of the cross, born of the cross, which turns in the direction where it does not find good which it may enjoy, but where it may confer good upon the bad and needy person."[7]

Such a gift makes no sense in the context of any of the sets of laws governing physical, chemical, biological, or human existence; it is counter-intuitive in those contexts. It can make sense only on the higher plane of Christ and his invitation to be absorbed into the greater good, the goal of evolution: utter and final unity in Him. "He is the image of the unseen God [who has] primacy over all created things . . . and all things are held together in him" (Colossians 1:15-17). This requires a humble act of acceptance, of acquiescence in response to an invitation; it is an "act of faith." The faith option then entails courage and requires great energy. It is not a falling into repose or restfulness, but rather a deeper involvement in the creative process than could be contemplated through any other means or manner of activity. "Faith is not an idle quality . . . [it is] trust in a thing we do not see, in Christ, who is present especially when he cannot be seen. . . . [F]aith . . . takes hold of and possesses this treasure".[8]

In the law of Christ we go beyond celebrating the dinosaurs and trilobites whose contribution to the biosphere was exuberance rather than continuity of DNA. We transcend appreciation of the loving, dynamic teacher who leaves no children but inspires generations of students. We now are absorbed in contemplation of the divine invitation, and caught up into the next evolutionary emergence: unification of all that exists in Christ, who is the guiding principle of creation and whose self-gift love (*agape*) transforms suffering and gives meaning to the struggle to exist, to grow, to survive, to contribute. Further, from this law of Christ we identify the principles guiding constructive participation in the process of evolution. *Agape* teaches us to live generously, creatively, sacrificially; thus we contribute to the trajectory toward unification of all things in Christ.

Dynamic love may be depicted as Christ casting fire on the earth (Luke 12:49; Matthew 3:11); he not only enlivens with the energy trapped by green plants in sugar molecules. Beyond that, he consumes us whole when we submit our creative energies to building the kingdom of God (which I take to mean the whole of creation). Every generous employment of our creativity is caught up by Christ in the project that is so much larger than anything we might be or even contemplate in our individual lives. We may speak of the emergence of the Christic plane of reality as *Christogenesis*.

We must stand in utter awe and humility before Christ who directs the symphony of universal progress while we are distracted by the details of the small portion in which we find ourselves for a fleeting moment. For instance, in tracing my own genealogy, I discovered that I am descended from Guillaume Couture (1617-1701) who came to New France with priest missionaries and eventually decided to work at building the colony within the secular realm rather than to take vows of celibacy. Had Couture decided otherwise, I would not exist as the individual I am because the peculiar mixture of DNA that makes me what I am, where I am, and when I am would never have come to be. Yet he could not have contemplated my existence!

# B. Reflections on Moral Dimensions from This Perspective

## 1. The Challenge

Whether and when and with whom to have children is not a new problem; it antedates modern problem-solving challenges, having been a prominent part of history in every culture. The concerns may have been political as in the effort to unify rival kingdoms, or personal as in the choice of the optimal dowry, or idealistic as in the romantic notion of being star-struck by the most stunning and remarkable mate. In each case people have labored over this point of choice in life. Nor have we reached a universally acceptable method of simplifying the problem. Some still submit willingly to arranged marriages, while others are horrified by the idea.

Modern scientific medicine has added a new interest and concern to this ancient problem. While it has long been held that one should choose a spouse wisely in order to improve (or at least not degrade) the family stock, we now really have ways of making some such choices. Having achieved this, we are sometimes ambivalent about applying the science to the actual decision. Many are dubious, for example, about the program of rabbinic influence used by orthodox Jewish communities. In that program, the rabbi keeps records of test results for carrier status of Tay-Sachs disease and other recessive disorders; when a young couple applies for marriage they are advised against a union if they are both carriers of the same genetic disorder.

Most modern religious and secular biases run against placing such life-decision-making power in the hands of outside authority; they are inclined to place it squarely in the hands of the prospective parents themselves. Arguments that they might lack a broad perspective or are blinded by their passions do not receive much respect. If we, nevertheless, are to take seriously our mission as created co-creators with God, we cannot escape the demands of responsibility that accompany the gifts of freedom in choice. We struggle to discover the path of creativity which expresses our unique gifts and opportunities, interests and abilities. We search for the path lighted by the Gospel which calls us to live generously, yes even sacrificially.

## 2. The Risk of Self-Giving

Reproductive decisions made by a committed Christian ought not to intend to leave behind carbon copies of myself so that at my death the world will not be deprived entirely of my wonderful presence. On the contrary, decisions should embody my desire to give of myself always, only, and entirely with the plan of making the best use of the opportunities given to me, to build the Body of Christ, to bring into ever greater visibility the Kingdom of God. I should be looking forward to my offspring being one of the ways in which I leave the world a better place for my having been here, by raising them to share my passion for Christ and for *sacrificial, generous, creative, and just living.*

I have often told my sons that the successful person is the one who recognizes and makes good use of his or her combination of ability, opportunity, and industry. Each human enters the world with some finite talent, a sort of "gift" (Matthew 25:14-30) or deposit by God into the fragile earthen vessel (2 Corinthians 4:7) that each of us is. The deposit is highly variable, since some are born geniuses while others have severely malformed central nervous systems and may never learn to speak. Each is given more or less opportunity to employ that gift or deposit; this, too, is highly variable since some are given the best private tutors while others must forage for food and are never taught an alphabet. Each, finally, makes some product from these talents and opportunities only in proportion to a certain willingness to labor. Since the result will not happen by accident or through the influences of entropy, it requires that energy be invested by the individual.

Marija Skoldowska Curie (1867-1934) could not have become one of the great scientists of our century if she had been born mentally retarded; she needed *ability*. Martin Luther would not have successfully launched a religious reformation if he had not been protected by friends who had the power to keep him safe while authorities sought his neck; capture and execution would have precluded *opportunity*. Charles Darwin could not have revolutionized biology without leaving the comfort of his British home to study personally the effects of Brazilian mosquito bites and to make observations of variation among species of finches on the remote Galapagos Islands; this required *industry*.

## 3. Dimensions of Genetic Responsibility

Confronted in our giftedness (ability and opportunity) with the responsibility to pour ourselves energetically into the project of making sound and generous reproductive decisions, we must assess various dimensions of responsibility. Space limits this discussion to a mere outline, but more in-depth discussion has been published previously.[9] The following are major dimensions of responsibility as I perceive the process:

### a. Between Spouses

The quality of relationship, and the sharing of goals, between spouses is a product of considerable time and effort, and prayer. Without these the relationship will not support the enterprise of building a family. A handicapped child challenges the spousal relationship. I think it possible to argue that there are genetic grounds for dissolution of a marriage that was not based on a certain minimum candor in regard to genetic background and knowledge, and the impact these may have on the quality of children produced.[10] The moral responsibility to share important genetic knowledge with a spouse or potential spouse is not a trivial or passing one; it is a radical responsibility which reaches to the core of the relationship.

## b. Between Parent and Offspring

Children make a demand on their parents for both nature and nurture, inborn giftedness and environmental opportunities, so that they may grow to be generous co-creators with God. Procreative decisions should take into account the needs of existing children, the reasonably projected future child-rearing resources, and the risks of impairment in contemplated future offspring. Seeking the best for a child includes consideration of genetic endowment and/or inborn limitations; these are as important as imparting high moral values. It is essential that this be fully appreciated. The goal is not antagonism between nature and nurture, but a desirable synergism.

## c. Between Nuclear and Extended Family

Some genetic disorders, having appeared in the offspring of one family member, pose a risk to the offspring of other family members. In the complexities of life we sometimes encounter sundered families where resentments interrupt communication and even may be deepened if long silence is broken by adverse genetic news. Sharing a warning with those at risk is a responsibility. A Christian should sense, and respond generously to, a duty to warn relatives at risk.

## d. Between Family and Society

An essential part of the opportunity each of us has for employment of our abilities is the social contract by which each should benefit from living at peace in a stable and organized society where it is possible to have leisure and quiet to exercise the spirit creatively. This opportunity creates a debt to society, a duty to consider the impact of personal decisions upon that complex fabric of social structure in which we thrive. On the other hand, one may be daunted by concern about ongoing employability, insurability for health and life policies, and the threat of discrimination against persons labelled as inferior due to findings in genetic testing. The revelation of genetic test results to others is thus a matter for caution. Participation in research, if it does not entail significant risk of harm, is a duty of the person who enjoys the benefits of modern medicine based on findings from research in which others have volunteered as participants. Our Christian sense of duty to live generously, creatively, even sacrificially would only serve to increase that sense of responsibility.

## e. Between Agent and Posterity

Contemplating the long-term consequences of my actions today is a relatively futile task, both because my own vision is so truncated (not only by lack of imagination or courage, but simply by the brevity of my own life), and because the intervening decisions and actions of others along the time line will alter or even obliterate my intended results. All my direct descendants, a century from now, might be destroyed in a single day of war or in an earthquake; whether a saint or a psychopath descends from me generations hence is beyond my ken. In the creative and generous exercise of my responsibility, I should remain humble in assessing the long-term impact. I should know better than to think that I can plan the future in detail, and should make the best decisions I can with the light of grace given to me today.

## 4. Some Considerations in Genetic Decision Making

The above dimensions of genetic responsibility identify certain considerations which I believe might occur during genetic decision making by a well-integrated and faithful moral agent. She or he can be expected to consider: (a) personal strengths and weaknesses of the individual and the couple (ability to meet foreseeable challenges); (b) the financial resources of the family; (c) the impact on existing children; (d) the benefits and burdens predictable in the future child/ren; (e) the impact on society; (f) the impact on the future gene pool; (g) the meaning of reproduction in the broad context of the evolutionary project of building up the Body of Christ (toward its ultimate unification). Such considerations may be given varying weights according to the perspectives of those making decisions.

# C. Reflections on Genetic Reproductive Technologies

"If God had intended for us to fly, She would have given us wings." This, or something like it, used to be uttered by people who considered the work of the Wright brothers (Orville 1871-1948; Wilbur, 1867-1912) to be a bane visited upon humanity (or who simply needed an excuse to hide their fear of flying). Today a similar attitude is sometimes encountered in reference to genetic diagnostic tests to determine abnormalities or predispositions. Since for most findings there are at present only limited options for intervention, some prefer not to look in order not to know. This prevents facing difficult choices.

We now have available predisposition testing to find a mutation which poses 40-80 percent risk for breast cancer and also high risk for ovarian cancer in the woman who has inherited it. We can offer presymptomatic testing to find a mutation which poses essentially 100 percent risk of developing a severe progressive neurodegenerative condition during the 4th or 5th decades of life. We offer diagnostic testing to discover whether a second trimester fetus is affected by genetic disease of more or less severity. Some people have an urgent inner need to know their status in such regards while others have the opposite sensation (a preference to remain uncertain of these things).

Where prenatal testing is concerned, the interface of technology with traditionally highly personal decisions may create especially difficult choices. The apparent *right* answer is often elusive. Should a woman whose baby is found to lack a brain continue the pregnancy and use the organs for donation to children awaiting transplant? Or is this an utilitarian approach that violates the integrity of her baby as an individual with integral value? Is it an intolerable burden for the mother to continue such a pregnancy to its natural outcome (loss of the baby at term)? Or does she have a duty to preserve her own equanimity and mental balance by requesting termination in order to put an end to fetal movements that are no longer a joy but a reminder of the inevitably impending loss?

Today it is commonplace for people who have entered pregnancy to take vitamin supplements and to seek medical (obstetric) consultation. Most of their friends and neighbors consider it a moral obligation that they take special care of the health of the prospective mother and observe precautions to protect and foster the growth of the unborn child. Thus, they are expected to avoid situations and behaviors that might compromise the outcome of the pregnancy: cigarette smoking, ingestion of large amounts of alcoholic beverages, overexertion, etc. Further, we are troubled to learn that someone we know in a pregnancy is not seeing her doctor regularly.

In our high technology society, people are coming to expect that an ultrasonographic fetal examination is performed; the assumption is, of course, that this will confirm the presumed normalcy of the pregnancy. But it should be obvious that many abnormal processes may be brought to light by such an examination. Since we know that observing ultrasound images advances the parental bonding, the discovery of an abnormality is now even more disturbing. Further, the grief over loss or impending loss, or even over confrontation by radical decisions, is thereby deepened. Since grief over pregnancy loss is typically not acknowledged by society in general,[11] those who find themselves in such a tragedy are frequently left without an opportunity to grieve effectively, and the technology which had been embraced because it was noninvasive and "safe" has served more to enmesh them than to help them. Thus there is grave potential danger in the use of such technology. Obstetricians should be keenly aware of these dynamics, and warn their patients of the dangers of ultrasound. This point receives less attention than it should, and—to make the situation worse—the church gives less effort than is warranted in the comforting of people who have experienced reproductive losses (either spontaneous or after agonizing decisions).

The issue becomes more complex when we are offered invasive methods of gaining information about possible abnormality in the pregnancy, such as amniocentesis or chorionic villus sampling. Much is made, in some circles, about the risk of complications of such procedures, yet in skilled and experienced hands they are very unlikely to cause any harm to the mother or the baby. For example, I have performed 2921 amniocenteses with loss of only three normal pregnancies as complication of the procedures; this 1:974 risk is far below the typical 1:180 risk of chromosome abnormalities which it is designed to detect.

Since any prenatal investigative tool has the purpose of allowing awareness of abnormality in the pregnancy rather than simply waiting for the natural outcome of the finite process, it is appropriate to reflect on what one does with the knowledge obtained. We should combat the naive assumption that these testing methods are useful only for identifying pregnancies to be targeted for termination. Such an assumption is a grave error because it overlooks the opportunity some families appreciate: to prepare themselves psychologically, financially, spiritually, and socially for the birth of a child with a handicap. In some few instances, it also allows for specific prenatal therapeutic efforts to be undertaken. In severe conditions, with survival impossible, it may provide the basis for "do not resuscitate" plans when delivery occurs.

On the other hand, since the challenge for the individual or couple is to make informed decisions about pregnancy, the prudent and faithful employment of technology is no small or simple matter. As I have tried to point out, always and in all possible settings, the response of the Christian must be guided and molded by a sincere and strenuous search for the path enlightened by sacrificial, creative, generous options for self-gift: the Christ-like action of faith. In any specific setting, the most creative option will not necessarily be obvious or easily discerned. In fact, the temptation of one person to tell another which course of action is best might be dangerous because the confrontation by God within the problem is an intensely personal salvific event.

It is also appropriate to sound warnings here, as many of my colleaegues in this book do. Lacking a firm religious commitment in decision making, people are at risk of falling blindly into the "free market eugenics" which worries some (see Peters, pp. 116 and 127). It is all too easy for us to be entrapped by given worldviews or careless use of words (see Hefner, p. 74 and Tiefel, p. 133) that mask the profound effects of our decisions. We then blunder into paths we did not intend but could have perceived by more disciplined and prayerful consideration. These decisions and actions have profound political and social meaning, the extent of which may not be appreciated without still further self-critical reflection (see Bettenhausen, p. 97). They pose pastoral challenges of fierce intensity (see Holst, p. 168) that must not be overlooked.

## D. Application of This Perspective to a Case

As a practicing clinical geneticist, I strive to help people faced with reproductive and other applicable options to achieve a high level of understanding of the issues confronting them. I attempt to do so without prescriptive or directive attitudes that might interfere with their reaching their own private and personal decisions. As such, I am somewhat uncomfortable with the following exercise that might seem to seek the "right answer" to a case study question. Of course, as a Christian I have attitudes and perspectives on the world which mandate certain modes of behavior. This potential conflict demands a synthesis which will support people in reaching decisions when confronted by the challenges of genetic disorders. To illustrate my methodology, I undertake a few comments on case number 1 in Kirstin Schwandt's chapter (p. 41).

"Sarah" was not well served by having her questions about the implications of the triple screen brushed off by her doctor at the outset. She should have been given or demanded more education prior to a decision on whether or not to have the screening performed, since the results often create anxiety about possible abnormalities in pregnancy. Apparently the prenatal team did respond promptly, so that Sarah and her husband were better prepared for the even more disturbing news they were about to learn from the amniocentesis.

This young family is confronted early and starkly to clarify their perspective on the gifts of life. Because persons with Down's syndrome usually are functioning members of families, giving and receiving love and laughter, but also handicapped persons whose future depends always on the help of others for survival, the decision on whether to continue the pregnancy is especially poignant. Families who state that their 20-year-old son with Down's syndrome is the greatest blessing ever to enter their lives may be sublimating their pain; or they may be entirely accurate. Often enough the influence of a handicapped sibling has elicited sensitivity and generosity in the other children of the family. But many families have been torn asunder by the stresses of raising a handicapped child.

I think that the demands of the Gospel are to choose and foster life, to live generously, to opt always for pouring oneself out for the other; in short, to listen to the promptings of God within a well formed conscience. This is very fine as a theoretical statement, and if a fellow Christian confided in me an inclination to act self-sacrificially in this setting I would encourage and support that plan; yet it may require too much heroism for me to urge it on one who finds it daunting. The presence of a handicapped person, loving but also very demanding toward those around him or her, may be quite creative in the Christian community, but any effort to measure this ultimately positive influence in advance is utterly futile.

So, we must advise Sarah and Allen of the dimensions of their responsibility (see section B.3 above) in reproductive decisions, which include (1) their relationship with one another, (2) the impact of decisions on existing or possible future children, (3) their roles as members of extended families, (4) their position in society at large, and (5) their influence on the future of humanity as long-range ancestors of future generations.

Sarah and Allen also should take into consideration (1) their finances, (2) their personal strengths and weaknesses, and (3) the impact of decisions on others who are not part of the decision process (see section B.4 above). Specifically, they must consider the difficulties of raising a child who is mentally retarded and whose best hope for the long-term future is to live in a group home under the supervision of another adult, and to be employed in a sheltered workshop doing menial tasks. How well will Sarah and Allen adapt to the stress of such a prospect? How will the child adapt? If they have any other children, how will this impact their lives? How will a handicapped child change their position in the extended family, in their town and larger social context? Who will bear the financial burdens of the extra assistance needed for a lifetime? Since people with Down's syndrome rarely reproduce, the long-term eugenic effect of having such a child is not meaningful.

If we move beyond general considerations, then the questions become more focused for a Christian couple making such decisions. All of this should occur in the context of their awareness of a call to creative and generous living that comes to them from the gospel; they should consider themselves invited to be created co-creators with God, to build the future of the world through their decisions and acts in response to the abilities, opportunities, and challenges they find before them.

If the fetus with an extra chromosome 21 is already a human long before being able to breathe independently, then how would termination of pregnancy manifest their sense of being called by the Gospel to generosity and creativity? Would it be an irretrievably evil option? If so, where are the roles of faith, of redemption, of forgiveness? How is Christ walking with them in this crisis of faith? As they pray for light, and call upon their faith community to pray with them, where will they discern the promptings of the Holy Spirit?

## E. The Problem of Evil in This Synthesis

The role of human creativity in evolutionary progress takes its place through the moral agency of the person who is capable of both sin and heroism. In the process of writing this chapter, I have been subject to friendly criticism for being an optimist, for believing that evolutionary progress is moving toward the ultimate goal of unification in and under Christ, the focal point of the universe. I understand and accept that a Christian should not be an empty-headed "Polyanna," but that we are called to live by faith in hope. Though unrepentant for my optimism, I am aware that the progress of evolution is not going forward in a single straight line, but that the flowing river has many eddies and lagoons; much water is lost along the way. It is to the most difficult of these questions that I would like to turn at the conclusion of this essay.

Evil is very much at work in the universal picture, on every plane of evolution; the role of evil in the evolutionary process is expressed as various forms of loss. The operation of evil on the physical plane is entropy, the basic tendency of molecules to move gradually toward even distribution in the space available to them (rather than to cluster in one region leaving the remaining space a vacuum). "Entropic doom" is the pessimistic notion that ultimately all matter will be evenly distributed throughout the universe, with no clusters of matter (stars, planets, nebulae). All energy then would be dissipated and all matter exist at the same (very low!) temperature, something close to 459 degrees below zero Fahrenheit. The notion of entropic doom runs counter to what I take to be the driving direction of evolution: the formation of planets and other bodies in which energy and matter are gathered. I do not believe that entropic doom will prevail, but entropy certainly is a power in the world as we find it.

Evil operates in the chemical world by disintegrating complex molecules, rendering them to simpler molecules and ultimately to individual elemental atoms. This dissipates the energy captured in chemical bonds and contributes to an entropy. This runs counter to what I take to be the forward direction of evolution, namely the formation of complex molecules as a substrate for the higher planes of the process. So, I do not believe it will prevail, though obviously there are many places in which it takes place every moment of history.

Any loss of life is, in this view, perceived as an evil event: the leopard starves to death, the jade plant withers for lack of water, the ant colony is destroyed in a rain storm, or the mastodon is hunted by humans into extinction. All these are manifestations of evil at work in the biosphere. They are losses to the process of diversification and complexification, and any loss in the process is undesirable. Here, however, we encounter an increasing complexity in thinking about the overall process, since the gazelle must die to feed the lion and the mastodon was hunted in order to feed and clothe the emerging human species. So the death of an individual, while a local evil in itself, might also contribute to the overall project toward the ultimate goal.

Evil enters the human plane whenever an individual or group elects to behave selfishly rather than to contribute to the group or individual advancement of others toward a more differentiated society with more educated persons who are free to exercise their talents. Destructive competition in the workplace, gossip, violence, and genocide are examples of evil at work against the progress of homogenesis. These are events associated with disordered human choices, which could have been made otherwise (generously and creatively). Even prior to that, we contend with the forces of evil tending toward entropic doom: aging, illness, infections, and accidents all take their tolls, and ultimately death comes despite all our best efforts to stave it off. These, too, are losses. I do not believe they are God's will for us, but rather distractions and detours which must be endured because we cannot exist as humans other than on the foundations of being biological and chemical and physical entities first, and subject to the laws of all those lower planes.

Unification of all things in Christ is the final goal of creation to which all things strive and "groan" (Romans 8:22-23); this is no small challenge or easy goal to achieve, but requires the utmost in effort and sacrifice. So any time that personal or corporate laziness prevails, progress toward the goal is lost or at least not advanced...and this is the manifestation of evil in the process of Christogenesis. It may appear on the personal plane as discouragement so deep that a person abandons all hope that the world is made to be good, and that God's creative power is moving it toward the goal of Christ. In such a case the person is tempted to blaspheme the Holy Spirit and to proclaim ultimate pessimism. On the larger scale, the evil forces within the layer of Christogenesis are at work systematically to deny the primacy of Christ by depriving whole populations of opportunities to advance (e.g., totalitarian regimes in which millions lack the Good News because those who proclaim it are killed, jailed, intimidated, or deported). Here we encounter the mystery whereby the blood of martyrs is the fertilizer by which the faith is nourished. We cannot understand this on any plane of thought other than faith posited in the risen Christ; I choose to believe that God's power directed toward the goal is greater than, and will finally overcome, even the most sinister of such evils.

## Summary

To summarize my perspective on the moral challenge to make reproductive or genetic decisions, I believe that God is at work in the evolution of the universe, driving and energizing it toward its final goal of unification in Christ. The energy transmitted by the Holy Spirit to this project is the gravitational attraction of one cosmic dust particle for another; it is the heat captured in chemical bonds; it is the spark of life which has the power of self-replication; it is the inspiration to plan and think and create; it is the willingness to sacrifice oneself for the good of others; it is the Life of the Body of Christ. Anything anywhere any time that operates to interrupt, reverse, or retard this progress is an entry of evil (reversal, loss) which may temporarily derail, detract, or discourage the process by removing some part of creation from its opportunity for forward progress. Yet while losses occur all around us constantly, still Christ is drawing all to Himself in the Parousia; when where and how, we have not the slightest idea.

I believe that each person confronted with a decision about genetic matters ought to approach it prayerfully to discern how the inspiration of the Holy Spirit is leading him or her toward the most creative and generous response to the challenge. How is She leading and supporting and guiding toward the most constructive choice intended to make Christ visible in the world, so that the final goal is advanced in the effort?

One of the most poignant manifestations of the faith I am espousing here is that we Christians believe that we shall see Him in the flesh, that we will be resurrected, joining Him forever. Yet we have no clear notion of how this will look. Surely it cannot be that we will look and sound and act as we are accustomed to doing during our brief sojourns on this planet, or that the goal of paradise is one of rest and repose. The reason for this is that we perceive divine purpose and power at work in the process by retrospective analysis. We still, however, cannot predict even the next step in evolution because the future of the process is potentiated by the present reality and there are many possible futures depending on decisions and random events that have not yet taken place.

As each molecule in my body is constantly being chemically degraded and replaced, the startlingly complex collection of materials currently occupying my chair was not here at all seven years ago. The molecules that made me then are now dissipated over the face of the earth as house dust and excretions (some left behind during visits to China, Mongolia, India, Thailand, Hungary, Greece, Rumania, Croatia, Italy, Denmark, Iceland, Canada, and various cities of the United States).

How (and out of which molecules) God will reconstitute a body for me at the end time is beyond my reckoning; how that body will be only glorious (lacking kidney stones, presbyopia and the other limitations imposed on this one) is also outside our contemplation. We cannot guess how God will provide wholeness to one whose temporary existence here was hampered by mental retardation or physical handicap, or the evil agency of persons who deprived the individual of food or education or other opportunities. We believe it will take place; we believe the promise of Christ.

It also should be clear from the foregoing pages that I believe our final goal will be challenging not only along the way, but that we will be caught up in a mysterious dynamism. It is a dynamism of complexity and beauty which are beyond any possible imagining while we are enmeshed in the daily routines and difficulties of living in cooperation with the gospel, as created co-creators. As God waits patiently for us to be ready for ever-more-thorough and dynamic incorporation into the Body of Christ, so we too must wait for God to reveal the fullness that lies before us (its seeds already borne but hidden within us).

# A PASTORAL PERSPECTIVE: COMPANIONSHIP BEYOND INNOCENCE

## Lawrence E. Holst

"For in much wisdom there is much grief; and he that increases knowledge, increases sorrow" (Ecclesiastes 1:18). In that single verse, the author captures the essence of our current genetics dilemma: increased knowledge expands moral choices and thereby imposes moral burdens upon the decision maker. And, indeed, our knowledge base in the field of genetic testing and screening is rapidly expanding. As a result, we are in the process of discovering what mutations underlie the multitude of genetic diseases (at this writing, believed to be in excess of 4,000!) and we are beginning to understand that there is a genetic component in many mental disorders and antisocial behaviors.

Such rapid developments are parting "the veil of innocence" by empowering us to understand more fully, and even to alter, what nature has given us. As a consequence, we as individuals and a society are faced with new possibilities, complex dilemmas, hard choices. This chapter is an attempt to provide a pastoral perspective for those seeking to provide care to loved ones and friends who will undergo genetic testing and will thereby experience "the parting of this veil." By focusing upon two hypothetical couples who elect to undergo such testing, and by exploring the dynamics and dilemmas they encounter, it is hoped that pastors—and others—will catch a glimpse of the rich opportunities for care in such real life situations. As these clinical vignettes unfold, it will become apparent how emotionally charged, morally ambiguous, and theologically provocative they can become.

The pastoral perspective proposed is one of a companion, or fellow sojourner, who walks caringly and sensitively with another through the often inexplicable, random genetic tragedies of life. Through such engagement, the care giver (pastor or otherwise) listens attentively to the voices of suffering, helps the patients to clarify carefully their needs, values, commitments, and moral options, and facilitates a process that hopefully will yield judgments and decisions consistent with the patients' professed beliefs. It is a perspective that attempts to hold in juxtaposition human responsibility and divine mercy. In any pastoral care, these must remain inseparable.

The first case is an example of difficulties that arise from the onset of genetic disease in adulthood.

Jane, age 27, is married and childless. She has just lost her mother to a disease known as Huntington's (see Powell, p. 25). It was hard for her to see her mother die such a prolonged and agonizing death. First there were the strange mood changes; then she could no longer talk or control her body movements. In the end, she was totally bedridden and could barely get enough food without choking.

But that was only part of Jane's agony. Following her mother's funeral, she had time to reckon with some of the potential implications for her own life. She learned from her doctor that Huntington's disease is inherited. In fact, as a so-called "dominant genetic illness," it requires only one parent carrying the mutated gene to pass it on to an offspring. This means that statistically Jane has a 50 percent chance of carrying the gene. Finally she learned that the disease is inevitably fatal, since there is no known cure for it. What can she do? Jane is informed that there is a test which can tell her—with a high degree of accuracy—if she, too, carries the mutation that has been identified as the source of Huntington's disease.

One would assume that Jane would jump at the chance to be tested. After all, "to be forewarned is to be forearmed." But she has mixed feelings. On the one hand, she would like to know so that she and her husband can plan appropriately for the future, including whether they should start a family. On the other hand, she wonders seriously if she might be better off not knowing, thereby maintaining "the veil of innocence" and letting be what is to be.[1]

As active members of St. Mark's Lutheran Church and knowing their pastor personally, Jane and her husband John decide to make an appointment and to seek the benefit of his counsel.

Genetic testing can be, and is often, done prenatally to determine the presence of a genetic disorder in a fetus, as we see in the second case.

Jennifer is 22, married, in good health and 18 weeks pregnant. A few days ago she learned that a much younger half brother (age 2) has been diagnosed with a disease she and her family had never heard of, the *Hurler-Scheie syndrome* (see Powell, p. 24). Understandably, her father and stepmother are devastated. They shared with Jennifer some of the things their child's pediatrician has told them about this disease: it is progressive and inevitably fatal, usually by age 10. There are as yet no known cures for it. It is characterized by multiple organ and tissue deterioration, limited mobility, gross facial features, hearing loss and mental retardation. And what was most startling for Jennifer, it is a gene which is passed on from generation to generation. Jennifer immediately contacts her obstetrician who tells her Hurler syndrome is an autosomal recessive disorder, which means that

*CONFRONTING PROFESSIONAL CHALLENGES*

both parents must carry the trait for an offspring to be affected. Therefore, since her biological father remarried, Jennifer has a 50 percent chance of being a carrier, even though she herself was spared the affliction.

Dramatically, a relatively blissful, much-anticipated pregnancy has been filled with fear and anguish. What should she do?

Her physician tells her that the usual process would be to test both her and her husband to see if both are carriers. But, since she is already well into her pregnancy, an immediate test could be done on the fetus which could determine the presence of Hurler syndrome. If the fetus tests positive, it would thereby confirm that both parents are carriers.

After painstaking discussions, in which they consider the pros and cons of knowing versus not knowing their fetus' genetic status, Jennifer and Tom agree to a fetal test. Reluctant to part "the veil of innocence" and risk even more devastating news, they agree that knowing would be much preferred to waiting out the pregnancy in suspense. Besides, they consoled themselves, there's not much chance (about 1 in 60) that Tom is a carrier and, even if he is, the risk of an affected child is 25 percent. After two anxious weeks awaiting lab reports, their worst fears are confirmed: defying the above odds, their child is diagnosed with Hurler syndrome. Since Tom, too, has now been confirmed a carrier it means that there is a 25 percent risk that any future offspring of this couple will be similarly afflicted.

This news suddenly thrusts them into yet another dilemma: Will they carry through with the pregnancy or elect to abort it?

Jennifer and Tom are crushed. In two and one-half weeks their world has been totally upended. They feel alienated from family and friends, even from the new life they are anticipating. Now it seems like a lose-lose situation: Either they end the pregnancy or have a child who will "be born dying." Not only must they concern themselves with this pregnancy, but they need to give serious thought to future ones. At this moment in their lives, church is about the farthest thing from their minds. As fringe members of Nazareth Lutheran Church, they barely know their pastor. However, news such as this travels fast in a small community. Their pastor hears of it and decides to take the initiative and contact Jennifer and Tom.

Though surprised to see her, the couple is pleased by their pastor's interest. Except for recent contacts with their doctors and a genetics counselor, they have kept much to themselves lately. This unexpected pastoral visit offers them a welcomed opportunity to process things more slowly and in the familiarity of their own home. After a lengthy, helpful meeting, Jennifer and Tom agree to meet again with their pastor in three days.

Neither of these cases has been overdramatized; in fact, they are becoming much too common. In both cases, genetic testing has provided these couples with enormously valuable information, but in so doing, it has also imposed upon them enormous burdens. Heart-wrenching decisions must now be made by each of them. What in the past would have "just happened," and been attributed to the whims of nature, cruel fate, bad luck, or God's will, can now be directly confronted *before the fact*!

# Pastoral Presence

## Contextual Factors

It is into such dynamic, anguishing situations that parish pastors (hospital chaplains and pastoral counselors) are finding themselves drawn . . . into that frenetic time period between the reception of potentially shattering information and the need to make vital, often irreversible, decisions. Indeed, into a time of crisis! Clergy are not new to crises. For countless generations, many in society have turned first to their pastors (priests/rabbis) in times of trouble. Clergy, in fact, have been regarded as society's premier crisis intervenors. This has been due, in part, to certain unique contextual factors inherent in their pastoral office—"customs of the discipline," as they have sometimes been defined. Some of these contextual features—so vital to effective crisis intervention—include, but are not limited to, the following:[2]

- *Location*: The parish pastor works in a specific and familiar location—the local parish. People affiliated with that building are likely to see it as a warm, secure place; one in which they have shared positive experiences: Sunday school, worship, baptisms, confirmations, weddings, and fellowship. Many confronted by the disorienting forces of a crisis are more likely to seek refuge in a site that is known.

- *Familiarity*: Because most of their functioning is so visible (preaching, teaching, administering, home and hospital visiting, community involvement), pastors are known to most of their parishioners. When a crisis occurs, rather than initiating still more new relationships, it is comforting for parishioners to know that a familiar person in their lives can be engaged.

- *Availability*: Because pastors are not engaged in a fee-for-service, Monday through Friday, 9 to 5 office practice, they have considerable time flexibility and mobility. They can respond in a timely fashion (if not immediately) and can often expend special time and energy, especially in the early phases of a crisis. Such immediate access is especially important to those who feel fragmented and immobilized by the sudden demands of a threatening situation.

- *Covenantal initiative*: Typically pastors do not sit in their offices and wait for people in need to come to them. By virtue of their calling, and a covenant established with their parishioners at the Rite of Installation, pastors have a broad license to enter into critical situations at their own initiative. In fact, clergy are expected to be present in such situations and are more likely to be criticized for their absence than for their "intrusions." As we saw in Jennifer's case, the pastor did not have to await an invitation or a formal referral. She heard of the couple's need and took the initiative via a home visit (an initiative, of course, that Jennifer and Tom could have spurned).

- *Detachment from the medical procedure*: Since pastors are not directly involved in any technical aspects of genetics testing or the communication of their results, they can bring a degree of neutrality and objectivity. With regard to any of the medical procedures, they have nothing to explain, justify or defend, which means they have the luxury of being able to focus their entire energy upon the involved parishioners, upon their perceptions of and responses to what is suddenly happening in their lives.

• *Continuity of care*: Of all the professionals providing care in such genetic crises, only the pastor's is ongoing and continuous. Their sustained visibility and availability provide innumerable opportunities—formal and informal—for meaningful interactions with those experiencing or having experienced such a crisis. No other caring profession works in a context that allows for such spontaneous, unscheduled, and random interactions.

• *Symbolic nature of their office*: No profession bears such a long history of mystical images and archetypes. Having seen their pastor fully robed in the pulpit proclaiming God's word or at the altar distributing Christ's body and blood, it is little wonder that parishioners often imbue them with divine authority. Oft-times these projected images suggest strength, safety, trust, and protection. The highly symbolic nature of their office and ministry invite such projections, whether or not deserved.

• *Represent the faith community*: Though pastors are not the only ones within a congregation who provide care and support to those in need (surely, within the Body of Christ, members provide them to one another), they are often seen as the visible embodiment of such care. Furthermore, in their designated role as the called spiritual leader of the congregation, they are often in the most strategic position to mobilize and direct the vast resources of that parish toward the care of those in need. So when those in crisis make contact with a pastor, they find themselves surrounded by a caring community which the pastor represents.

Lest we overidealize, each of the above-mentioned contextual forces has a potential downside. For instance, *prior contacts* between pastor and parishioner may have left a bad impression. Such encounters may have suggested to the parishioner that the pastor is moralistic, shallow, insensitive, untrustworthy to keep a confidence, or ineffectual . . . hardly a person to be trusted in a crisis.

The "right" of *covenantal initiative* may be seen by some as an unwelcome intrusion, a violation of their privacy. Even in situations where the pastor's self-initiated presence might be welcome (as it was to Jennifer and Tom), such initiative can draw the pastor into an assortment of vague and muddled relationships, where goals and limits are not defined and where the pastor's zeal to help gets far ahead of the parishioner's readiness to be helped. Part of the skill in such covenantal initiative is for the pastor to facilitate ever so subtly and gently a shift to the psychological initiative by the parishioner. When this happens, parishioners reach a point when they are able to assume important responsibilities in the crisis; for example, recognizing it as theirs and being motivated themselves to work toward some kind of meaningful resolution. Until and unless this shift from the pastor's covenantal initiative to the parishioner's personal responsibility occurs, little can be expected by way of effective pastoral care.

Likewise, the pastor's ready *availability* and *ease of access* can be deliberately or indeliberately abused by parishioners, thereby fostering unhealthy and unhelpful overdependence. When this occurs, responsibility for appropriate action is transferred to the pastor. Assuming such responsibility for the parishioner might seem momentarily helpful—even compassionate—but it is of little lasting value. In becoming the "solution" for another's problem, a pastor has ceased to be realistically helpful because that allows little opportunity for the person to grow and mature. In a zeal to help others, pastors can easily do too much of the wrong thing.

The pastor's *detachment* from the delivery of genetic testing and medical services is also a mixed blessing. While providing a much-needed outside view, pastors may be seen by parishioners as being too far removed from the complexities of their clinical situation and thereby irrelevant to their immediate needs.

Finally, the *symbolic nature* of the pastoral office may invite considerable distortion. Parishioners may unintentionally (often unconsciously) project negative images of God onto their pastor: fear, distrust, anger, or guilt. Or they may impute to that clergy figure magical powers in the form of unrealistic expectations ("make this awful test result go away," "get my husband to change his mind," tell us "the right thing to do"), which, when unmet, are seen as their pastor's unwillingness not his/her inability. While some pastors may be flattered by being credited with such powers, and try to fulfill them, relationships built upon such distortions will be of little therapeutic value.

What we have been addressing are some of the contextual factors in parish ministry which have often enhanced the pastor's role as crisis intervenors. Of course, context alone does not insure pastoral effectiveness; but it is a start. The remainder of this chapter will explore ways in which that context can be infused with knowledge about, and sensitivity to, genetic testing and those who undergo it. Hopefully, the merging of context with such clinical skill will result in more effective pastoral crisis intervention.

## The Pastoral Entree

Regardless of how the pastor engages the parishioner-patient (whether by one's own initiative or in response to a call or referral), it is vital that the pastor be carefully attentive to the parishioner's perception of his/her unique situation—a situation he/she probably never before faced. Clinical facts can be later corroborated with the parishioner's medical team; of more importance at the outset is how and what the parishioners are perceiving and feeling. How are they giving voice to their suffering? Though we all suffer at one time or another, we experience it very individually and specifically. Eric Cassell, a physician ethicist, defines suffering as the interior response to "anything that threatens the intactness and integrity of the person."[3] It occurs when anything in which a person has made a significant emotional investment is threatened. Examples include: a threat to body image by disfigurement or aging; functional capacities compromised by a chronic illness; optimism and security usurped by a feared disease; cherished dreams abandoned because of positive test results; the hope for healthy, normal children sacrificed to the diagnosis of genetic disease.

Suffering results from real or feared losses which are influenced by one's values, which in turn are related to one's personal faith and meanings. As such, suffering is very much a religious/moral issue having to do with our priorities and sources of self-worth, meaning, and fulfillment. To listen carefully and sensitively to "the voices of suffering" is a demanding task. To be invited into another's pathos is to tread on sacred ground; it is to engage another at the very core of their existence for it is in suffering that one's deepest fears and most profound hopes are inextricably bound.

This becomes clear as we consider our cases. A portion of Jane's suffering is obvious since her future health and life, as well as her reproductive choices, are being threatened. These in turn will provoke pain in other dimensions of life that will be uniquely experienced by her and Tom. Likewise, a portion of Jennifer's suffering is obvious since she must determine the future of her current pregnancy; but she, too, must look ahead at her reproductive options. Will she want to endure the anxieties and uncertainties of future pregnancies? If not, then what? These threats and uncertainties will have a profound effect upon both couples' self-images, goals, and parental ambitions.

In such struggles, the questions exceed the answers. But the pastor's task is not to explain the unexplainable; rather it is to share as deeply as is humanly possible in the afflictions of those who suffer and to help them find meaning in it for their lives. Hopefully, in the process, the sufferer will be reassured that such struggles in life do not diminish one's worth or dignity as a person created and redeemed of God.

## What Can The Pastor Do?

Once such entree has been made and the pastor has some sense of the suffering being voiced, what then? The easiest answer is that the pastor renders pastoral care. Which is what?

Care is something universally needed in every moment of human existence. No one takes care of oneself in every respect. Care is mutual; everyone at some point or another is both a giver and receiver of care. Care is both attitude (being positively disposed toward another) and action (concrete acts or behaviors intended to enhance another's well-being).

Care becomes pastoral when its power and focus are centered upon the one in need, but is also mindful of a force that transcends all humanity. Paul Tillich described pastoral care as "a helping encounter in the dimension of ultimate concern." Its function is "to communicate the power of the Divine, which conquers all forces of non being;" and its power "mediates the courage to accept finitude and the anxieties of creatureliness."[4] Ronald Cole-Turner and Brent Waters put it somewhat similarly: "The pastor's task is to engage in conversation that enables a deeper, clearer understanding and response, one that is open to the possibility of God's presence, healing and blessing."[5]

In his letter to the Philippians 1:9-10, Paul wrote: "It is my prayer that love may abound more and more, with knowledge and all discernment so that you may approve what is excellent." Though not intended as a blueprint for pastoral care, these few words contain applicable wisdom. "Knowledge" and "discernment" can be understood to mean: sorting through the profusion of technical clinical data (much of it new and complex for both the parishioner-patient and the pastor); exploring the meaning and specific relevance for this new-found situation; carefully clarifying the issues and options that are realistically available; making moral judgments that appear consistent with one's faith and identity as a follower of Jesus Christ; and implementing a decision that seems to best fulfill one's loyalties, relationships, and responsibilities in life—one that the parishioner can "approve as excellent."

Granted, in the ebb and flow of crisis intervention, the pastor cannot always structure dynamic interpersonal encounters so neatly. In fact, flexibility and responsiveness are much preferred (and, in the end, more effective) than imposing such a pat format upon a therapeutic interaction; but at least St. Paul opens up here a broad framework for pastoral care.

Never will a pastor be working alone with a parishioner who has been or will be a participant in genetics testing. There will be a clinical team of physicians, nurses, genetics counselors, social workers, and laboratory personnel. In fact, in most instances, the pastor will appear well after that team has begun its work, and will have to play "catch up." (Chapters 1 and 2 of this book are specifically intended to help fill that knowledge need.)

Communication with members of that team will be imperative if the pastor's involvements are to be relevant and integrated. It would be a disservice to the parishioner-patient if the pastor tried to avoid, compete with, or totally subjugate oneself to the genetics team. Words like complement, support, and mutuality better describe the preferred pastoral involvement. Such interaction is more likely to be relevant if the pastor has at least a rudimentary awareness of genetics testing, its vocabulary, methodologies and broad implications for patients. Admittedly, it is a complex and ever-changing field of knowledge and there is no expectation that a pastor will, or should, attain expertise in the field. Still a rudimentary awareness will enable the pastor to provide more astutely what perhaps no one else in the parishioner's situation is equipped or inclined to provide, *spiritual care*. Once the technical data have been deciphered and the clinical options carefully delineated by the genetics specialists, many nonmedical questions tend to arise for patients— questions that are more philosophical and theological in nature: "Why me?" "Am I being tested or punished by God?" "Are these random genetic events part of a Divine plan, or accidents beyond God's control?" "Is there anything in the Bible or my faith tradition that can tell me what to do?"

While such questions do not alter the test results or their grave possibilities, they are important to how parishioner-patients will respond to such tests. And while pastors are not the only ones who can address such questions, in the economy of role ascriptions they are seen as most likely to have expertise in such areas.

# Back To Jane And Jennifer

### Jane: To Test or Not to Test?

As was noted, Jane is faced with a decision to undergo a laboratory test that can tell her if she is carrying the Huntington's disease mutation. Since Huntington's is a dominant genetic disorder requiring only one parent to pass it on, her chances of a negative test result are one in two. If she is found to be carrying the gene, then she will know two more things: she will get Huntington's disease (probably in middle age) and any of her offspring will run the same 50 percent chance of inheriting it. Unlike many other decisions in genetics testing, this decision does not have to be made immediately. The gravity of potential consequences will not disappear, but she and John do have time to sort things out.

When the couple meets with their pastor to begin the sorting out process, they bring him up to date clinically. They have learned that a mutation in one gene means that the body produces an abnormal protein that leads to a breakdown in that part of the brain that controls movement. Further, Jane shares that if the mutation is identified in her, there is very little she can do. Not only is there no cure, but no test can determine when the disease will strike (only that it surely will in time) or how quickly it will take over her body. The only real use of the test at this time is to provide Jane and John important information.[6]

Their first question to the pastor: Is it better to know or not to know? The consequences of a positive result are so devastating, would they be better off just letting nature play it out? During the ensuing silence, the pastor recalls some familiar words of Thomas Gray:

> Why should we know our fate
> Since sorrow never comes too late;
> Such thought would destroy our paradise.
> Where ignorance is bliss, 'tis folly to be wise.[7]

Jane's mind, however, is moving in a different direction: "Isn't there something in the Bible about truth making us free?"[8] The pastor acknowledges that there is, in the Gospel of John, but he also concedes that it is among the most commonly misquoted texts in the Bible. This saying of Jesus, he continues, has two parts, the first being a condition for the second: "If you continue in My word, you are My disciples, and you will know the truth" (John 8:32). It is this truth which comes by faith that frees us from evil, sin, and death.

As the pastor further explores the verse, it becomes clearer to Jane and John that it is this ultimate truth in Christ that sets us free. The pastor cautions that the kind of verifiable information, or truth, that comes from a genetic test may be both liberating ("It will show you where you stand with regard to Huntington's disease") or enslaving ("It has the potential of dominating your lives"). But, the pastor cautions, it is not the kind of truth to which the Gospel of John points. That truth, he adds encouragingly, can undergird us regardless of what things like genetic tests reveal or whatever tragedies life presents to us.

Having attempted to distinguish between proximate and ultimate truth, the pastor ponders aloud: "What effect will such proximate knowledge derived from a genetic test have for your lives—freeing or enslaving? Will it be an opportunity to put life in a larger perspective and move on? Or a noose of bitterness and self-pity?" At this point, neither Jane nor John is sure. They agree these are questions worth raising since they give them an opportunity to play out both alternatives in their minds and, more importantly, to begin assessing their coping resources.

The pastor inquires as to how they have handled similar situations (albeit not as grave as this one) in the past. What did each do that was helpful or destructive? What would each need from the other, if the news is bad? The pastor cautions that no one knows fully how they will react to anything, but past reactions do give us some clues.

With the encouragement of the pastor, Jane and John begin to speculate together on the various possibilities that may lay ahead for them. If the tests are negative, will Jane feel "survivor's guilt," since her mother suffered so? If she could stop worrying about Huntington's disease, are there other issues in her life she has been avoiding? Finding out she does not have this fatal disease may be happy news, but it may not necessarily make her a happy person, the pastor cautions.

On the other hand, knowing she has the disease may not be as devastating as she feared. In fact, she may find it a relief finally to put it to rest. It may free them both to appreciate each day as it comes and to make fuller use of the time they have left together. While their days will be fewer in number, they might be fuller.

The pastor reminds them that some results of a positive test finding can be anticipated, even though no one can predict all of the problems. For instance, how should they handle such information? Who else should know? Do they tell other members of their family? Her employer? Her insurance company? Jane and John realize that some of these decisions may not be entirely within their control. Test findings go into medical records, which can be accessed by both Jane's employer and health insurance company. Such medical data could cause her to lose her job, which would be illegal (the Americans with Disabilities Act, a 1990 federal law, forbids discrimination against persons who are disabled), but it could still happen; or it could cause her to lose her health insurance as has happened to others in similar situations. Though Jane has been told that a cure for Huntington's will no doubt come some day, she realizes that it is not something she can realistically count on in her lifetime.

Lurking just beneath the surface for this couple is the question of God's involvement. Does such genetic randomness mean God lacks either power or compassion, that God either cannot or will not control such details of the universe?

The pastor acknowledges that the problem of suffering in God's created world is a complex one. At an *intellectual level*, he concedes, the Bible is not very helpful. That is, the "why" questions are never fully addressed: Why me? Why this? Why now? In fact, he offers, there is no single, dominant motif for suffering in the Bible, but there are several.[9] Each motif, or theme, represents a particular way people of God tried to make sense out of their suffering in their time. But no single motif, he suggests, is adequate to explain all suffering, including Jane's and John's.

The best we can do, he advises, is to affirm the fact that most suffering is a mystery. We do not fully know why it comes, when it comes, or to whom it comes. In the chaos and randomness of this world, bad things happen to all of us, though not equally or with the same intensity. But suffering happens, frequently because of human sin, but quite often in spite of human involvement. Acknowledging this may not be very satisfying, the pastor admits, because it leaves so many questions unanswered; but it may be as close to the truth of human suffering as we mortals can ever expect to get.

However, the pastor reassures the couple that while the Scriptures may be inconclusive at an intellectual level, they are immensely helpful at a spiritual level.[10] At this level, the Bible is far less concerned with *why* suffering occurs than with *how* we sufferers can endure it and even transcend it. At this level, we are reminded that God cares about and indeed suffers with us; and that God does not inflict suffering. Therefore we need not flee from God as an enemy but cling to God as a companion-in-suffering. "What's more," the pastor concludes, "at this level, the Bible reassures us that suffering—no matter how devastating, untimely, or cruel— never has the last word in life, nor can it ever separate us from God's steadfast love and mercy."

The pastor admits that while all this will not spare us suffering, nor explain it when it comes, it may help us to overcome the terrible loneliness, despair, guilt, and bitterness that are often the most burdensome accompaniments of human suffering. In the end, the pastor declares, the Bible's greatest help for Jane and John in these perilous times is to put their potential travails in perspective: While they are immediately cataclysmic, eternally they are of little consequence because "nothing in all creation can separate us from God's love in Jesus Christ" (Romans 8:39).

In this clinical vignette, the pastor walked with Jane and John to the threshold of a very important event in their lives, one fraught with potential agony. He did not tell them what to do, for he realized—as did they—that whether or not Jane consented to a genetic test, the clinical realities would not be altered. It boiled down to whether it would be best for them to know or not know. There was no moral value at stake; it was a matter of what each felt capable of handling at the time. More important than their eventual decision was what happened within them emotionally and spiritually in and through this crisis. What the pastor tried to do was to frame the clinical issues in the broader context of God's grace and their ultimate destiny as God's people.

Whether or not Jane and John agree to test, they and their pastor know that serious questions and decisions await them, not the least being how to live within the fragility of life. In reality, their lives are no more fragile now than before they learned of the very real possibility of Huntington's disease, it is only that their *awareness* of life's contingencies has intensified. In their late 20s, this couple is suddenly face-to-face with some very sobering realities.

They will not be the same people ever again, even if the Huntington's disease threat can be put to rest. In many ways, their relationship with their pastor will never be the same now that they have invited him into this most private and painful journey. Having engaged each other in this dynamic way, they will most surely reconnect whether or not Jane and John's *anticipatory* grief turns suddenly into real grief.

## Jennifer: To Abort or Not?

Unlike Jane, in Jennifer's case there is the urgency of decision. Following the prenatal test, she is now 20 weeks pregnant, with a fetus already diagnosed with Hurler syndrome, a disfiguring, dysfunctional, and fatal childhood disease. Time is especially short if an abortion is to be considered.

Because we have so few cures for so many prenatally diagnosed diseases, it is very difficult to separate genetics testing from abortion. This is not to suggest, however, that consent to prenatal testing predisposes couples like Jennifer and Tom to abort their pregnancy. Some may simply want the test in order to prepare themselves and their families for what is to come. Certainly that is valid enough reason. It is this chapter's stance that each couple has the legal option and moral responsibility to make its own decision on abortion, without any external coercion and in a way that is consistent with their own values, religious convictions, personal resources, and limits. Consequently, the pastoral approach to abortion offered in this chapter is consistent with that stance.

Abortion, of course, is not a new dilemma, but genetic testing has thrust it into a new context (see Peters, p. 121, and Tiefel, p. 144, for expanded discussions on this). For Jennifer and Tom, it is not the usual societal debate of pitting the "rights" of the mother to control her body vs. the "rights" of the fetus to be born. Indeed, for this couple it centers on the predicted suffering of their newborn who has been diagnosed with a painful, fatal disease, and their conflicting parental duties both to protect life and to prevent suffering, whenever possible.[11]

In this second meeting with their pastor, this parental conflict was center stage. The couple conceded that it would be impossible to validate both parental duties in the decision they must now make; one duty (or good) had to be sacrificed to the other. If they were to continue the pregnancy, they would knowingly subject their child to inevitable (and avoidable) suffering; if they terminate the pregnancy, they would end the life of their child almost before it started. The couple readily admitted it was a forced option of the worst sort—a tragic choice.

By electing to lift "the veil of innocence," they now face a dilemma very few before them have had to face: *the pressure of knowingly giving birth to a genetically defective offspring.*[12] Such pressure is changing the moral definition of parental responsibility because it offers couples like Jennifer and Tom a parental option of "quality control." (See Lebel, p. 158, for another view of these dimensions.)

No doubt, the pastor lamented, Jennifer and Tom are nostalgic for those "good ol' days" when things were not so complicated by this level of knowledge and when couples like themselves were "passive" participants in the reproductive process except for mate selection and the decision to have sexual intercourse. When things went wrong it was nobody's fault, just bad luck, cruel fate. Parents were pitied because there was nothing they could have done rather than scorned because they failed to exercise their option to abort such a fetus.

To put the moral conflict in a somewhat different context, the pastor cited ethicists who have approached the issue of prenatal genetic knowledge differently. First she referred to Barbara Katz Rothman who has argued that such increased knowledge has offered couples like Jennifer and Tom *"the illusion of choice"* (emphasis added).[13] But in reality, Rothman laments, more freedom has turned out to be less by making it increasingly difficult for prospective parents to commit themselves to an unborn child whose diagnosis is not yet assured, and to exercise their freedom not to abort when the diagnosis is bad. As Rothman notes, to fail to abort a knowingly genetically disordered child is seen by society as poor judgment. Jennifer and Tom could certainly identify with her observation.

Secondly, the pastor called attention to Ronald Cole-Turner and Brent Waters who take a different approach. Where prenatal diagnosis is more advanced than treatment, they assert that abortion may be seen as a recognition of our *human limits.*[14] That is, since we cannot heal diseases like Hurler syndrome, they suggest that we may morally decide to do the next best thing and eliminate the child's pending suffering by terminating the pregnancy. Rather than seeing it as an arrogant misuse of parental power, Cole-Turner and Waters propose that we see it instead as a *"confession of our weakness"* (emphasis added).[15] In other words, why should parents like Jennifer and Tom with such devastating information be deprived of a less than perfect choice (such as abortion) until a better one (such as a cure for Hurler syndrome) comes along?

The couple seemed momentarily overwhelmed by such divergent data. The pastor allowed time for reflection. In a few moments Jennifer broke the silence: "But what does our church say about abortion?"

While not surprised by the question, the pastor paused to gather her thoughts. "Yes, our church has spoken on this topic; but nothing it has said prescribes what the two of you should do in your unique situation. Nevertheless, the church has put some important thoughts in perspective which may help you to decide with more confidence."

The pastor then made reference to "The Social Statement on Abortion" adopted by the Evangelical Lutheran Church in America in 1991, which—among other things—declares:

> The act of intentionally terminating a developing life in the womb is an issue about which members of the Evangelical Lutheran Church in America have serious differences.
>
> All human beings, created in God's image, have intrinsic value and dignity and are to be treated with respect.
>
> As such, there is, therefore, a strong Christian presumption to preserve and protect life.
>
> Yet, there may be compelling circumstances wherein abortion may be an option of last resort, yet seen always as a tragic option. What is determined to be a morally responsible decision to abort in one situation may not be in another.[16]

In explaining the Statement the pastor noted that reasons given for such a decision may include: a threat to the woman's life, a pregnancy resulting from rape or incest, circumstances of extreme fetal abnormality which will result in severe suffering and very early death of the infant.

Jennifer, listening intently, interrupted: "Pastor, we partly fit that last category, but our doctors have told us that our child could live 8-12 years, and that most children with Hurler disease, despite their suffering, are usually placid, easily manageable, and very lovable. It all gets confusing; I'm not sure what's right."

Their pastor readily acknowledged that Jennifer and Tom faced pain no matter what they decided. If they continued the pregnancy, they would have a child, but certainly not the child they hoped for. If they aborted, they would give up a life they could have loved and raised, if even for a brief time and under adverse circumstances.

The pastor conceded that the United States Supreme Court's decision on abortion in 1973 (Roe vs. Wade) has increased the burdens upon people like Jennifer and Tom by shifting abortion from the legal to the moral realm.[17] Now the question is not: "Do I have a right to terminate my pregnancy?" but "Can I justify it morally?" By taking it out of the courts and thrusting it upon individuals, it is couples like Jennifer and Tom who must assess their total situation, balance the factors and do what is ethically appropriate in terms of their multiple relationships with God, each other, their unborn child, their larger family and the broader community.

"Yet, Pastor, the only reason we're even considering abortion is because of the suffering our child will go through. Is there such a thing as a life not worth living?"

The pastor sensed immediately their quandary: Is a life that knowingly will be fraught with suffering, and surely will end in childhood death, preferred to a life not lived at all. The issue was not new to the pastor. She had often confronted situations where a parishioner in prolonged pain, and with little prospect of a medical recovery, would opt to discontinue further life-sustaining treatments and be allowed to die. Such a choice, in such circumstances, clearly expressed a preference for death rather than a life of chronic suffering. But these were usually adults, who had experienced years of life and who were now making a conscious, deliberate choice *for themselves*, whereas Jennifer and Tom were facing a life-or-death decision on behalf of their unborn child who had never lived.

"That is a tough question you raise," the pastor replied. "Though you already know that Hurler syndrome will inflict sharp limits on the scope, depth, and length of your child's life, no one fully knows how such an existence will affect that child, yourselves, or any other children you may have," the pastor continued.

"Oh, I'm quite certain Tom and I would be up to the demands imposed by this child's disease, but we would feel so responsible for his pain, just as we would feel responsible for his death if we choose to abort," Jennifer lamented.

"I know neither of you wants to be responsible for your child's progressive, unremitting suffering nor for a death by abortion, but I think we need to look beyond those dual tragedies," the pastor advised. "I know some of us in this world see death as the ultimate enemy and seek to avert or delay it at all costs, even the cost of continued suffering; likewise, there are those who perceive suffering as humankind's worst fate and seek to escape it at all costs, even the cost of an earlier-than-necessary death, or failing to bring a fetus to birth. But our Christian faith does not confine itself to those tragic realities. It sees neither suffering nor death as life's greatest enemies—nor, for that matter, life as our most precious gift. Separation from God is our greatest enemy and eternal redemption in Jesus Christ is our greatest gift," the pastor proclaimed. The couple was attentive but offered no comment.

"While suffering and death are unwelcomed intruders and remain constant earthly companions, Christ's resurrection puts them both in their proper place—to be taken seriously but not to be given more than their due," the pastor continued. "You might recall those powerful words written by the Apostle Paul in his letter to the Romans: 'I am sure that neither death, nor life, nor things present, nor things to come, nor powers, nor height, nor depth, nor anything in all creation, will be able to separate us from the love of God in Christ Jesus'"(8:38-39).

Momentarily the couple was pensive. "I appreciate how you have helped us put such difficult matters in perspective," Tom responded, "but it sounds as though you're advising us to abort our child."

"I didn't intend to, but I guess we have spent more time discussing the parental duty to prevent suffering where possible than we have its parallel duty to protect life. Reverence for life—all life—has been an important principle in our Christian tradition throughout its history. This includes unborn life. The Bible reminds us that human life is a mysterious, awesome gift of God and as such it is endowed with worth and dignity. You might recall that beautiful passage in one of the Psalms: 'You formed my inward parts, you knit me together in my mother's womb' (139:13); and the prophet Jeremiah quotes God as claiming: 'Before I formed you in the womb, I knew you.' (1:5)."

"Reverence for life is a basic tenet of our faith," the pastor continued, "because life is not self-derived, it is a gift of God. That fetus in your body, Jennifer, has the God-given potential to develop into a human being."

"We truly believe that," Tom lamented, "but our child will be born into such a difficult life, with an incurable disease that will burden him for however long he lives."

"True enough," the pastor responded, "and that places a heavy moral burden upon you both. I know you love that child already and want to do what you think is best. Regardless of what you decide to do, your unborn child—even though, as you say, genetically deprived—is a gift of God's creation and, as such, is quite irreplaceable. Though the two of you may choose to, and are able to, have more children, none will ever replace this child."

"We needed to hear that, Pastor, to help us keep things in focus," Jennifer interrupted. "It reminds us of how unique and precious our child really is. Right now I wish that's all we knew and nothing else about our child."

"I know, that's what makes it so tough," the pastor said. "Your new-found knowledge has delivered cruel news and agonizing options. Now you must try, as best you can, to put all these factors together, sort them out, and do what you feel as people of God will be best for all concerned."

"That's what we want to do, Pastor, to do what we think God wants us to do," Jennifer exclaimed frustratingly; "but either choice seems selfish on our part—to carry through the pregnancy so that we can have a child for a few short years, even though that child will spend those years in suffering; or to abort, take the life of the child, so that our lives will be easier."

"It's true," the pastor agreed, "selfishness and love get so easily intertwined in our decisions that it's sometimes difficult to tell them apart. That's why it's so important that you help one another to explore carefully your motives. Distortion and self-deception can be ever so subtle. But given your situation and all its complicated dimensions, I doubt that you can make a decision that will seem to you to be totally just and right, that will validate all of your moral values." The pastor continued, "Given our human nature, it's doubtful such a point is ever reached. All too often in life, we have to balance our values and make critical decisions before we feel totally adequate and morally certain."

"That's reassuring for Tom and me who have to make the decision," Jennifer responded. "But I have another question, Pastor; what about our child . . . what happens to it in all this?"

The pastor replied: "That is the crux of the matter, isn't it? You are deciding for someone else who can't voice an opinion, who nevertheless suffers the consequences for that decision. Getting back to St. Paul, he wrote some other powerful words in that same epistle to the suffering people in the congregation at Rome: 'whether we live, or whether we die, we are the Lord's . . . for Christ is the Lord of the dead and the living'" (Romans 14: 8-9). "According to these words, your child remains in

God's loving care no matter what you decide," the pastor said reassuringly. "I know this doesn't banish your dilemma, nor lessen the pain of your decision, but hopefully it puts it in the proper context of God's loving and eternal care for us."

Tom pondered for a moment and exclaimed: "In some ways you've made it easier for us, in other ways you've made it more difficult, but you've been helpful."

On that note they parted with the agreement to meet again in four days, after Tom and Jennifer had another meeting with their genetics counselor.

## Jennifer and Tom: To Have or Not to Have Children

When the couple returned for their agreed-upon follow-up session, they told the pastor that before they could reach a decision whether to abort or not, they had another important issue to discuss: their future reproductive choices. Before they decided what to do about this pregnancy, they wanted to consider subsequent pregnancies.

Now that they had already conceived one fetus with Hurler's syndrome, what were the odds for another? Yesterday the genetics counselor told them: 25 percent. Their reaction was mixed: shocked it could happen again, and yet relieved that at least they had a fighting chance to produce a healthy child.

What now? That's the question Jennifer and Tom pursued with the counselor. From notes she had taken at the session, Jennifer counted up for the pastor four possible options open to them, with yet an assortment of variables:

1. They could continue with the usual procreative possibilities and try to have another child. In any subsequent pregnancy, they could agree to fetal testing and thereby subject themselves to the same moral dilemma they are now facing; or they could elect to suspend all testing and simply accept what nature gives them.

2. They could discontinue all efforts to produce their own biological child and adopt.

3. They could employ *artificial insemination*, whereby pre-screened donor semen would be injected into Jennifer's vagina. If conception occurs, she and the anonymous donor would provide the genetic material for the subsequent pregnancy; but she and Tom, of course, would rear the child.

4. They could employ *in vitro* fertilization (IVF), which means literally "fertilization in a glass." First done in 1978, they learned, it has become increasingly common, with an estimated 33,000 births resulting from it in the U.S. alone. Egg and sperm from Jennifer and Tom are fertilized outside Jennifer's uterus, a cell from the fertilized embryo is then tested for the presence of Hurler's syndrome and, if healthy, is transferred to Jennifer's uterus. Hopefully, this will result in a normal child. Through this process, Jennifer and Tom would share fully in the genetic structure of the child. They also noted that donor eggs or sperms could be substituted in this process, giving them further options.

The couple seemed overwhelmed by the plethora of reproductive options. "The good news," Tom exclaimed, "is that we'll be able to remove any doubts about Hurler's syndrome."

"Yes, that is good news," the pastor retorted: "Is there any bad news in all this?"

The couple turned to each other, betraying some uneasiness with the question.

Jennifer responded first: "It's all so new and scary . . . it all seems so cold and impersonal. It's not the way we'd really want it." Tom echoed her concerns and added one of his own: "I'd feel funny knowing that Jennifer is carrying a child from a stranger's sperm . . . almost as if the child wasn't mine."

"Then, too, it's expensive, with no guarantees it will work," Jennifer added. After a pause she continued: "I, too, would feel strange carrying someone else's child than Tom's, almost as if I'd been unfaithful. I'd feel equally awkward carrying another woman's egg in my body even though it had been fertilized by Tom's sperm."

"I guess we're back with the same question, Pastor. What does the church say about all this?" Tom queried.

"The issues don't get any easier, do they?" the pastor mused. She then went on to underscore the concerns they had already voiced. Any "mixing-and-matching" techniques which employ donor specimens invite potential, troublesome, though not insurmountable, issues. A third party enters into a heretofore exclusive psycho-physical-spiritual marital relationship. The pastor cautioned that this could lead to alienation and suspicion, as well as to feelings of inadequacy in the partner who is not directly involved in the conception, which, in turn, can threaten the marital solidarity.

Such threats and fears can carry over into the rearing of the child, she further cautioned. If, for instance, donor sperm is employed, Tom might feel a stranger to the new life developing in Jennifer's womb and feel cheated that he is not a part of it. This asymmetry may cause Tom to feel the child is more Jennifer's than his, and harbor resentment toward it.

"It's not something that is morally forbidden by the church, but it certainly ought to be entered into with very careful consideration," the pastor cautioned. The couple nodded in agreement. "What about using Tom's semen and my egg. Does that make a difference?" Jennifer asked. "Well, it has the advantage of biological and psychological symmetry—you're both biologically involved in the pregnancy from conception to delivery. Of course, that doesn't guarantee success or happiness, but it does blunt some of those potential problems we discussed," the pastor replied.

Sensing they were nearing the end of the session and that further discussion on reproductive options could be pursued in more depth later, the pastor opted to conclude this session by attempting to put the couple's reproductive dilemma into a broader, theological perspective. She did this by calling attention to two very important teachings of the Christian Church: The concepts of *Parenthood* and *Vocation*.

Of the former, she shared the Bible's two-dimensional view of parenthood: it is regarded as an extremely important role, she told them, otherwise the authors of Scripture would never have employed it as a metaphor for God's relationship with humanity; and yet, the biblical focus of parenthood is upon nurturing, not genetic bonds.[18]

Among other things, she continued, this means that neither the method of conception nor the fact of biological parentage is so ethically critical as the willingness to assume nurturing responsibility for the born child. Therefore, adopting, or conceiving a child by donor semen and eggs, need not in itself compromise Jennifer and Tom's true parenthood covenant, which is that of nurturing. "The church holds that parenting is fundamentally an emotional-social-spiritual function," the pastor concluded.

Then the pastor lifted up one of the major contributions of the 16th century Protestant Reformation, namely the doctrine of *Christian Vocation,* or *Calling.* Contrary to the common assumption, she advised, vocation is not limited to occupation. Certainly, it includes work (if one is employed), but it embraces much more; it includes all of the "stations" or "offices," all of the places and roles of responsibility which people have.[19]

In a very real sense, the pastor continued, a Christian calling or vocation may be seen as a concrete way in which we live out our baptismal covenant in the mundane sectors and duties on earth, as spouses, parents, neighbors, friends, citizens, and workers. It is through such roles that Christians are called to serve God and neighbor.[20]

She pointed out that Martin Luther wrote about our vocations as "masks" behind which God has chosen to care for the creation: "What else is all our work to God—whether in the fields, in the garden, in the city, in the house, in war, or in government—but just such a child's performance, by which He wants to give His gifts in the fields, at home, and everywhere else? These are masks of God, behind which He wants to remain concealed and do all things."[21]

Of particular relevance to Jennifer and Tom is the fact that parenthood is, indeed, a Christian vocation—and a very important one—but not one *required* of a follower of Jesus Christ. Parenthood is but one of many callings, duties, and responsibilities available to us.

In fact, the pastor concluded, what is absolutely vital about our Christian vocations is not what we do, or where we do them, but that we live them out faithfully, diligently, and lovingly in service to God and neighbor. A faith active in love will strive earnestly to discern what is "right, good, and fitting."[22]

Though these last moments in the session seemed a bit tutorial, the pastor wanted to conclude the session by calling attention to these age-old concepts in order to dispel two possible *false* illusions Jennifer and Tom might have about their current reproductive dilemma: namely, (a) that parenthood is a requirement for them as Christians; and (b) that true parenthood—if it occurs—requires biological procreation by them.

# The Human Quandary and the Gift of Faith

From these two clinical situations, one can readily see that a vital part of pastoral care is to provide "emotional and spiritual companionship" to those in crisis by helping them: (a) to give voice to their suffering; (b) to discern and clarify their options; and (c) to make decisions that seem most appropriate to, and consistent with, their identity as people of God. In both cases, three factors became readily apparent.

## 1. The ambiguity and anguish in each situation

For both couples, it was not so much a case of trying to distinguish good from evil, but of choosing between competing goods, competing claims and loyalties, all of which could not be equally validated in a single decision. For instance, Jennifer and Tom could not protect the life of their fetus while also protecting their child from suffering. Given the fetal diagnosis, one good had to give way to another. Which good would it be? They could not have it both ways; and once the choice was made, its alternative was thereby negated. Likewise, Jane and John faced a dilemma: they could not both know and not know their genetic future. They couldn't pursue the benefits of a good test outcome without running the risk of bad news. In both cases, the couples had to choose without knowing fully the future consequences of their choices, and in both cases their decisions were irreversible.

This is not to suggest that all options in such situations are equally valid or that choosing between moral goods is unimportant. It does suggest that pastors be cautious about prescribing specific courses of action. Unless, in the pastor's judgment, there is a clear moral violation at stake, or a selected option constitutes a potential threat to the parishioner's well-being, or the parishioner appears emotionally incapable of making a decision at this time, it is best that such decisions be made by the participants in the crisis so that those decisions and their potential consequences can be fully owned by them. What the pastor can do is to reinforce the broader context in which such decisions are made: the parishioner's confessed allegiance to Jesus Christ. While the pastor may concede that the will of God is never absolutely clear, the pastor must also insist that it is absolutely clear that the will of God be sought.[23] As St. Paul wrote centuries ago; "seek to discern what is the will of God, what is good and acceptable . . . " (Romans 12:2).

## 2. The anguish of decision making is due, in part, to the peculiarity of human nature

God has endowed us with the freedom and power to make decisions, but has not endowed us with the wisdom to see all of the possible contingencies in the future, nor the power to guarantee the outcomes we intend. And, as we know from personal experience, every decision has an infinite array of potential outcomes that we humans can never fully know or anticipate. That is part of the agony of decision making: to have responsibility without full knowledge and empowerment.

As a result, hindsight quickly exposes our lack of insight, our poor judgment, and our unfortunate decisions. What is more, we and others suffer because of them.

Tragically, what we intended in a decision sometimes gets completely reversed and what we tried to avoid may come to pass. Good intentions, worthy motives, and even God's goodness, do not suspend the relentless sequence of cause and effect. Forces in life easily get out of our control.

Because of such contingencies, neither couple could make their decision with absolute certainty. If Jane and John opt to forsake parenthood because of the threat of Huntington's disease, she may live symptom-free into her seventies and sorely regret their choice to remain childless. Jennifer and Tom may opt to abort, be unable ever to conceive again, and thereby forfeit the only opportunity of parenting nature ever bequeathed to them. Neither couple has sufficient capacity to make a decision today that they will never regret in the future. Such human limitations infused their dilemmas with considerable agony that neither pastor could fully dispel.

## 3. What makes this human quandary tolerable is God's infinite grace

Without question, the greatest news of our faith is that God has made us, redeemed us, and continues to care for us. Yet that is the crux of the matter: *We are not only anguished, bewildered, limited decision makers; we are also redeemed decision makers.*

Though our decisions are never free of sin, we as the makers of those decisions are free from the anxious drive to be perfect, to do deeds that will somehow make us right with God. For these couples to be "right" or "wrong" in their decision—to test or not, to abort or not, to have a child via IVF or not—will not make them "right" or "wrong" with God. That issue has already been settled, by God, on God's terms, at Calvary. There is no way they, or any of us, can add to or diminish this reality.

This does not lessen moral accountability. If anything, it heightens it. Martin Luther wrote: "We Christians are perfectly free, lord of all, subject to none; but we are also perfectly dutiful servants of all, subject to all."[24] Nor does it obviate the earthly consequences of our choices. Rather, it means that our eternal salvation is not contingent upon them. Hopefully, the Janes, Johns, Toms, and Jennifers of this world will bracket their penultimate decisions within this ultimate context: that is, to see them as terribly important, with potentially vast earthly consequences, but as not the last word. That *word*—a word of grace—has already been spoken by God, which is why the Gospel is always more gentle with us than we are with ourselves.

Luther once advised Christians "to sin boldly." But he added: "Rejoice in Christ even more boldly for He is victorious over sin, death, and the world."[25] It would appear Luther is advising us to discern carefully our moral situations, then decide and act with boldness. This boldness is rooted not in the infallibility of our moral discernments but in God's sustained forgiveness. Because of this, we Christians must always co-mingle human responsibility with God's mercy. They are and must remain inseparable. Jane, John, Jennifer, and Tom might not make the wisest decisions in their current dilemmas, nor refrain from second guessing the decisions they make. But they have this going for them: No matter how they, or their decisions, turn out in this world, God's grace abounds.

# NOTES

## Introduction
*Roger A. Willer*

1    Charles Siebert, "Living With Toxic Knowledge," *New York Times Magazine* (September 17, 1995).

2    "A Social Statement on Abortion," Evangelical Lutheran Church in America, approved at 2nd biennial Churchwide Assembly (September 1991). This statement exemplifies the point. It is a relatively recent document that sketches the church's general position on abortion and does touch on some matters relevant to genetically informed medicine. It does not, however, address the specific issues or concerns prompted by the advent of genetic knowledge.

3    "A Social Statement on Caring for Creation: Vision, Hope and Justice," as adopted by the ELCA Churchwide Assembly (August 1993), 3.

4    "A Social Statement on The Church in Society: A Lutheran Perspective," adopted by the ELCA Churchwide Assembly (August 28- September 4, 1991), 3.

5    Ibid, 5.

6    "Policies and Procedures of the Evangelical Lutheran Church in America for Addressing Social Concerns," as adopted by the ELCA Churchwide Assembly (August 1997), 3. This book exemplifies the Sphere Two resource described in that document. Such resources intend to promote "open-ended deliberation on specific contemporary social concerns without the pressure of legislative decision or community consensus."


## Personal Stories: Cases from Genetic Counseling
*Kirstin Finn Schwandt*

1    Lori B. Andrews, Jane E. Fullarton, Neil A. Holtzman, Arno G. Motulsky, ed., *Assessing Genetic Risks: Implications for Health and Social Policy* (Washington, D.C.: National Academy Press, 1994), 14.

2    Martin Luther, "Preface to the Psalms," In *The Reformation Writings of Martin Luther*, II, Bertram Lee Woolf, ed. (London: Lutterworth Press, 1956), 267-71.

3    George W. Forell, *Faith Active in Love* (Minneapolis: Augsburg Publishing House, 1954), 104.

4    Martin Luther, "Preface to the Epistle of St. Paul to the Romans," In *The Reformation Writings of Martin Luther,* II, Bertram Lee Woolf, ed. (London: Lutterworth Press, 1956), 284-300.

5    Martin Luther, "Sermons on the Catechism," In *Luther's Works*, 51, Sermons: I, John Doberstein, ed. (Philadelphia: Muhlenberg Press, 1959), 162-93.

6   Martin Luther, "Whether One May Flee From a Deadly Plague," In *Luther's Works*, 43, Gustav K. Wienke, ed. (Philadelphia: Fortress Press, 1968), 122.

7   Ibid, 124.

8   Ibid, 126.

# Genetics in the Marketplace: A Biotech Perspective
*John Varian*

1   S. Wiggins, P. Whyte, et al., "The Psychological Consequences of Predictive Testing for Huntington's Disease," *New England Journal of Medicine*, 327 (1992), 1401-1405.

2   Biotechnology Industry Organization (BIO), *BIO Policy Statement Regarding Genetic Privacy*, Approved by BIO Board of Directors on September 18, 1996.

3   K. B. Lee, Jr., and G. S. Burrill, *The Industry Annual Report on Biotech 95: Reform, Restructure, Renewal* (Palo Alto: Ernst & Young LLP, 1994), 52.

4   G. S. Burrill, and K. B. Lee, Jr., *The Industry Annual Report on Biotech 94: Long-Term Value, Short-Term Hurdles* (San Francisco: Ernst & Young LLP, 1993), 56-57.

5   Cancer Facts and Figures, 1997, American Cancer Society.

6   D. Ford, D. F. Easton, et al., "Risks of Cancer in BRCA1-Mutation Carriers," *Lancet,* 343 (1994), 692-695.

7   D. F. Easton, D. Ford, et al., "Breast and Ovarian Cancer Incidence in BRCA1-Mutation Carriers," *American Journal of Human Genetics*, 56 (1995), 265-271.

8   R. Wooster, S. L. Neuhausen, et al., "Localization of Breast Cancer Susceptibility Gene BRCA2 to Chromosome 13q12-13," *Science*, 265 (1994), 2088-2090.

9   C. Mettlin, C. R. Smart, "Breast Cancer Detection Guidelines for Women Aged 40-49 Years," *CA Cancer J Clin*, 44 (1994), 248-255.

10  P. J. Couch et al., "BRCA1 Mutations in Women Attending Clinics That Evaluate the Risk of Breast Cancer," *New England Journal of Medicine*, 335 (1997), 1409-1415.

11  National Cancer Institute: Surveillance, Epidemiology and End Results Program, 1995.

12  D. Schrag, K. M. Kuntz, et al., "The Value of Prophylactic Mastectomy and Oophorectomy for Women at High Risk for Breast Cancer," *Medical Decision Making Quarterly* (Oct-Dec 1996).

13  D. Ford, D. F. Easton, et al., "Risks of Cancer in BRCA1-Mutation Carriers," *Lancet,* 343 (1994), 692-695.

14  T. Katsuya, et al., Association of Angiotensinogen Gene T235 Variant with Increased Risk of Coronary Heart Disease," *Lancet,* 345 (1995), 1600-1603.

15  A. D. Hingorani, J. Haiyan, et al., "Renin-angiotensin System Gene Polymorphisms Influence Blood Pressure and the Response to Angiotensin Converting Enzyme Inhibition," *Journal of Hypertension*, 13 (1995), 1602-1609.

16  T. Katsuya, et al., "Association of Angiotensinogen Gene T235 Variant with Increased Risk of Coronary Heart Disease," *Lancet*, 345 (1995), 1600-1603.

17  Focus Groups conducted by BIO in 1995. The focus groups were held in Atlanta, Georgia, and Fredericksburg and Tyson's Corner, Virginia.

18  S. L. Sherman, J. C. DeFries, I. I. Gottesman, J. C. Loehlin, J. M. Meyer, M. Z. Pelias, J. Rice, I. Waldman, "Behavioral Genetics '97: ASHG Statement. Recent Developments in Human Behavioral Genetics: Past Accomplishments and Future Directions," *American Journal of Human Genetics*, 60, 6 (1997), 1265-1275.

# The Genetic "Fix": Challenge to Christian Faith and Community
*Philip Hefner*

1  Charles Siebert, "Living with Toxic Knowledge," *New York Times Magazine,* December 17, 1995.

2  Joseph Sittler, *The Sittler Speeches,* ed. Phil Schroeder (Valparaiso, Ind.: Center for the Study of Campus Ministry, 1978).

3  Ronald Grimes, *Ritual Criticism* (Tuscaloosa: University of Alabama Press, 1990), 164.

4  Wolfhart Pannenberg, "The Doctrine of the Spirit and the Task of a Theology of Nature," *Beginning with the End: God, Science and Wolfhart Pannenberg,* eds., Carol Rausch Albright and Joel Haugen (Chicago: Open Court, 1997), 65-79.

5  Paul Tillich, *The Shaking of the Foundations* (New York: Charles Scribner's Sons, 1948), 153-63.

6  Philip Hefner, *The Human Factor* (Minneapolis: Fortress Press, 1993), 23-54.

7  I am indebted to my colleague, Walter Michel, for this term.

8  Theodore Hiebert, *The Yahwist's Landscape: Nature and Religion in Early Israel* (New York: Oxford University Press, 1996).

9  Lysaught, Mary Therese, "Sharing Christ's Passion: A Critique of the Role of Suffering in the Discourse of Biomedical Ethics from the Perspective of the Theological Practice of Anointing of the Sick." Unpublished Ph.D. dissertation in the Department of Religion in the Graduate School of Duke University, 1992. Chap. 4.

10  *The Oxford Dictionary of the Christian Church*, eds., F. L. Cross and E.A. Livingstone (London: Oxford University Press, 1974), 1218-20.

11  Ibid.

# Genes in Society: Whose Body?
*Elizabeth Bettenhausen*

1  Dorothy L. Sayers, *Whose Body?* (New York: Avon Books, 1961), 127.

2  Ibid, 50f.

3  Ibid, 166.

4  Doris Teichler Zallen, *Does It Run in the Family? A Consumer's Guide to DNA Testing for Genetic Disorders* (New Brunswick, NJ: Rutgers University Press, 1997), 129. This is a clear, thoughtful, and very helpful work that treats many complex issues from the experience of families involved in genetic testing and interviews with genetic professionals.

5  Associated Press, "Drug Experiments on Boys Criticized," *The Boston Globe*, 18 April 1998, A3.

6  See LeRoy Walters and Julie Gage Palmer, *The Ethics of Human Gene Therapy* (New York: Oxford University Press, 1997), especially Chapter 2: Somatic Cell Gene Therapy. (Hereafter cited as *Ethics of Human Gene Therapy.*)

7  James E. Bowman, "Genetic Screening: Toward a New Eugenics?" *"It Just Ain't Fair" The Ethics of Health Care for African Americans,* ed. Annette Dula and Sara Goering (Westport, CT: Praeger, 1994), 166f. (Hereafter cited as *Ethics of Health Care*). See also Steve Jones, *The Language of Genes* (New York: Anchor Books, 1993). (Hereafter cited as *Language.*)

8  *Ethics of Health Care*, 166.

9  *Ethics of Human Gene Therapy*, 161.

10  Ibid, 91.

11  Ibid, chapters on germ-line gene therapy and enhancement genetic engineering; Leroy Hood, "Biology and Medicine in the Twenty-first Century," *The Code of Codes: Scientific and Social Issues in the Human Genome Project,* ed. Daniel J. Kevles and Leroy Hood (Cambridge, MA: Harvard University Press, 1992). *(Hereafter cited as Code of Codes.)* According to an Associated Press report in *The Boston Globe,* 5 June 1998: A17, "In an experiment, Duke University scientists were able to change sickled blood cells into normal cells using proteins that correct mutated genetic instructions" in RNA. Genetic therapy for sickle cell anemia will perhaps be a possibility.

12  Gina Kolata, "Genetic Testing Fall Short of Public Embrace," *The New York Times National,* 27 March 1998, A16. On the studies: "Beth Newman, et al., "Frequency of Breast Cancer Attributable to BRCA1 in a Population-Based Series of American Women," *Journal of the American Medical Association,* 25 March 1998, 915-921; Kathleen E. Malone, et al., "BRCA1 Mutations and Breast Cancer in the General Population," *Journal of the American Medical Association,* 25 March 1998, 922-929; Fergus J. Couch and Lynn C. Hartmann, "BRCA1 Testing—Advances and Retreats," *Journal of the American Medical Association,* 25 March 1998, 955-956.

13  Elizabeth Bettenhausen, "Hagar revisited: Surrogacy, Alienation, and Motherhood," *Christianity and Crisis,* 4 May 1987, 157-159. See also Gena Corea, *The Mother Machine: Reproductive Technologies from Artificial Insemination to Artificial Wombs* (New York: Harper & Row, 1985); Meg Stacey, "The New Genetics: A Feminist View," *The Troubled Helix: Social and Psychological Implications of the New Human Genetics,* ed. Theresa Marteau and Martin Richards (Cambridge University Press, 1996). (Hereafter cited as *Troubled Helix.*)

14  Dorothy Nelkin and M. Susan Lindee, *The DNA Mystique: The Gene as a Cultural Icon* (New York: W. H. Freeman, 1995), (Hereafter cited as *DNA Mystique*) 47. See also Philip Kitcher, *The Lives to Come: The Genetic Revolution and Human Possibilities* (New York: Simon & Schuster, 1996), Chapter 7 (Hereafter cited as *Lives to Come*); Ruth Hubbard and Elijah Wald, *Exploding the Gene Myth* (Boston: Beacon Press, 1997), Chap.11. (Hereafter cited as *Exploding.*); Eric Lander, "DNA Fingerprinting: Science, Law, and the Ultimate Identifier" in *Code of Codes.*

15  Massachusetts 1997 Session Laws, Chapter 106, "An Act Relative to the Enhancement of Forensic Technology," Capt. 22E, State DNA Database, Section 1.

16  Ibid, Section 3.

17  *Ethics of Human,* 162; *Language,* 23f.

18  Evelyn Fox Keller, "Nature, Nurture, and the Human Genome Project" in *Code of Codes,* 298.

19  John D'Emilio and Estelle B. Freedman, *Intimate Matters: A History of Sexuality in America* (New York: Harper & Row, 1988), 86.

20  *DNA Mystique,* 112. Philip Kitcher states the issue only in passing in reference to the burdens and benefits. "Members of ethnic groups most at risk for stigmatization and other adverse effects through the dissemination of genetic information are also least likely, as things now stand, to benefit from genetic testing" (78). The lack of resources needed to meet their interests is the reason mentioned, and Kitcher later points out:

> If prenatal testing for genetic diseases is often used by members of more privileged strata of society and far more rarely by the underprivileged, then the genetic conditions the affluent are concerned to avoid will be far more common among the poor—they will become "lower-class" diseases, other people's problems. Interest in finding methods of treatment or for providing supportive environments for those born with the diseases may well wane (198).

This does not attend explicitly to ethnic identity or "race" as correlating with privilege.

21  Dorothy Roberts, *Killing the Black Body: Race, Reproduction, and the Meaning of Liberty* (New York: Pantheon, 1997), 261 (Hereafter cited as *Killing the Black Body*). See also Patricia Hill Collins, *Black Feminist Thought* (London: HarperCollins Academic, 1990).

22 Ibid, 292.

23 The poll was reported in a four-part series, "Rethinking Integration," *The Boston Globe,* 16 September 1997 (margin of error: 5 percent). The greatest difference was in response to questions on affirmative action, which was supported by 71 percent of blacks and only 42 percent of whites. However, another question posed a very troubling agreement. "Do you think whites and blacks really understand each other?" Sixty-one percent of blacks and whites answered No. At the same time, 86 percent of whites and 87 percent of blacks have "developed friendships with people of another race."

24 *Killing the Black Body,* 268.

25 Ibid, 269.

26 Jefferson M. Fish, "Mixed Blood," *Psychology Today,* Nov/Dec 1995, 58.

27 Ibid, 58.

28 Ibid, 80. See also F. James Davis, *Who is Black? One Nation's Definition* (University Park, Penn.: The Pennsylvania State University Press, 1991).

29 *Exploding,* 149.

30 *Language,* 208.

31 *Exploding,* 149.

32 Ibid, 149.

33 Harlan Levy, *And the Blood Cried Out: A Prosecutor's Spellbinding Account of the Power of DNA* (New York: Basic Books, 1996), 56.

34 Ibid, 123f.

35 *DNA Mystique,* 115.

36 *Exploding,* 152.

37 Associated Press, "Drug Experiments On Boys Criticized," *The Boston Globe,* 18 April 1998, A3. An excellent, detailed study regarding genetic research and racism is Hannah Bradby's "Genetics and Racism" in *Troubled Helix,* 295-316.

38 Hank Greely, "Mapping the Territory," *Utne Reader,* March-April 1996: 87-88. (Hereafter cited as "Mapping.")

39 Harriet A. Washington, "Piece of the Genetic Puzzle Is Left Out," *EMERGE,* September 1997, 30.

40 Luigi Luca Cavalli-Sforza, statement in hearing before the Committee on Government Affairs of the Senate of the United States on 26 April 1993, 30.

41 Ibid, 31.

42 Robyn Nashimi, statement in hearing before the Committee on Government Affairs of the Senate of the United States on April 26, 1993, 19.

43 Ibid, 19.

44 Andrew Kimbrell, "High Tech Piracy," *Utne Reader,* March-April 1996, 86.

45 "Mapping," 88.

46 Christopher J. L. Murray and Alan D. Lopez, "Global Mortality, Disability, and the Contribution of Risk Factors: Global Burden of Disease Study," *The Lancet,* 17 May 1997, 1436-1442.

47 Ibid, 1441.

48 Ibid, 1439, Table 2.

49 Blumenthal, Causino, and Campbell, *Nature Genetics,* 16 May 1997, 104+. See also Eric G. Campbell, et al., "Relationship Between Market Competition and the Activities and Attitudes

of Medical School Faculty," *The Journal of the American Medical Association*, 16 July 1997, 222-226.

50   Ibid, et al., 104.

51   Richard Saltus, "Tailor-made Drugs," *The Boston Globe* 20 April 1998, C1.

52   Ibid, C2.

53   *Exploding*, 27.

54   Ibid, 61.

55   *Lives to Come*, 268.

56   Elizabeth Bettenhausen, "Ethical Issues in Postmenopausal Pregnancy and Birth," IN/FIRE ETHICS, Vol. 3 Issue 1, 1994 (Hereafter cited as *Ethical Issues.*); "Hagar Revisited," *Christianity and Crisis*, 4 May 1987.

57   *Ethics of Human Gene Therapy*, 75.

58   *Ethical Issues*, 5.

59   *DNA Mystique*, 39.

60   Ibid, 41f.

61   "The Judgment of Martin Luther on Monastic Vows," 1521, *Luther's Works*, AE 44, trans. and ed. James Atkinson (Philadelphia: Fortress Press, 1966), 301.

62   Martin Luther, "The Blessed Sacrament of the Holy and True Body of Christ, and the Brotherhoods," 1519, *Luther's Works*, AE 35, trans. Jeremiah J. Schindel and ed. E. Theodore Bachman (Philadelphia: Muhlenberg Press, 1960), 61f.

63   Martin Luther, "To the Councilmen of All Cities in Germany," 1524, *Luther's Works*, AE 45, trans. Albert T. W. Steinhaeuser and ed. Walther I. Brandt (Muhlenberg Press, 1962), 356, 367.

64   Additional useful books for this conversation are: Richard M. Lerner, *Final Solutions: Biology, Prejudice, and Genocide* (University Park, Penn.: Pennsylvania State University Press, 1992); Marque-Luisa Miringoff, *The Social Costs of Genetic Welfare* (New Brunswick, New Jersey: Rutgers University Press, 1991); Roger Shinn, *The New Genetics* (Cleveland: Pilgrim Press, 1996); Elizabeth L. Marshall, *The Human Genome Project: Cracking the Code Within Us* (New York: Franklin Watts, 1996).

## Love and Dignity: Against Children Becoming Commodities
*Ted Peters*

1   The material for this chapter is partially adapted from research supporting my earlier book, *For the Love of Children: Genetic Technology and the Future of the Family* (Louisville: Westminster/John Knox Press, 1996).

2   See: Daniel J. Kevles, *In the Name of Eugenics* (Berkeley and Los Angeles: University of California Press, 1985).

3   "I would look to the history of the U.S. eugenics movement as a source for values and actions to be avoided," writes Thomas Shannon. "For that history reveals a very dark side of our society with respect to treatment of both groups and individuals." "Genetics, Ethics, and Theology: The Roman Catholic Discussion," in *Genetics: Issues of Social Justice*, ed. by Ted Peters (Cleveland: Pilgrim Press, 1998), 173.

4   "Although the old eugenic generalizations have been cast off, the logic behind them persists, refueled by evidence from diagnostic tests and justified in terms of efficiency, effectiveness, and cost." Dorothy Nelkin and Laurence Tancredi, *Dangerous Diagnostics* (New York: Harper, Basic Books, 1989), 13.

5    "Genetic tests could foster a new eugenics in which pressure is exerted on women whose offspring would be at risk to avoid their conception or birth." Neil A. Holtzman, *Proceed with Caution: Predicting Genetic Risks in the Recombinant DNA Era* (Baltimore and London: Johns Hopkins University Press, 1989), 8.

6    A "genetic test" can be defined as the "analysis of human DNA, RNA, chromosomes, proteins, and certain metabolites in order to detect heritable disease-related genotypes, mutations, phenotypes, or karyotypes for clinical purposes." *Promoting Safe and Effective Genetic Testing in the United States: Final Report of the Task Force on Genetic Testing*, ed. by Neil A. Holtzman and Michael S. Watson (Washington: NIH-DOE Working Group on Ethical, Legal, and Social Implications of Human Genome Research, September 1997), xi; 9. "Genetic screening" refers to the use of genetic testing to "search within a population for persons possessing certain genotypes." Ibid., xii.

7    Martin Luther, "Table Talk" No. 1607, *Luther's Works*, 55 Volumes (St. Louis: Concordia, and Minneapolis: Fortress, 1955-1967), 54:158.

8    "Draft of Statement on Genetic Discrimination in Health Insurance," Directorate for Science and Policy Programs, American Association for the Advancement of Science, 1200 New York Avenue NW, Washington DC 20005.

9    "Designing Genetic Information Policy: The Need for an Independent Policy Review of the Ethical, Legal, and Social Implications of the Human Genome Project," Sixteenth Report by the Committee on Government Operations (Washington: U.S. Government Printing Office, April 2, 1992), 15, 19.

10   Ibid, 21.

11   Michael S. Yesley, "Genetic Privacy, Discrimination, and Social Policy: Challenges and Dilemmas," *Microbial and Comparative Genomics*, 2:1 (1997), 19-35.

12   *Genetic Information and Health Insurance*, NIH Publication No. 93-3686 (Washington: National Center for Human Genome Research, May 10, 1993), 2. In the more recent report, *Promoting Safe and Effective Genetic Testing*, we find this: "No individual should be subjected to unfair discrimination by a third party on the basis of having had a genetic test or receiving an abnormal genetic test result. Third parties include insurers, employers, and educational and other institutions that routinely inquire about the health of applicants for services or positions." xiv.

13   Karen Lebacqz documents just why genetic privacy is doomed to failure due to technical and social forces, and then adds that the very idea of genetic privacy will only add to disproportionate discrimination against the poor and marginalized of our society. "It is not technically feasible to trust privacy to ensure that information gained from the Human Genome Project does not result in discrimination. Further, under present circumstances it is not socially feasible. Medical information has a gatekeeping function in our society. There will be pressures to use this information to reduce costs for a number of social services and business ventures such as insurance. This is built into the very structure of our social arrangements." "Genetic Privacy: No Deal for the Poor," in Peters, ed., *Genetics*, 250.

14   Sheryl Stolberg, "Insurance Falls Prey to Genetic Bias," *Los Angeles Times*, (March 27, 1994), A20.

15   Scott B. Rae, "Prenatal Testing, Abortion, and Beyond," in *Genetic Ethics: Do the Ends Justify the Genes*, ed. by John F. Kilner, Rebecca D. Pentz, and Frank E. Young (Grand Rapids, Michigan: Eerdman's, 1997), 140. (Hereafter cited as *Genetic Ethics*.)

16   Ibid, 140.

17   Choice of language here is important, though in itself not morally decisive. Bioethicist John C. Fletcher reminds us that "abortion kills the fetus, an act that cannot be disguised by applying such qualifying terms as 'selective', 'elective', or 'therapeutic,' or referring to the act as 'termination of pregnancy.'" "Moral Problems and Ethical Guidance in Prenatal Diagnosis," in Aubrey Milunsky, editor, *Genetic Disorders and the Fetus* (New York and London: Plenum

Press, 2nd ed., 1986), 824. George McKenna observes that even those who favor abortion want it to be "safe, legal, and rare." Why rare? He takes note of expressions substituted for the word "abortion" such as "termination of pregnancy," as well as references to abortion clinics as "reproductive health clinics." He asks whether this language is trying to cover up something troubling. "The obvious answer is that abortion is troubling because it is a killing process. Abortion clinics may indeed be places of healing and care, as the Planned Parenthood counselor maintains, but their primary purpose is to kill human fetuses." "On Abortion: A Lincolnian Position," *The Atlantic Monthly*, 276:3 (September 1995), 54. The language battle here described is fought at the professional and ideological level. The genetic counselor confronts women or couples dealing with existential decisions at a personal level. At this level human intuition seems to presume that the unborn fetus is a person deserving regard if not devotion. This can remain true even when the decision to abort is made.

18    "Over 95 percent of such couples do not need to consider elective abortion. The few who are initially ambivalent almost invariably move to terminate the pregnancy following detection of a serious fetal defect." Milunsky, *Genetic Disorders and the Fetus*, 9. Genetic disorder is not the only grounds for selective abortion. Increasingly pregnancy reduction has become a normative practice. When twins or triplets or more embryos are discovered implanted in the mother's womb and it is thought that not all can be brought to viability, the number of fetuses will be reduced in order to increase the chance that one or perhaps two will survive in healthy fashion. Rather than use the term "abortion," this is called "selective feticide" in behalf of "selective birth." Ibid., 830.

19    Compassion need not be applied only to the unborn child in question, but rather to all involved. John C. Fletcher warns that "choosing not to abort in pregnancies of high genetic or social risk can result in serious harm for the woman, the couple, the family, and the affected individual...with consequences that cannot be put aside by referring to the outcome as a 'gift of God' or as an event that draws family members together." Milunsky, *Genetic Disorders and the Fetus*, 824.

20    Currently half of all pregnancies in California are terminated by abortion. The vast majority are due simply to the choice of the mother, not for medical reasons. If this continues, then the total number of abortions may not rise dramatically due to genetic selection, just the number in this category.

21    See Ted Peters, "My Genes Made Me Do It!" *The Lutheran*, 8:3 (March 1995), 25-27.

22    Marsha Saxton, "Prenatal Screening and Discriminatory Attitudes About Disability." *Genewatch*, 4:1 (1987), 8-10; cited by Holtzman, *Proceed with Caution*, 216.

23    Caring for discarded or marginalized persons is the clear Christian mandate. It is the work of redemption in a world that is already a mess. At a more abstract level, the ethicist can ask: Should we create a mess? To this Paul Ramsey answers: No. "Men and women have no unqualified right to have children. The treatments for the prevention of cystic fibrosis, Huntington's chorea, achondroplasia, some forms of muscular dystrophy, PKU, amaurotic idiocy, and other chromosomal abnormalities...are continence, not getting married to a particular person, not having any children, using three contraceptives at once, or sterilization." *Fabricated Man: The Ethics of Genetic Control* (New Haven: Yale, 1970), 120.

24    Despite his emphasis on the creativity of the human being, the eminent mid-century Roman Catholic theologian Karl Rahner thought he saw in the prospect of genetic intervention the delusional motive to control what cannot be controlled. He wrote that "genetic manipulation is the embodiment of the fear of oneself, the fear of accepting one's self as the unknown quantity it is." What tempts us to engineer our evolutionary future through genetics is "despair because [we] cannot *dispose* of existence." "The Problem of Genetic Manipulation," *Theological Investigations*, IX (New York: Seabury Press, 1976), 245, italics in original.

25    Michael S. Beates, "God's Sovereignty and Genetic Anomalies," in *Genetic Ethics*, 53.

26    Ibid, 57.

27  Allen D. Verhey, "Playing God," in *Genetic Ethics*, 66.

28  Ibid, 68.

29  Ibid, 70.

30  Ibid.

31  Laurie Zoloth-Dorfman, "Mapping the Normal Human Self: The Jew and the Mark of Otherness," in Peters, ed., *Genetics*, 192.

32  Rae, *Genetic Ethics*, 140.

# Individualism vs. Faith: Genetic Ethics in Contrasting Perspectives
*Hans O. Tiefel*

1  President's Commission for the Study of Ethical Problems in Medicine and Biomedical and Behavioral Research, *Screening and Counseling for Genetic Conditions: A Report on the Ethical, Social, and Legal Implications of Genetic Screening, Counseling, and Education Programs*, February 1983, p. 37.

2  Ibid.

3  Philip Hefner, *The Human Factor: Evolution, Culture, and Religion* (Minneapolis, Minn.: Fortress Press, 1993), pp. 38f.

4  Gilbert Meilaender, *Bioethics: A Primer for Christians* (Grand Rapids, Michigan: Eerdmans, 1996), p. 54.

5  Evangelical Lutheran Church in America, "A Social Statement on Abortion," September 1991, pp. 3f.

6  Ibid, p. 7.

7  Stanley Hauerwas, *A Community of Character: Toward a Constructive Christian Social Ethic* (Notre Dame and London: University of Notre Dame Press, 1981), p. 198.

8  Joseph Pieper, *About Love*, trans., Richard and Clara Winston (Chicago: Franciscan Herald Press, 1974), p. 19; quoted in the context of prenatal screening by Gilbert Meilaender, *Bioethics*, p. 49.

9  "A Social Statement on Abortion," p. 7.

# A Geneticist's Synthesis: Evolution Faith, and Decision Making
*Robert Roger Lebel*

1  Plato. *Cratylus*, 402.

2  Martin Luther (1521), "Commentary on Psalm 68," *Luther's Works*, Volume 13, 4-6. Jaroslav Pelikan and Helmut Lehmann, eds. American Edition (Philadelphia and St. Louis: Fortress Press and Concordia Publishing House, 1955-1984). (Hereafter cited as *Luther's Works*.)

3  Victor A. McKusick, *Mendelian Inheritance in Man*, Twelfth Edition (Baltimore: Johns Hopkins University Press, 1998).

4  I. Thompson, *The Audubon Society Field Guide to North American Fossils* (New York: A.A. Knopf, 1990).

5  Christopher Stringer and Robin McKie, *African Exodus* (New York: Henry Holt and Company, 1997), 115-148.

6    Pierre Teilhard de Chardin, *The Phenomenon of Man*, Transl. Bernard Wall (New York: Harper & Row, 1959).

7    Martin Luther (1518), "Heidelberg Disputation," *Luther's Works*, 31, 57.

8    Martin Luther (1535), "Lectures on Galatians," *Luther's Works*, 26, 129-130.

9    Robert Roger Lebel, "Genetic Decision-Making: Parental Responsibility," *Linacre Quarterly* Vol. 43 No. 4 (1976), 280-291.

10   Robert Roger Lebel, "Genetic Grounds for Annulment." *The Jurist 36*, 3/4 (1976), 317-327.

11   Robert Roger Lebel, B. Rafael Elejalde, Maria Mercedes de Elejalde, "Pregnancy Loss and Unsanctioned Grief," in *Unrecognized and Unsanctioned Grief*, VR Pine et al. (eds.), 41-46, (Springfield: Charles C. Thomas, 1991).

# A Pastoral Perspective: Companionship Beyond Innocence
*Lawrence E. Holst*

1    Catherine Baker, *Your Genes, Your Choices: Exploring the Issues Raised by Genetic Research* (Washington, D.C.: American Association for the Advancement of Science, 1997), 14. (Hereafter cited as *Your Genes, Your Choices*).

2    For more information see David Switzer, *The Minister as Crisis Counselor* (Nashville: Abingdon Press, 1974), 65-68.

3    Eric Cassell, "The Nature of Suffering and the Goals of Medicine," *New England Journal of Medicine*, 306, 11 (March, 1983), 639.

4    Paul Tillich, "The Theology of Pastoral Care," *Pastoral Psychology*, 10, 97 (October, 1959), 22.

5    Ronald Cole-Turner and Brent Waters, *Pastoral Genetics: Theology and Care at the Beginning of Life*, (Cleveland: The Pilgrim Press), xiii. (Hereafter cited as *Pastoral Genetics*.)

6    *Your Genes, Your Choices*, 22-23.

7    Mortimer J. Adler and Charles Van Doren, eds., *Great Treasury of Western Thought* (New York and London: R. R. Bowker Co., 1977), 439.

8    J. Robert Nelson, *On the New Frontiers of Genetics and Religion* (Grand Rapids, Michigan: Eerdmans, 1994), 77.

9    For a fuller description see Daniel J. Simundson, *Faith Under Fire: Biblical Interpretations of Suffering* (Minneapolis: Augsburg Publishing House, 1980).

10   Ibid, 15-16

11   Ronald Cole-Turner, "Religion and the Human Genome," *Journal of Religion and Health*, 31, 2 (Summer 1992), 165-166.

12   *Pastoral Genetics*, 59.

13   Gilbert Meilander, "Mastering Our Genetics: When Do We Say No?" *The Christian Century* (October 3, 1990), 873.

14   *Pastoral Genetics*, 109-110.

15   Ibid.

16   "A Social Statement on Abortion," adopted at the 2nd Biennial Churchwide Assembly of the Evangelical Lutheran Church in America in Orlando, Florida, September 4, 1991, 1-11.

17   Franklin E. Sherman, "The Problem of Abortion after the Supreme Court Decision," Division for Mission in North America, Department for Church and Society, Lutheran Church in America, 1974, 10-11.

18    Karen Lebacqz, *Genetics, Ethics and Parenthood* (New York: Pilgrim Press, 1988), 22.

19    Marc Kolden, "Christian Vocation in Light of Feminist Critiques, *Lutheran Quarterly*, 71. (Hereafter cited as *Christian Vocation.*)

20    "The Church in Society: A Lutheran Perspective," a social statement of the Evangelical Lutheran Church in America adopted at the Second Biennial Churchwide Assembly, September 1991, 4. (Hereafter cited as *Church in Society.*)

21    Martin Luther, *Luther's Works*, American Edition, 55 volumes, edited by Pelikan and Lehmann, (St. Louis and Philadelphia: Concordia Publishing House and Fortress Press, 1955), 14:114 (as quoted in *Christian Vocation*).

22    *Church in Society*, 4.

23    James H. Burtness, "A Statement on Abortion" (Received by Eighth General Convention of The American Lutheran Church and transmitted to member congregations for study) 1976, 31.

24    Martin Luther, "The Freedom of the Christian," *Luther's Works*, American Edition, 31 (Philadelphia: Muhlenberg Press, 1957), 344.

25    Martin Luther, *Luther's Works*, American Edition, 48 (Philadelphia: Fortress Press, 1986), 282.

# GLOSSARY

**Acquired mutations**: gene changes that arise within individual cells and accumulate throughout a person's lifetime; also called somatic mutations. (See Hereditary mutation.)

**Alleles**: variant forms of the same gene. Different alleles produce variations in inherited characteristics such as eye color or blood type.

**Alzheimer's disease**: a disease that causes memory loss, personality changes, dementia, and ultimately death. Not all cases are inherited, but genes have been found for familial forms of Alzheimer's disease.

**Amino acid**: any of a class of 20 molecules that combine to form proteins in living things.

**Amniocentesis**: prenatal test in which a needle is inserted into the womb and into the fluid in which the fetus floats. A few milliliters of fluid are withdrawn for testing.

**Anencephaly**: severe type of neural tube defect in which the top of the brain fails to develop.

**Autonomy** (as a moral category): the power of self-rule or direction; independence from outside guidance. A dominant category of Enlightenment thinking.

**Autosomal disease**: disease related to a gene located on an autosome; it may be either dominant or recessive. (See Dominant allele and Recessive allele.)

**Autosomal recessive disorder**: disorder in which both alleles of an autosomal gene are erroneous.

**Autosome**: any of the non-sex-determining chromosomes. Human cells have 22 pairs of autosomes.

**Base pairs**: the two complementary, nitrogen-rich molecules held together by weak chemical bonds. Two strands of DNA are held together in the shape of a double helix by the bonds between their base pairs. (See Chemical base.)

**BRCA1**: a gene that normally helps to restrain cell growth.

**BRCA1 breast cancer susceptibility gene**: a mutated version of BRCA1, which predisposes a person toward developing breast cancer.

**Brief Order for Confession and Forgiveness**: a short order of worship in the Lutheran Book of Worship in which participants confess their sin and receive the assurance of God's forgiveness.

**Carrier**: a person who has a recessive mutated gene, together with its normal allele. Carriers do not usually develop disease but can pass the mutated gene on to their children.

**Carrier testing**: testing to identify individuals who carry disease-causing recessive genes that could be inherited by their children. Carrier testing is designed for healthy people who have no symptoms of disease, but who are known to be at high risk because of family history.

**Catechism of the Book of Common Prayer**: the manual of basic Christian instruction found in the Anglican Church's (Church of England) authorized worship book.

**Cell**: small, watery, membrane-bound compartment filled with chemicals; the basic subunit of any living thing.

**Chemical base**: an essential building block. DNA contains four complementary bases: adenine, which pairs with thymine; and cytosine, which pairs with guanine. In RNA, thymine is replaced by uracil.

**Chromosomes**: structures found in the nucleus of a cell, which contain the genes. Chromosomes come in pairs, and a normal human cell contains 46 chromosomes—22 pairs of autosomes and two sex chromosomes.

**Clone**: a group of identical genes, cells, or organisms derived from a single ancestor.

**Cloning**: the process of making genetically identical copies.

**Crossing over**: a phenomenon, also known as recombination, that sometimes occurs during the formation of sperm and egg cells (meiosis); a pair of chromosomes (one from the mother and the other from the father) break and trade segments with one another.

**Cystic fibrosis**: an inherited disease in which a thick mucus clogs the lungs and blocks the ducts of the pancreas.

**Cytoplasm**: the cellular substance outside the nucleus in which the cell's organelles are suspended.

**Dementia**: severe impairment of mental functioning.

**DNA**: the substance of heredity; a large molecule that carries the genetic information that cells need to replicate and to produce proteins.

**DNA repair genes**: certain genes that are part of a DNA repair pathway; when altered, they permit mutations to pile up throughout the DNA.

**DNA sequencing**: determining the exact order of the base pairs in a segment of DNA.

**Dominant allele**: a gene that is expressed, regardless of whether its counterpart allele on the other chromosome is dominant or recessive. Autosomal dominant disorders are produced by a single mutated dominant allele, even though its corresponding allele is normal. (See Recessive allele.)

**Enlightenment**: historically speaking, a period from the middle of the 17th century until roughly the turn of the 19th; during this period a European philosophical movement flourished concerned with the critical examination of established doctrines, authority, and institutions from the point of view of rationalism. Broadly speaking, the term designates views from that period that are widely held to be the dominant shapers of the modern world. Immanuel Kant (1724-1804) is a representative figure known for summarizing the meaning of Enlightenment as the courage to "think for yourself."

**Enzyme**: a protein that facilitates a specific chemical reaction.

**Eschatological**: (See Eschatology.)

**Eschatology**: derived from the Greek word for "last things"; in Christian theology it refers to any discussion of or beliefs about the final events and destiny of the individual and creation in God's purposes.

**Eucharist**: from the Greek word for "thanksgiving," it designates the Christian sacrament involving bread and wine. Roughly equivalent terms include Holy Communion, the Lord's Supper, and the Sacrament of the Altar.

**Eugenics**: literally it means "good genes"; the term can simply indicate the study of hereditary improvement by genetic control. It usually, however, refers to any intentional strategy to direct human evolution through encouraging the transmission of "desired" traits while discouraging the "undesired" ones. Such strategy could include selective mating, prenatal testing, selective abortion, forced sterilization, ethnic cleansing, or others.

**Expression**: (See Gene expression.)

**Expressivity**: the degree to which a gene produces an observable effect or characteristic.

**Fen-phen**: popular drug combination of fenfluramine and phentermine used to reduce appetite for weight loss. Fenfluramine was pulled from the market in 1997.

**Fenfluramine**: (See Fen-phen.)

**Gamete**: reproductive cell such as sperm or egg containing a half-copy of the genome.

**Gene**: a unit of inheritance; a working subunit of DNA. Each of the body's 50,000 to 100,000 genes contains the code for a specific product, typically, a protein such as an enzyme.

**Gene deletion**: the total loss or absence of a gene.

**Gene expression**: the process by which a gene's coded information is translated into the structures present and operating in the cell (either proteins or RNAs).

**Gene mapping**: determining the relative positions of genes on a chromosome and the distance between them.

**Gene testing**: examining a sample of blood or other body fluid or tissue for biochemical, chromosomal, or genetic markers that indicate the presence or absence of genetic disease.

**Gene therapy**: treating disease by replacing, manipulating, or supplementing nonfunctional genes.

**Genetic linkage maps**: DNA maps that assign relative chromosomal locations to genetic landmarks—either genes for known traits or distinctive sequences of DNA—on the basis of how frequently they are inherited together. (See Physical maps.)

**Genetics**: the scientific study of heredity; how particular qualities or traits are transmitted from parents to offspring.

**Genome**: all the genetic material in the chromosomes of a particular organism.

**Genome maps**: charts that indicate the ordered arrangement of the genes or other DNA markers within the chromosomes.

**Genotype**: the actual genes carried by an individual (as distinct from phenotype—that is, the physical characteristics into which genes are translated).

**Germ cells**: the reproductive cells of the body, either egg or sperm cells.

**Germline mutation**: (See Hereditary mutation.)

**Hereditary mutation**: a gene change in the body's reproductive cells (egg or sperm) that becomes incorporated in the DNA of every cell in the body; also called germline mutation. (See Acquired mutations.)

**Human genome**: the full collection of genes needed to produce a human being.

**Human Genome Project**: an international research effort (led in the United States by the National Institutes of Health and the Department of Energy) aimed at identifying and ordering every base in the human genome.

**Huntington's disease**: an adult-onset disease characterized by progressive mental and physical deterioration; it is caused by an inherited dominant gene mutation.

**Hurler-Scheie syndrome**: an autosomal recessive disorder caused by inadequate production of an enzyme protein, characterized by facial and dental malformations, dwarfism, blindness from cataracts, and progressive dementia beginning at a few months of age.

**Immunology**: the study of the immune system which fights infection.

**Imprinting**: a biochemical phenomenon that determines, for certain genes, which one of the pair of alleles, the mother's or the father's, will be active in that individual.

***In vitro* fertilization**: any of a number of methods of treating infertility by initially combining sperm and egg outside the body.

**Inborn errors of metabolism**: inherited diseases resulting from alterations in genes that code for enzymes.

**Lecsch-Nyhan syndrome**: a genetic disorder due to lack of an enzyme, characterized by self-mutilation by biting.

**Linkage analysis**: a gene-hunting technique that traces patterns of heredity in large, high-risk families, in an attempt to locate a disease-causing gene mutation by identifying traits that are co-inherited with it.

**Molecule**: a group of atoms arranged to interact in a particular way; one molecule of any substance is the smallest physical unit of that particular substance.

**Mutation**: a change in the number arrangement, or molecular sequence of a gene.

**Neoplasm**: abnormal new growths, either malignant cancers or benign tumors.

**Newborn screening**: examining blood samples from a newborn infant to detect disease-related abnormalities or deficiencies in gene products.

**Norm** (as a moral term): a pattern, precept, or rule for decision and action. In this usage the term does not refer to what may be statistically standard or normal practice; it refers instead to a principle for regulating or judging conduct.

**Norm** (as a medical term): a typical, average, or standard characteristic or behavior.

**Nucleotide**: A subunit of DNA or RNA, consisting of one chemical base plus a phosphate molecule and a sugar molecule.

**Nucleus**: the cell structure that houses the chromosomes.

**Oncogenes**: genes that normally play a role in the growth of cells, but when overexpressed or mutated, can foster the growth of cancer.

**Parousia**: from Greek, literally "presence" or "arrival"; in Christian theology it designates the future return of Christ in glory when God judges all and brings an end to the present world order.

**Penetrance**: a term indicating the likelihood that a given gene will actually result in disease.

**Pharmacogenetics**: the study of genetically controlled variations in individual responses to drugs or products that use genetic susceptibility as part of the rationale for their use.

**Pharmacogenomics**: (See Pharmacogenetics.)

**Phenotype**: the observable characteristics of gene expression. (Compare with genotype.)

**Phenylketonuria** (PKU): an inborn error of metabolism caused by the lack of an enzyme, resulting in abnormally high levels of the amino acid phenylalanine; untreated, PKU can lead to severe, progressive mental retardation.

**Physical maps**: DNA maps showing the location of identifiable landmarks either genes or distinctive short sequences of DNA. The lowest resolution physical map shows the banding pattern on the 24 different chromosomes, the highest resolution map depicts the complete nucleotide sequence of the chromosomes.

**Predictive gene test**: test to identify gene abnormalities that may make a person susceptible to certain diseases or disorders.

**Prenatal diagnosis**: examining fetal cells taken from the amniotic fluid, the primitive placenta (chorion), or the umbilical cord for biochemical, chromosomal, or gene alterations.

**Probe**: a specific sequence of single-stranded DNA, typically labeled with a radioactive atom, which is designed to bind to, and thereby single out, a particular segment of DNA.

**Prostate Specific Antigen** (PSA): cell marker measured by blood test that can be used to screen men for prostate cancer.

**Protein**: a large, complex molecule composed of amino acids. The sequence of the amino acids— and thus the function of the protein—is determined by the sequence of the base pairs in the gene that encodes it. Proteins are essential to the structure, function, and regulation of the body. Examples are hormones, enzymes, and antibodies.

**Protein product**: the protein molecule assembled under the direction of a gene.

**Recessive allele**: a gene that is expressed only when its counterpart allele on the matching chromosome is also recessive (not dominant). Autosomal recessive disorders develop in persons who receive two copies of the mutant gene, one from each parent who is a carrier. (See Dominant allele.)

**Recombination**: (See Crossing over.)

**Reproductive cells**: egg and sperm cells. Each mature reproductive cell carries a single set of 23 chromosomes.

**Restriction enzymes**: enzymes that can cut strands of DNA at specific base sequences.

**RNA**: a chemical similar to DNA. The several classes of RNA molecules play important roles in protein synthesis and other cell activities.

**Screening**: looking for evidence of a particular disease such as cancer in persons with no symptoms of disease.

**Sequencing**: (See DNA sequencing.)

**Sex chromosomes**: the chromosomes that determine the sex of an organism. Human females have two X chromosomes; males have one X and one Y.

**Sickle-cell anemia**: an inherited, potentially lethal disease in which a defect in hemoglobin, the oxygen-carrying pigment in the blood, causes distortion (sickling) and loss of red blood cells, producing damage to organs throughout the body.

**Somatic cells**: all body cells except the reproductive cells.

**Somatic mutations**: (See Acquired mutations.)

**Survivor's guilt**: refers to the experience described by survivors of a misfortune in which a friend or family member is lost to disease or calamity. It is usually described as a sense of being somehow responsible for the event or culpable for remaining alive or free from the harm.

**Tay-Sachs disease**: an inherited disease of infancy characterized by profound mental retardation and early death; it is caused by a recessive gene mutation.

**Toxic Knowledge**: genetic information about a statistically probable onset of, or disposition to, a disease or disorder for which there is no cure.

**Transcription**: the process of copying information from DNA into new strands of messenger RNA (mRNA). The mRNA then carries this information to the cytoplasm, where it serves as the blueprint for the manufacture of a specific protein.

**Translation**: the process of turning instructions from mRNA, base by base, into chains of amino acids that then fold into proteins. This process takes place in the cytoplasm, on structures called ribosomes.

**Translocation**: the swapping of a genetic material from one chromosome to another.

**Trisomy**: three copies of a chromosome per cell, which causes disease. Trisomy 18 is one example. Trisomy 21 (three copies of chromosome 21) is also known as Down's syndrome.

**Variable number of tandem repeats** (VNTR): some sequences of DNA are repeated many times in a row. The number of repeats may not be identical in offspring. This can lead to disease and can be used in forensics to identify individuals.

**X chromosome**: a sex chromosome; normal females carry two X chromosomes.

**Y chromosome**: a sex chromosome; normal males carry one Y and one X chromosome.

*Some of the genetic definitions here are courtesy the National Institutes of Health, National Cancer Institute.*

# INDEX

# S

Sacramentals, 87
St. Augustine, 87
St. Paul, 131, 150, 154, 174, 181, 182, 186
Sample acquisition, 32—33
I Samuel 13; 17, 35—36
Saxton, Marsha, 125
Sayers, Dorothy, 94—95
Schizophrenia, 56
Schwandt, Kirstin Finn, 69, 99, 100, 123, 139, 141, 151, 162
Science, 133—135
    and Christian worldview, 151—157
    laws of biology, 153—154
    laws of chemistry, 152
    laws of physics, 152
    and problem of evil, 164—165
Scientific language, 133—135
Scientists
    professional responsibility, 27
    reasons for studying genetics, 25—26
Screening; see Carrier screening; Genetic screening
Selective abortion, 6, 125, 126—127
Self-giving, risk of, 157—158
Self-realization, 132
Sex selection, 102
Sexual reproduction, 18
    transmitting genetic information, 21
Shephelah, 35—36
Sickle cell anemia, 25, 44
    carrier screening for, 40—50
    and discrimination, 99
Single-gene disease, 118
Single gene errors
    dominant/recessive genes, 23—24
    examples, 24—25
    genes and alleles, 23
Single point mutations, 25
Social dignity, 96—97
Social Statement on Abortion, 7, 147, 180
Social well-being, 111—113
Society, and procreative decisions, 159
Soul, and cloning, 22
Speciation, 154
Sperm bank, 117
Spina bifida, 31
Spiritual care, 174
Spontaneous pregnancy loss, 22
Spousal reproductive decisions, 158
Symbolic nature of pastoral office, 171, 172

# T

Tay-Sachs disease, 50, 79, 127
Tentative pregnancy, 144—147

Therapeutic drugs
    development of, 64—65
    effectiveness, 71
Tiefel, Hans O., 64, 124, 162, 178
Tillich, Paul, 173
Toxic knowledge, 6, 30, 55
Traits, penetrance, 29
Translocated chromosomes, 22—23
Trilobites, 154
Trinucleotide repeat sequences, 25
Triple marker screen test, 30, 40—43
Trisomy 22, 31
Turner Syndrome, 22, 34

# U

Ultrasound, 31, 33, 161
United States Supreme Court, abortion ruling, 180

# V

Value judgments, 29, 33—34
Variability, 29
Variagenics, 111
Varian, John, 26, 29, 96, 110—111, 120
Verhey, Allen D., 126
Vocation, 185

# W

Washington, Harriet, 107—108
Waters, Brent, 173-174, 179
Watson, James, 17, 27
Well-being
    global, 109—111
    personal/social, 111—113
"Whether One May Flee From a Deadly Plague" (Luther), 58
Whole chromosomes, 21—22
Whose Body? (Sayers), 95
Woods, Tiger, 104
Working Group on Ethical, Legal, and Social Implications of the Human Genome Project, 120
Worldview
    Christian-scientific, 151—158
    dilemmas inherent in, 77—79
    fix-it mentality, 78—79
    and genetic testing, 73—79
    ideas on sex, race, and culture, 104—106
    media image of nature, 74—76
    rooted in human nature, 76—77
Wright, Orville, 160
Wright, Wilbur, 160

# X-Z

X chromosome, 22
Y chromosome, 20—21
Zallen, Doris Teichler, 97